TWENTIETH-CENTURY CATHOLIC THEOLOGIANS

Praise for Twentieth-Century Catholic Theologians

"With characteristic lucidity and insight, Fergus Kerr narrates the story of twentieth-century Catholic theology. This illuminating and compelling account will surely be appreciated by a wide ecumenical readership."
David Fergusson, University of Edinburgh

"An engaging biblio-biographical study designed to show the critical influence of ten theologians in transforming twentieth-century Catholicism. Kerr's keen sense for trajectories reveals how startling has been the transformation – more than half had been disciplined by Vatican authorities. In the face of these lives, no one will ever be able to doubt the potential for intellectual regeneration, while the rich perspective they offer may also help defuse trivial tensions exacerbated by needless ideological polarization. This narrative of theology-in-action is meant for literate faithful as well as pastoral workers from acolyte to bishop."
David Burrell, University of Notre Dame

"Kerr, with his usual oblique fluency, miraculously manages to include an attention to nuance and telling detail within a short general account that is unerringly focussed on what, in the previous century of Catholic thought, is still likely to matter in the current one. This volume will surely become the standard introduction to its subject matter."
John Milbank, University of Nottingham

"This volume offers analysis of some of the most significant theologians of the last hundred years by a theologian widely regarded as the most knowledgeable and insightful academic in the field. Simply invaluable."
Alan Torrance, St. Andrews University

TWENTIETH-CENTURY CATHOLIC THEOLOGIANS

From Neoscholasticism to Nuptial Mysticism

Fergus Kerr

Blackwell Publishing

BLACKWELL PUBLISHING
350 Main Street, Malden, MA 02148-5020, USA
9600 Garsington Road, Oxford OX4 2DQ, UK
550 Swanston Street, Carlton, Victoria 3053, Australia

First published 2007 by Blackwell Publishing Ltd

3   2007

Library of Congress Cataloging-in-Publication Data
Kerr, Fergus.
Twentieth-century Catholic theologians: from neoscholasticism to nuptial mysticism /
Fergus Kerr.
p.   cm.
Includes bibliographical references and index.
ISBN 978-1-4051-2083-8 (hardback: alk. paper) – ISBN 978-1-4051-2084-5 (pbk: alk. paper)
1. Catholic Church—Doctrines—History—20th century.   2. Theologians.   I. Title

BW1751.3.K47 2007
230'.20904—dc22

                                                2006004748

A catalogue record for this title is available from the British Library

Set in 10.5 pt Bembo
by The Running Head Limited, Cambridge, www.therunninghead.com

For further information on
Blackwell Publishing, visit our website:
www.blackwellpublishing.com

CONTENTS

Preface   vii

1 Before Vatican II   1

2 Marie-Dominique Chenu   17

3 Yves Congar   34

4 Edward Schillebeeckx   52

5 Henri de Lubac   67

6 Karl Rahner   87

7 Bernard Lonergan   105

8 Hans Urs von Balthasar   121

9 Hans Küng   145

10 Karol Wojtyla   163

11 Joseph Ratzinger   183

12 After Vatican II   203

   Appendix: The Anti-modernist Oath   223

   Index   226

PREFACE

'There is no doubt that the outstanding event in the Catholic theology of our century is the surmounting of neo-scholasticism', so Walter Kasper declared, in 1987.[1] Anyone who began ordination studies in 1957, as I did, would agree. That the century ended with a reaffirmation of nuptial mysticism by influential theologians, we did not anticipate.

'Neo-scholasticism', Kasper explains, 'was the attempt to solve the modern crisis of theology by picking up the thread of the high scholastic tradition of mediaeval times. The aim was to establish a timeless, unified theology that would provide a norm for the universal church. It is impossible to deny this attempt a certain grandeur. But in the long run a restoration of this kind was bound to fail'.[2] For one thing, neoscholastic Catholicism depended on 'metaphysics', and developments both within Catholic theology and outside led to 'the breakdown of metaphysics in their classic form'. By classical metaphysics Kasper means 'the study of the final, all-determining and cohering foundations, wisdom about the oneness and wholeness of reality'. In Catholic theology, this study was essential: 'In the total theological tradition hitherto, metaphysics with its universal categories had provided the instrument with which to render in the medium of thought a theologically appropriate and reflective account of God, the one reality that – itself all-comprehending and all-determining – yet transcends all else'.

Obviously, in selecting some eminent theologians to discuss, many others are left aside, including those writing in Italian and Spanish, a deplorable omission. Also, the neoscholastic theologians who resisted the trend should

---

[1] *Theology and Church* (London: SCM Press 1989): 1.
[2] Cf. James A. Weisheipl, 'Neoscholasticism and Neothomism', *New Catholic Encyclopedia* (New York: McGraw-Hill 1967), vol. 10: 337.

have been examined on their own and for their own sake. Since they published mostly in Latin, their work is now largely unread. Regrettably, they appear here only as spectral adversaries, no doubt caricatured as adversaries in controversy often are. Some of the theologians highlighted here suffered harassment by neoscholastic colleagues and ecclesiastical superiors. The Roman Catholic Church, one should not forget, is a church of extremes: tolerant of forms of devotion barely distinguishable from 'superstition', with pastoral care sometimes verging on 'tyranny', and often ferocious in resisting intellectual innovation.[3] Moreover, the fate of theologians cannot be separated from power struggles within the Church, or from events in the wider world: the First World War, the rise of fascism and Soviet communism, the Second World War, and the Cold War. These are only alluded to when they brush the lives of our subjects. While neoscholasticism will not be restored in the foreseeable future, the philosophical problems for theology raised during the modernist crisis in the first decade of the twentieth century seem as troublesome as ever. Whether the counter-cultural emphasis on a certain nuptial mysticism, in ecclesiology and theological anthropology and elsewhere in Catholic Christian doctrine, will carry us far into the new century, remains to be seen.

These chapters derive mostly from lectures at Blackfriars, Oxford. Versions of chapter one were offered as the Saint Thomas Aquinas Lecture at the National University of Ireland, Maynooth, in March 2005; at the joint meeting of the Society for the Study of Theology and the Irish Theological Society at Drumcondra, in April 2005; and as the Glasmacher Lecture at Saint-Paul University, Ottawa, in November 2005. The chapter on Joseph Ratzinger derives from the address which I gave when receiving the Yves Congar Award at Barry University, Florida, in October 2005, while the chapter on Yves Congar comes from the Discern Annual Lecture 2005 at the Institute for Research on the Signs of the Times in Malta. My thanks go to Dr Thomas A.F. Kelly, Dr Paul D. Murray, Dr Richard Feist, Dr Ed Sunshine and Fr Mark Wedig op, and Fr Joseph Inguanez, respectively, for these invitations, and much enjoyable hospitality.

Several friends have read parts of the text. Vivian Boland op, Neil Fergu-

---

[3]   Cf. John Henry Newman's Preface to the Third Edition (1877) of *Lectures on the Prophetical Office of the Church viewed relatively to Romanism and Popular Protestantism*, in *The 'Via Media' of the Anglican Church*, edited by H.D. Weidner (Oxford: Clarendon Press 1990): 10–57, in which he sees the dynamic in the Church in terms of the threefold functions of worship, theology and rule, the first tending to 'superstition and enthusiasm', the second to 'rationalism', and the third to 'ambition, craft and cruelty', each corrected by the others ideally in 'a truce or a compromise' – 'tyranny' is Newman's word.

son OP and Rebecca Harkin read the text in draft, for which I thank them, while of course declaring them free of blame for blemishes that remain and for prejudices of mine that were not overcome. I am grateful to my friend Jacinta O'Driscoll OP for essential technical assistance and to Eileen Power for her careful and sympathetic copy-editing. I cannot resist adding a word of thanks to Larry Page and Sergey Brin, founders of the Internet search engine Google, without which my claims to learning would be even more tenuous.

Chapter One

BEFORE VATICAN II

According to Pope John Paul II, writing in 1998, 'the more distinguished of the Catholic theologians of this century, to whose reflections and researches Vatican II owes so much', were all 'educated in the school of the Angelic Doctor'.[1]

Reason under Oath

The essential thing, for Catholic theologians born between 1890 and 1940, was that they should be grounded in 'thomistic philosophy'. This was to inoculate them against infection by the idealist, subjectivist and positivist philosophies, which were held to have created 'the modernist crisis'.[2]

According to Canon Law, clergy were required to attend lectures in philosophy and theology, delivered in Latin, by professors who treated everything according to the method, doctrine and principles of the Angelic Doctor, Saint Thomas Aquinas.[3] Moreover, all clergy, pastors, seminary professors and so on, swore the Anti-modernist Oath imposed in 1910 (see

---

[1] Pope John Paul II, Encyclical Letter *Fides et Ratio*, 15 September 1998 (numerous editions): §§57–9.

[2] The literature is immense: see Darrell Jodock (ed.) *Catholicism Contending with Modernity: Roman Catholic Modernism and Anti-Modernism in Historical Context* (Cambridge: Cambridge University Press 2000).

[3] No one imagined that lay men, let alone women, could be theologians, though consider Mary Daly (born 1928), who took a different turn, but whose doctorates in philosophy and theology with the Dominicans at the University of Fribourg, Switzerland, are good examples of neoscholasticism: *The Problem of Speculative Theology* (Washington: Thomist Press 1965) and *Natural Knowledge of God in the Philosophy of Jacques Maritain* (Rome: Officium Libri Catholici 1966).

appendix). The philosophy examinations, to be passed before students proceeded to theology, were framed in terms of the Twenty-four Thomistic Theses.[4]

Paradoxically, the revival of Thomistic philosophy in the wake of Leo XIII's directive, intended to keep modern philosophy out of Catholicism, and especially German Romanticism, kept to very much the same canons of rationality as we find in the Enlightenment. The Enlightenment ideal was to attain timeless, universal and objective conclusions by exercising a unitary and ahistorical form of reasoning.[5] Similarly, neoscholastic theology 'identified truth and life with immutability and rationality; it opposed being to history and ignored concreteness in human life and in the economy of salvation'.[6] For neothomists, as for Enlightenment philosophers, appealing to experience, tradition and historical studies was the wrong way to get to truth.

The word 'modernism' settled in Catholic parlance in the early twentieth century, for example in the encyclical *Pascendi Dominici Gregis* issued by Pope Pius X in 1907. Setting aside the absurdly bombastic style of papal documents in those days, the modernism which the encyclical attacks is amazingly like postmodernism: 'Postmodernity is a style of thought which is suspicious of classical notions of truth, reason, identity and objectivity, of the idea of universal progress or emancipation, of single frameworks, grand narratives or ultimate grounds of explanation'.[7]

The Anti-modernist Oath asserts the Roman Catholic Church's commitment to intellect, and articulates fears of the effects in theology of anti-intellectualism. The existence of God, it is asserted, may be known for certain and proved by arguments from cause and effect. That is to say, we are not dependent on faith, feeling, intuition or instinct, for this belief. There are objective external criteria for the truth of Christianity; it is not all a matter of subjective psychological states. The institution of the Church, including the papacy, was founded by Jesus Christ, historically, prior to his death. There is no such thing as 'evolution of doctrine', if by this is meant change in meaning. Faith is not a 'blind feeling'; it is real assent to true propositions. Those who swear this oath endorse the anti-modernist utterances of Pope Pius X, especially in relation to 'the so-called history of dogmas'. There is no distinction between what the historian may say and

---

[4]   See www.vaxxine.com/hyoomik/aquinas/theses.eht for Latin text and translation.
[5]   Alasdair MacIntyre, *Three Rival Versions of Moral Enquiry* (London: Duckworth 1990): 65.
[6]   Thomas F. O'Meara OP, *Thomas Aquinas Theologian* (Notre Dame, IN, and London: University of Notre Dame Press 1999): 171.
[7]   T.F. Eagleton, *The Illusions of Postmodernism* (Oxford: Blackwell 1996): vii.

what the believer says, as if the truths of faith might differ from the truths of historical fact. We do not accept biblical exegesis that is supposedly 'neutral' and 'scientific'. Finally, we are most of all concerned to uphold the notion of there being *absolute* and *unchangeable* truths.

The Thomistic Theses

It is easy to see what the problem was: *the nature of truth*. Whether imposing a framework for the study of philosophy in the form of the Twenty-four Thomistic Theses was a wise move might well be questioned. To what extent the average seminary philosophy course actually conformed to the pattern seems doubtful. Most seminarians – straight from school – were in any case never destined to be competent in philosophy. They could do little more than learn the arguments off by heart, to reproduce in the brief (always oral) examinations.

The course was divided into ontology, cosmology, psychology and theodicy: dealing, then, with being, nature, soul and God, respectively.

The point of the eight theses in ontology was to secure the difference between that which is pure act and that which is composed of potency and act. Prior to any consideration of the biblical doctrine of creation, that is to say, the student learns how to explain that there is a radical difference in being between God and everything else. God is not a being in the same way as we are; God is identified as 'pure act of being', *ipsum esse subsistens*, dependent on no entity or event to be God. There is no potentiality in God; that would mean God required some other entity or event to complete Him. There is no 'possibility' in God, potential that needs to be realized. This is a matter of rational demonstration; not something we take on faith.

Some beings composed of potency and act are corporeal, and some of these have souls, as the five theses in cosmology maintain. Basically, the point here was to secure proper understanding of the (relative) autonomy of the natural order, with its intrinsic teleology. This was important: the physical world had to be shown to work on its own natural principles – it was not sustained by regular infusions of divine grace, it was not a permanent miracle. In short, natural science is possible. In some ways, cosmology was the decisive element of the curriculum which secured the Aristotelian basis of neoscholastic Thomism.

The theses in psychology maintain that the human soul is by nature immortal (Thesis 15); there is no body/soul dualism (16); yet the intellect operates independently of any bodily organ (17); our minds have direct knowledge of the natures of things (20); and the will is subordinate to the intellect (21).

The whole course culminates in the three theses in theodicy: the existence of God is demonstrable by cosmological arguments (22); the divine nature is appropriately identified as pure act or subsistent being (23); God alone may be said to create (24).

Much might be said about these theses. As the standard course books would show, cosmology included consideration of such terms as substance and accident, form and matter, the philosophical terminology required (for example) for the doctrine of transubstantiation. Theodicy, obviously, covers only the opening moves in natural theology – not extending to justifying the ways of God in the light of the problem of evil.

In psychology, the programme was to expound the metaphysical arguments that prove that we have immortal souls – it is not just a matter of faith, or intuition. Independently of whether we are to be raised from the dead, there are metaphysical arguments that demonstrate human immortality.

Second, our knowledge of things is of things as they are, not only of how they seem – we are not prey to varieties of phenomenalism that lay us open to the anxieties over whether we have knowledge of anything outside our own heads.

Finally, the existence of God is philosophically demonstrable. Here again, we are not dependent on intuitionism, *a priori* considerations or mere faith. It is possible to *reason* one's way to the truth that God exists – this is not a truth that we learn from the testimony or on the authority of others, nor one that wells up from within, as the product of instinct, feeling or intuition.

In short, theologians were expected to take their stand on the realist metaphysics, philosophy of science, epistemology and natural theology, framed no doubt somewhat abstractly by the Thomistic Theses – which nonetheless show that the Christian faith, at least in its Catholic form, is not against all reason. On the contrary, as every Thomist knows, 'Grace does not obliterate nature but perfects it, just as natural reason subserves faith and the natural inclination of the will yields to charity' (*Summa Theologiæ* 1a. 1, 8 ad 2m).

In their own way, the pastors of the Roman Catholic Church were determined to uphold the claims of reason against a generation of theologians whom they suspected of opting rather for the authority of intuition, testimony, tradition, and especially 'experience'.[8] The history of twentieth-century Catholic theology is the history of the attempted elimination of

---

[8]   Alessandro Maggiolini, 'Magisterial teaching on experience in the twentieth century: from the Modernist crisis to the Second Vatican Council', *Communio* 23 (1996): 224–43.

theological modernism, by censorship, sackings and excommunication – and the resurgence of issues that could not be repressed by such methods.

Modernism

The easiest access to the problem set by theological modernism is *Medievalism*, the very readable book published in 1908 by the former Jesuit George Tyrrell (1861–1909).[9] Born in Dublin, raised Anglican, he became a Catholic in London in 1879 and entered the Society of Jesus. Set to teach philosophy to Jesuit students he was soon transferred to other duties (journalism, conducting retreats), on the grounds that he was sponsoring 'pure Thomism' rather than the required 'Suárezianism'. His writings became steadily more unorthodox. He was expelled from the Society in 1906. He died of Bright's disease, 'fortified by the rites of the Church', absolved by three priests, denied a Catholic funeral (however) by the bishop since none could say that he 'recanted'.[10]

Cardinal Mercier, Archbishop of Malines and Primate of Belgium, had addressed his flock on the subject of modernism.[11] Why, when he assures them that the heresies, principally in France and Italy, had scarcely a single adherent in Belgium, remains mysterious. Modernism, anyway, Mercier says, is the view that believers draw the object and motive of their faith from themselves, denying historically revealed truth and thus also the teaching authority of the Church. Modernism is a form of Protestantism: faith understood as 'private judgment'. This Protestant spirit has infected Catholic consciousness. Mercier singles out 'the English priest Tyrrell'. Again, why he did so, since few churchgoers in Belgium could have known of his existence, let alone of his writings, remains puzzling.[12]

Undaunted, indeed exhilarated, by this personal attack, Tyrrell, with

---

[9] Third revised and enlarged edition 1909 reprinted with foreword by Gabriel Daly (Tunbridge Wells: Burns and Oates 1994).

[10] Cf. Ellen M. Leonard, *George Tyrrell and the Catholic Tradition* (London: Darton, Longman and Todd 1982); Nicholas Sagovsky, *'On God's Side': A Life of George Tyrrell* (Oxford: Clarendon Press 1990).

[11] Désiré Mercier (1851–1926), the first professor of Thomist Philosophy at Louvain, was an ardent promoter of neoscholasticism and a valiant opponent of the German occupation of Belgium in 1914–18. He set up the Malines Conversations 1921–5, cut short by his death, to respond to the Anglo-Catholic reunion initiative.

[12] Abbot Columba Marmion of Maredsous had approached Mercier about accepting Tyrrell for incardination in Malines diocese; grateful for Mercier's interest, Tyrrell would not accept his conditions (no preaching or publishing).

Mercier's permission, translated the pastoral so that he could reply. After some polite remarks he went on the offensive: 'In spite of all their theological heresies and divisions, the religious interest still lives and grows in Protestant countries, whereas it languishes and dies among Catholics under this modern craze for centralization and military uniformity'.[13] Whatever the Cardinal says, it is the vitality of faith that is the source and criterion of doctrinal truth, which is not the same thing as individual subjectivity. Indeed, if there is a subjectivism threatening the Church, it is the 'individualistic conception of papal authority'. Since 1870, catechisms and seminary textbooks have been revised to impose the heresy of ultramontanism — 'to destroy the constitution of the Church; to make ornamental nonentities of the bishops; and to substitute, as the rule of faith, the private judgment of the Pope instead of the public judgment of the whole Church as represented by the entire episcopate'.[14] The lay Catholic's place is not just 'to receive the faith passively as one receives a traveller's tale of regions beyond his ken; a tale which he repeats to others word for word for what it is worth, but with no guarantee of personal experience or conviction'. On the contrary, 'the laity are part of the Church': 'You forget that every baptized Christian is commissioned apostle and teacher; and as such is no mere telephone, but must speak from the fulness of a living personal interest in the truth of his religion'.[15] Of course there is a distinction between the 'Church Teaching' and the 'Church Taught' — the hierarchy and the faithful. However, priority lies with 'a Divine Tradition of which the entire Church, and not merely the episcopate, is the organ and depositary'. 'Tradition is the faith that lives in the whole Church and is handed down from generation to generation, of which the entire body, and not a mere handful of officials, is the depositary and organ of transmission. Of this rule and law the Holy Spirit diffused in the hearts of the faithful is the author; the episcopate merely the servant, the witness, the interpreter'.[16] Tyrrell attacks the 'new theology', according to which a bishop in his diocese is merely the delegate or vicar of the Bishop of Rome. He defends the Church of England ('We have much to learn from her'). He mocks the idea that he is 'leader' of any movement. Finally, his 'method of immanentism', which Mercier denounces, is indebted, not to crypto-Kantian Protestantism, as alleged, but to the *Exercises* of St Ignatius of Loyola.[17]

---

13   *Medievalism*: 43.
14   Ibid: 50.
15   Ibid: 59.
16   Ibid: 61.
17   Ibid: 104.

Tyrrell writes with gusto. He was a journalist, not a scholar, as he might have agreed. In *Through Scylla and Charybdis* (1907) he sympathizes with a symbolic approach to religious truth, which deprives the concept of truth of its meaning; and in the posthumous *Christianity at the Cross-Roads* he envisages Christianity as developing into a universal religion. In these books he moves well beyond Catholic orthodoxy. In *Medievalism*, however, he raised real questions, albeit in an inflammatory manner. They would have to be dealt with: governance in the Church; the dignity and role of laity; and the concepts of experience and tradition as loci of truth.

He was not forgotten at Vatican II. On 1 October 1963, in a powerful speech, Ernesto Ruffini, Cardinal Archbishop of Palermo, a major figure at the Council, informed the assembly that the idea of the Church as a sacrament came from Tyrrell. He was probably indebted to Joseph C. Fenton, the most eminent American theologian at the Council, who complained that the whole of the first chapter of *Lumen Gentium*, the document on the nature of the Church, was composed in the language of Tyrrell. That the Church as hierarchical institution (chapter 3) should be treated after the Church as mystery (chapter 1) and as people of God (chapter 2) would surely have seemed to Tyrrell a good way of laying out the doctrine. That the likes of Ruffini and Fenton, significant members of the ultramontanist minority at Vatican II, should find *Lumen Gentium* to reek of modernist heresy is, however, a salutary thought.[18]

Alternatives to Neoscholasticism

Even during the decades when Thomist philosophy was mandatory, many significant theologians worked on quite different lines. In Germany, for example, neither Karl Adam (1876–1966) nor Romano Guardini (1885–1968) was Thomist, in any sense.

Karl Adam, trained as a patristic scholar at the University of Munich, with books on Tertullian's concept of church (1907) and Augustine's doctrine of the eucharist (1908), taught all his life at Tübingen. Building on the legacy of the Catholic Tübingen School,[19] he presented the Church as primarily a

---

[18]   G. Alberigo and J.A. Komonchak (eds.) *History of Vatican II*, vol. III *The Mature Council Second Period and Intersession September 1963–September 1964* (Maryknoll, NY: Orbis, and Leuven: Peeters 2000): 50 (Ruffini), 30 (Fenton).

[19]   For the Catholic Tübingen School see James Tunstead Burtchaell csc, in Ninian Smart and others (eds.) *Nineteenth Century Religious Thought in the West* (Cambridge: Cambridge University Press 1985): 111–39.

community, indeed as 'mystical body of Christ', contrasting this quite deliberately with the prevailing neoscholastic image of the Church as a 'perfect
society', and, on the other extreme, with liberal Protestantism's fuzzy eccle-
siologies. In the 1920s he contributed to the development of 'kerygmatic
theology', *Verkündigungstheologie*, in this instance steering between the syl-
logistically expounded Christology of neoscholastic textbooks and the 'life-
of-Jesus research' of liberal Protestantism.

Adam, delated to Rome (need it be said?), revised several of his books to
reduce suspicions of his orthodoxy. Like others in the Tübingen tradition,
with its Romantic emphasis on community, he was attracted, initially, in the
early 1930s, to the patriotism and family values proclaimed by the National
Socialist German Workers' Party. Too old to play a part in the run-up to
Vatican II, his books nevertheless helped to prepare some of his compatriots
for the unexpectedly radical event.[20]

Romano Guardini, Italian by birth, grew up in Mainz.[21] He studied at
Freiburg im Breisgau and Tübingen, before going to the diocesan seminary,
where he found the neoscholastic textbooks insufferable. Back in Freiburg
for doctoral studies, he worked on Bonaventure's teaching on redemption.[22]
This choice of topic, and unconcealed scorn for neoscholasticism, prevented
his being appointed, as he had expected, to teach in the diocesan seminary.
Anyway, parish ministry soon gave way to military service as a medical
orderly (1916–18). In 1918, through his sympathy with the Benedictine-
inspired liturgical movement in Germany, he published his first, immensely
influential book, *Vom Geist der Liturgie*. He was involved with the Catholic
youth movement, centred at Burg Rothenfels. In 1923, he accepted a newly
established chair in Berlin, though his Protestant colleagues were so un-
welcoming that he agreed to the fiction that he was a visiting professor from
Breslau. In March 1939, the Nazi regime abolished the post, forbade his
ministry with youth, and in 1941 banned him from speaking in public.
Among the first academics to be reinstated, he taught at Tübingen, before
joining the philosophy faculty at the University of Munich, where he
remained until retirement in 1962. He took part in the pre-Vatican II
liturgy commission though not in the Council itself. While seeing that the

---

[20] See Robert A. Krieg, *Karl Adam: Catholicism in German Culture* (Notre Dame, IN, and
London: University of Notre Dame Press 1992).
[21] See Robert A. Krieg, *Romano Guardini: A Precursor of Vatican II* (Notre Dame, IN, and
London: University of Notre Dame Press 1997).
[22] Supervised by Engelbert Krebs (1881–1950), who conducted his friend Heidegger's
wedding in 1917; primarily a medievalist, he was removed from teaching by the Nazis in
1938.

Council accepted much of the agenda that he had stood for all his life, he was sceptical about the likely results. He refused Pope Paul VI's invitation to become a cardinal.

Immensely influential, with dozens of books, Guardini never engaged with historical-critical biblical exegesis. He wrote about the Church without referring to Vatican I. He wrote manifestly Catholic theology without frequently citing papal encyclicals, as was the style of the day. Relating theology to culture and literature, he wrote on Dostoevsky, Pascal, Dante, Hölderlin, Rilke, and much else.

That neither Karl Adam nor Romano Guardini belonged to any religious order, is no accident – nor that they had tenure in German universities.

Neoscholasticism

In most seminaries and universities throughout the Catholic world, however, philosophy and theology were taught strictly *ad mentem Sancti Thomæ.* The best account, by Anthony Kenny, recalls his experience at the Gregoriana, the great Jesuit university in Rome, from 1949 to 1956.[23] He recalls Paolo Dezza, the Professor of Metaphysics: 'sitting totally motionless, he enunciated rheumily, in a barely audible voice, theses about the analogy of being and the varieties of potentiality and actuality'. Later, in his theology years, so Kenny reports, neither the Bible nor the *Summa Theologiæ* was much studied. He did not appreciate Bernard Lonergan then as he did later, for his Aquinas books: he 'lectured with an air of boredom that quickly communicated itself to his audience'. He recalls Maurizio Flick on the theology of grace, 'the best lecturer I have heard in a lifetime of lecture-going' (no small compliment from an Oxford don).

Classes were huge. No one studied primary sources. Cyclostyled lecture notes became available as technology advanced. The bright students relied on secondary literature, in Latin, such as the textbooks of Gredt[24] and Billot.

Joseph August Gredt (1863–1940), born in Luxembourg, a Benedictine monk, studied in Rome with Dominican Thomists such as Alberto Lepidi, and Tommaso Zigliara. He taught philosophy in Rome for 40 years. Interested in physics and biology, he became a legend for his two-volume textbook, *Elementa philosophiæ aristotelico-thomisticæ*, 1899 and 1901, reissued in expanded editions into the 1960s, 'the classical textbook of thomistic

---

[23] *A Path from Rome: An Autobiography* (London: Sidgwick and Jackson 1985): 47 (Dezza), 77 (Lonergan), 77 (Flick).
[24] Cf. A.W. Müller, in *New Catholic Encyclopedia* VI (1967): 725.

philosophy', still in use 20 years after his death. Gredt's position was worked out in opposition to external-world scepticism and the other problems of post-Cartesian philosophy. The problematic should not be unfamiliar to student theologians.

Louis Billot (1846–1931), a French Jesuit, taught for years in Rome. He is perhaps best remembered for resigning as Cardinal in 1927, unable to accept the papal condemnation of the ultra-rightwing movement *Action Française*. Billot's books, massive and well documented, from his *De Verbo incarnato* (1892) onwards, constitute by far the most impressive body of Catholic theology as it existed at the beginning of the twentieth century, covering all the main topics. Neglected, if not completely forgotten, Billot's work would need to be explored in any attempt to write a balanced and comprehensive history of modern Catholic theology, which would do justice to all sides.

Thomism at the Angelicum

The model Thomist – not only in Dominican mythology – was Réginald Garrigou-Lagrange.[25] Born in 1877, he had a conversion, while a medical student, through reading work by Ernest Hello (1828–85), the somewhat maverick, radically conservative ultramontanist Breton writer. He joined the French Dominicans, studied and taught at Le Saulchoir before moving to Rome, where he lectured at the Collegio Angelico, the Dominican university, from 1909 until he retired in 1960. He supervised the doctoral research of M.-D. Chenu and the future Pope John Paul II. He gave the retreat in Paris which attracted Yves Congar to leave the diocesan seminary in order to join the Dominicans. He was a controversial figure, much admired but also often caricatured, even demonized. His big book on God, for example, is not as dreadful as some have asserted: 'the God of the Bible and the Gospel has been reduced to a *caput mortuum* of frozen abstractions . . . overwhelmingly boring . . . nothing but a gigantic and futile exercise in tautology'.[26]

For Garrigou-Lagrange, Thomas Aquinas's work – chiefly the *Summa*

---

[25] Cf. Richard Peddicord, *The Sacred Monster of Thomism: An Introduction to the Life and Legacy of Reginald Garrigou-Lagrange* OP (South Bend, IN: St Austin's Press 2005).
[26] Thus Louis Bouyer (1913–2004), formerly a Lutheran pastor, priest of the French Oratory, himself a major theologian, Newman scholar and liturgist, who never endured seminary neoscholasticism: cf. *The Invisible Father: Approaches to the Mystery of the Divinity* (Edinburgh: T&T Clark 1999): 248.

Theologiæ – was an unsurpassed and unsurpassable speculative theological achievement. It might, and indeed should, be studied in the light of the clarifications offered by a select band of sixteenth-century commentators. There was, however, no point in paying much attention to how his thought interacted with that of his contemporaries or how it was shaped by his inheritance from earlier Christian thinkers (let alone Jewish and Muslim ones). On the other hand, good students should work on Aristotle and Aquinas's commentaries on Aristotle. Otherwise, knowing nothing of Aquinas's grandeur as a metaphysician, they would misunderstand him completely.

Natural Metaphysics

There was no way of entering Catholic theology without first doing philosophy – learning to master the doctrine laid out in the 'perennial philosophy', and, secondarily, laying bare and refuting all the wrong philosophies. In the key text, *La synthèse thomiste* (1946) we can see Garrigou-Lagrange at his most characteristic.[27]

As regards the positive exposition, the author insists that, in Aristotle, Aquinas discovered the 'natural metaphysics of human intelligence', a metaphysics which, beginning with sense experience, rises progressively until it reaches God, *actus purus* and *noesis noeseos*, 'sheer being' in Aquinas's phrase, and 'self-knowing' in Aristotle's. As this argument unfolds it delivers a philosophy of being, an ontology, differing entirely from philosophies of appearance (phenomenalism), of becoming (evolutionism), and of the ego (psychologism). Phenomenalism is still on the market, the others we might be inclined to relabel as process thought and subjectivism; but the main aim of philosophical studies for neophyte theologians had to be to establish for themselves a moderate form of metaphysical, epistemological and moral realism.

Being, reality, which is what intellect first apprehends, is not the being of God, nor the being of the cognizing subject, Garrigou-Lagrange insists. In other words, he suspects that the neophytes are strongly tempted to think that either God or oneself is the primary datum of knowledge. Against this, so he contends, we have to see that being, reality, exists in the sense-perceptible world. This means that knowledge of God's existence and nature is mediated: in knowing things in the world we can argue from effect

---

[27] *Reality: A Synthesis of Thomistic Thought* (St Louis, MO: Herder 1952): the rest of this chapter summarizes this book.

to cause – but it is the world that we know in the first place. We do not have some basic innate knowledge of God nor any knowledge of our own consciousness, prior to our engagement with things in the world we inhabit. It is only by reflection on its own act of knowing things that the intellect comes to know the existence of its cognitive acts and thus of its being a subject, a centre of consciousness.

The 'moderate realism' of Aristotle and Aquinas is in harmony with common sense, which is to say: our natural, spontaneous knowledge. This harmony appears most clearly in the objective validity of first principles, which are laws, not of the mind only, mere logical laws, nor laws restricted to phenomena, merely experimental, as the neophytes seem to be inclined to believe – rather, these are necessary laws of being, objective laws of all reality, of all that is or can be.

Rising immediately from the idea of being is the first principle, which is the principle of non-contradiction: the articulation of opposition between being and nothing. 'Being is not nothing', we may say; 'one and the same thing, remaining such, cannot simultaneously both be and not be'. Positively considered, then, this is the principle of identity: 'If a thing is, it is: if it is not, it is not'. To this principle of non-contradiction is subordinated the principle of sufficient reason: 'Everything that is, has its *raison d'être*, in itself, if of itself it exists; in something else, if of itself it does not exist'.

These are the principles of our natural intelligence, first manifested in that spontaneous form of intelligence which we call common sense, that is, the natural aptitude of intelligence, to judge things sanely – *before we have been initiated into a certain philosophical culture.*

Exposition of the principles of ontology takes up the greater part of Garrigou-Lagrange's book. It cannot be said to be easy going. On the contrary, it seems, at least to an analytic philosopher's eye, all too much like the exposition, highly abstract and syllogistic, of a set of quasi-Euclidean theorems. The communication of metaphysical principles seems very much like setting out the rules of a game. From the point of view of a more text-based way of studying philosophy, metaphysics seems treated like a kind of mathematics. On the historical side, concepts seem to come from nowhere, they have no background or context. One way to keep one's head up, however, is to keep reminding oneself that, for Garrigou-Lagrange, the abstract structure which he expounds is actually intended to seem perfectly natural, once we clear away the mistaken philosophical theories which distort and occlude our common sense. His metaphysics, one may say, is intended to let things appear to us as they would if our minds were not clouded by philosophical theorizings.

Alternative Philosophies

This becomes much easier to grasp when we come to the three principal tendencies that characterize contemporary philosophy, as Garrigou-Lagrange lists them:

1   agnosticism, which includes the neo-positivism of Carnap, Wittgenstein, Rougier, and of the group called the Vienna Circle, which is the nominalism of Hume and Comte rehashed.[28] Here, too, belongs the phenomenology of Husserl, which holds that the object of philosophy is the immediate datum of experience. All these philosophies are concerned, then, not with being, reality, but with phenomena, 'appearances'.
2   evolutionism, which, in the wake of Hegel, takes the form of idealism, represented by Gentile in Italy, and by Leon Brunschvicg in France; and when given a twist towards the empirical, coming out as the creative evolution of Bergson.
3   the modern German school – rather a mixed bag, it has to be said – voluntarism as in Max Scheler; natural philosophy in Driesch, who (however) leans on Aristotle; and ontology in Hartmann, who gives a Platonic twist to Aristotle's metaphysics – accordingly, for a Thomist like Garrigou-Lagrange, these philosophies are worth engaging with, precisely where they limp towards Aristotle and Plato.

Garrigou-Lagrange's map of modern philosophy need not be accepted in every detail. Nonetheless, as a rough guide, he is by no means completely at sea. On the contrary, he had a more informed and better-balanced picture than many philosophers, let alone Thomists, had at the time.

Theology without Thomistic Philosophy

What goes wrong when Catholic theologians turn away from metaphysics? Lip service is, of course, paid to Thomas Aquinas, Garrigou-Lagrange says, sarcastically. Catholic theologians have to pretend to be Thomists. Yet, he asks rhetorically, is one a Thomist by accepting the dogmas defined by the Church, while following Descartes on the spiritual life – by privatizing one's relationship with God? Or while, with Hume, denying the principle of

---

[28]   Louis Rougier (1889–1982), the French link with the Vienna Circle, a sort of logical empiricist, organized the Paris International Congress of Scientific Philosophy 1935.

causality and hence the validity of cosmological proofs for the existence of God?

Ah – we might naively ask – are not the truths of common sense a sufficient foundation for Catholic philosophers and theologians? Indeed they are, Garrigou-Lagrange replies, warming to his theme – the problem is that the truths of common sense are too often overlaid by modern philosophical theorizings. The minds of neophyte theologians, so he thinks, are so soaked in phenomenalism, idealism, positivism, pragmatism, and so on, that, without serious engagement with these philosophies, they remain under their spell, which means in the end that they discount reason.

He then goes off into something of a rant. When theologians choose history of doctrine as their specialism, and abandon metaphysics, which he seems to regard as the unavoidable effect, then relativism creeps into the teaching of doctrine. Pope Pius X was right to highlight, in many Catholic theologians, in his day, a gaping void: the lack of philosophy. Nearly fifty years later, in the 1950s, so Garrigou-Lagrange thinks, the same void lies gaping open.

Recently, for example, Garrigou-Lagrange reports, one theologian has asserted that, while speculative theology no doubt produced beautiful systems in the Middle Ages, it no longer has a role: serious work is now all in positive theology – historical scholarship, that is to say – rather than in metaphysical system-building. Another proposes to put the treatise on the Trinity before the *de Deo uno*, which in any case he would cut down to size. As regards the relationship between nature and grace, another would return to what he holds to be the true position of the Greek Fathers before the time of Augustine – as if the labours of Aquinas, and seven centuries of Thomists, were of no value! For the likes of Garrigou-Lagrange, there was no point in studying earlier authors whose work was absorbed into, or rendered redundant by, Aquinas's achievement.

Pragmatism is a great temptation: 'A doctrine according to which truth is a relation, entirely immanent to human experience, whereby knowledge is subordinated to activity, and the truth of a proposition consists in its utility and satisfactoriness'.[29] Dogma becomes a norm, regulatory, a practical prescription: 'In your relations with God, act as you do in your relations with people'. Dogma, that is to say, would not be true by its conforming to transcendent divine reality, but by its relation to the internal religious experience of the person. 'The dogmas of faith are to be retained only in the practical sense, i.e.: as preceptive norms of action, but not as norms of belief' – which is a thesis that has been condemned by the Church (§1371).

---

[29] *Reality*: §1367. Subsequent page references for quotations are given in the text.

Garrigou-Lagrange becomes extremely eloquent. Are we to suppose that the dogma of the Incarnation affirms that Jesus is God, a statement of fact – or a pious exhortation, that we must act towards Jesus 'as if' he were God? Is Christ really present in the eucharist, or do we only act as if he were so? Succumbing to the allurements of pragmatism, he fears, we forget how to understand dogmas defined by the Church as true, immutable, and as conforming to the extramental reality, which they express. What they express is not our religious experience. As regards the dogma of the Incarnation, Garrigou-Lagrange asks, with rough humour, 'Who can claim to *experience* the hypostatic union?' We may experience, not the mystery itself, but its effects in us – if you like: 'The Spirit Himself giveth testimony to our spirit that we are the sons of God' (§1384). Thomas Aquinas would agree to that, no doubt allowing that the Spirit evokes in us a filial affection, which (if you like) you may say you 'experience'. Yet even this 'experience', Garrigou-Lagrange says, deflatingly, would be difficult to distinguish from mere sentimental affection.

Bemused by this pragmatist conception of truth, another theologian has claimed that theology is at bottom a spirituality, which has found concepts adequate to its religious experience. This position comes from the German Romantic Tübingen School, and especially from Johann Adam Möhler. Here, however, as we shall see in the next chapter, Garrigou-Lagrange is attacking his former student Marie-Dominique Chenu. This is the claim that Thomist theology would be the expression of Dominican spirituality, Scotism that of Franciscan spirituality, Molinism that of Ignatian spirituality, and so on. These three schools of spirituality, it would be said, are tolerated in the Catholic Church, and so the theologies, which are their conceptual expressions, each being in conformity with the particular religious experience, which is its source, would all be equally 'true'. At times, however, Garrigou-Lagrange protests, these theologies contradict one another – what is to be said about this?

This 'spiritualization' of theology, reducing it to a religious experience, deprives it of all 'scientific' objectivity. This is the morass into which we are led if we abandon the notion of truth as conformity with objective reality, proposing rather to define truth as conformity with constantly developing experience, moral and religious. To abandon the traditional conception of truth as correspondence with reality is to unsettle all foundations, not only in theology, in metaphysics, but also in the sciences, and in faith: 'The enthusiasm of hope and charity, if it is not to remain a beautiful dream of religious emotion, must rest on a faith which is in conformity with reality, not merely with the exigencies of our inner life, or even with our best intentions'.

Back, then, to where we were before, so Garrigou-Lagrange counsels us. Action, practice, experience, can never be the first criterion of what is true. Rather, the first criterion must be ontological, that objective reality from which reason draws first principles. The first act of the intellect is to know, not its own action, not the ego, not phenomena, but objective and intelligible being (§1398).

Unless would-be theologians free themselves of the philosophies by which Garrigou-Lagrange takes it for granted they are captivated, their theology will inevitably subvert true Catholic doctrine.

Conclusion

Much more might be said, of course. Garrigou-Lagrange published many books on dogmatic theology and spirituality. His exposition of Thomistic philosophy of being, one may concede, is so abstract as to be almost impossible for beginners nowadays to get into. What he perhaps intended as merely a supplementary historical sketch of the types of philosophy in vogue when he was writing is a far more accessible point of entry into the questions about truth and reality, realism, idealism, phenomenalism, and so on, which any would-be Catholic theologian still needs to sort out. Ironically, when this inveterate adversary of the historico-contextualist approach considers the philosophical options adopted by philosophers in his own day, he becomes a model of how to engage with the philosophical issues about being, truth, and so on, which may perhaps always remain on the theologian's agenda, but which, in any case, haunt the theologies we are now to examine. The next step is to consider how differently the thought of Thomas Aquinas was approached by Garrigou-Lagrange's pupil: Marie-Dominique Chenu.

Chapter Two

MARIE-DOMINIQUE CHENU

While Garrigou-Lagrange wanted him to remain in Rome, in 1920, as his assistant at the Angelicum, the young Chenu chose rather to return to Le Saulchoir, the French Dominican college then in exile in Belgium.[1] The younger man wanted to develop a radically different way of reading Thomas Aquinas from the one inculcated at the Angelicum. The conflict of interpretations which divided them so bitterly soon emerged.

Marcel-Leon Chenu was born on 7 January 1895 at Soisy-sur-Seine, and died in Paris on 11 February 1990. His parents, bakers near Corbeil, eventually running a metalworking business, were never free of financial anxieties. His maternal grandparents, state school teachers, especially his grandmother, encouraged his aptitude for study. As a 15-year-old, visiting Le Saulchoir, he fell in love with what he saw as 'a very beautiful liturgy with a life of study and a community discipline'.[2] He just missed meeting Garrigou-Lagrange, already gone to Rome. In 1913, after some months in a diocesan seminary, he was clothed as a Dominican friar, receiving the name Marie-Dominique, according to the custom in those days. Unfit for military service, he was packed off to Rome in late 1914, with others, when the German advance into Belgium led to the suspension of teaching at Le Saulchoir. Thus Chenu completed the whole seven years of neoscholastic philosophy and theology at the Angelicum. Réginald Garrigou-Lagrange supervised his doctorate dissertation. In Latin, of course, it is an analysis of

---

[1] Despite Pope Leo XIII's call to French Catholics to support the Republic they failed to do so, leading, especially under Emile Combes, prime minister 1902–5, to a serious attempt to destroy the power of the Church, and to the exile of religious orders.

[2] For details see Christophe F. Potworowski, *Contemplation and Incarnation: The Theology of Marie-Dominique Chenu* (Montreal and Kingston: McGill-Queen's University Press 2001), with bibliography listing 1,396 items.

what Aquinas says about contemplation, motivated, however, by the desire to challenge the assumption (then), allegedly, that spirituality is primarily to do with a person's soul and overcoming sin, rather than concerned with contemplative self-submission to the objectivity of God.[3] In effect, this reconstruction of Aquinas's account of contemplation was designed to retrieve a theocentric conception of Christian spirituality over against modern, at any rate late nineteenth-century, concentration on the state of the individual's spiritual progress.

After these years in Rome, which he found uncongenial, Chenu was impatient to get back to Le Saulchoir. His reluctance to work with Garrigou-Lagrange, however, suggests that he already had a different way of expounding Aquinas in mind. Back at Le Saulchoir, his first course (to fellow Dominicans little younger than himself) was on 'the patristic sources of the thought of St Thomas'. This was not unprecedented, and in any case he was charged with teaching the history of doctrine, not with any of the main courses on dogmatic and moral theology. These were, of course, taught by more experienced professors, and took the form (well into the 1960s) of line-by-line exposition of the *Summa Theologiæ*, with reference to the commentary by Cajetan but with little or no allusion to the sources of Aquinas's views, in patristic or other literature.

In ten years, what began as an ancillary course by a junior professor entirely redirected the way of reading Aquinas. In 1936–7 Chenu lectured on Bonaventure's *Itinerarium Mentis in Deum*: obviously not only relating Aquinas to his greatest contemporary but also implying that, in its own quite different way, the *Summa Theologiæ* could, and should, be read as a kind of 'journey of the mind into the divine mystery'.[4] Just as challengingly, we find Chenu lecturing, in 1938–9, on 'Augustine and Denys: the two Platonisms of St Thomas'.[5] The difference between the theologies of Aquinas and Bonaventure expressed a difference in 'spiritualities'. The contribution of Denys and Augustine was as significant as that of Aristotle in shaping Aquinas's work. In these, and several other ways, Chenu's ancillary course edged out the standard way of expounding Aquinas. From the start he broke completely with the style of expounding the Thomist synthesis as practised by Garrigou-Lagrange.

---

[3] '*De contemplatione* (Angelicum 1920), La Thèse inédite du P. M.-D. Chenu', edited by Carmelo Giuseppe Conticello, *Revue des Sciences Philosophiques et Théologiques* 75 (1991): 363–422: extracts, with commentary.
[4] For the finest account along these lines: A.N. Williams, 'Mystical Theology Redux: The Pattern of Aquinas's *Summa Theologiæ*', in *Modern Theology* 13 (1997): 53–74.
[5] Cf. Fran O'Rourke, 'Aquinas and Platonism', in Fergus Kerr OP (ed.) *Contemplating Aquinas: On the Varieties of Interpretation* (London: SCM Press 2003): 247–79.

In effect, Chenu was denying any need to master Thomistic philosophy before being allowed to enter into Aquinas's work as a whole. Older colleagues at Le Saulchoir, as well as Garrigou-Lagrange, were dismayed at what seemed to them neglect of speculative theology in favour of ('mere') historical scholarship, the slippery slope to relativistic notions of truth and thus to modernism. Chenu was undismayed. In 1937 he issued a manifesto: *Une École de théologie: Le Saulchoir.* He had just passed the STM examination, the highest degree within the Dominican Order. He had been appointed Regent, head of the college. At 42 he was on the brink of great things. The college itself had just been granted the right to award pontifical degrees, in addition to internal Dominican qualifications. The result of his manifesto, however, was a summons to Rome in 1938 to be interrogated by a handful of his fellow Dominicans, headed by Garrigou-Lagrange. They bullied him so severely that: 'I gave in to a sort of psychological pressure, I let myself be intimidated. One of them − no doubt to pacify Roman irritations − asked me to sign a series of ten propositions. I signed'.[6]

Clearly, as a glance at them shows, in their fabulous absurdity, the propositions reveal the senior Dominicans' fear that Chenu's emphasis on recreating the historical context meant that truth was not 'absolute and immutable'; that theology was only an expression of religious experience and not a 'true science'; and so on. It may seem incredible that grown men would come up with the proposition that 'It is glorious for the Church to have the system of Saint Thomas as truly orthodox', and suchlike, and

---

[6]   The ten propositions Chenu signed were as follows: 1 Formulæ dogmaticæ enunciant veritatem absolutam et immutabilem. 2 Propositiones veræ et certæ, sive in philosophia sive in theologia, firmæ sunt et nullo modo fragiles. 3 Sacra Traditio novas veritates non creat, sed firmiter tenendum ut depositum revelationis, seu complexum veritatum divinitus revelatarum, clausum fuisse morte ultimi apostoli. 4 Sacra Theologia non est quædam spiritualitas quæ invenit instrumenta suæ experientiæ religiosæ adæquata; sed est vera scientia, Deo benedicente, studio acquisita, cujus principia sunt articuli Fidei et etiam omnes veritates revelatæ quibus theologus fide divina, saltem informi, adhæret. 5 Varia systemata theologica, quoad ea in quibus ab invicem dissentiunt non sunt simul vera. 6 Gloriosum est Ecclesiam habere systema S. Thomæ tamquam valde orthodoxum, i.e. veritatibus Fide valde conforme. 7 Necesse est veritates theologicas per S. Scripturam et traditionem demonstrare, necnon earum naturam et intimam rationem principiis et doctrina S. Thomæ illustrare. 8 S. Thomas, etsi proprie theologus, proprie etiam philosophus fuit; proinde, philosophia eius in sua intelligibilitate et veritate non pendet ab ejus theologia, nec enunciat veritates mere relativas sed absolutas. 9 Theologo in processu scientifico suo valde necessarium est metaphysicam S. Thomæ adhibere et ad regulas dialecticæ diligenter attendere. 10 De aliis scriptoribus et doctoribus probatis servandum est moderamen reverentiale in modo loquendi et scribendi, etiamsi in quibusdam defectum inveniuntur. The Latin needs no translation; it would sound even more absurd in English; the text is in the hand, it is said, of Michael Browne (see facsimile, *Une École de théologie: le Saulchoir* (Paris: Cerf 1985): 35).

badger Chenu into putting his signature to such poppycock – but that is symptomatic of the theological pathology of those days.

Chenu's critics, besides Garrigou-Lagrange, included Mariano Cordovani (1883–1950), then recently appointed Master of the Sacred Palace, personal theologian to the pope; and Michael Browne (1887–1971), Rector of the Angelicum and future Master of the Dominican Order and a leader of the ultramontanist minority at Vatican II. These three were formidable theologians, determined enemies of any tendency in Catholic theology that could be accused of modernism, and very capable exponents of the Aristotelian-Thomist synthesis. Their views were certainly representative of the majority of Chenu's fellow Dominicans at the time.

In 1942, in German-occupied Paris, Chenu heard on the radio that his little manifesto was now on the Index of Prohibited Books.[7] Thomas Philippe, formerly a colleague at Le Saulchoir but teaching in Rome since 1936, arrived with authority from the Master of the Order to deprive Chenu of his post as Regent at Le Saulchoir (back in France, in the south-east suburbs of Paris, since 1938), denouncing him explicitly as a 'modernist', for playing down the role of reason in doing theology, and advocating the study of Tübingen School theologians, in particular of Johann Adam Möhler.[8]

Chenu never again taught at Le Saulchoir. Friends got him a post at the École des Hautes Études in Paris, which only confirmed the judgement that, while perhaps suited to historical research, he was not a reliable exponent of Aquinas. By then, however, as a friar-preacher, he was involved with the beginnings of the worker-priest movement, and its attempt to evangelize the anti-clerical industrial suburbs of Paris. Eventually, in 1953, Chenu was among the French Dominicans disciplined by the Master of their Order (Suárez), supposedly to save them from worse treatment by the Vatican.[9]

Never an official 'expert' at Vatican II, but employed as adviser to French-speaking African bishops, Chenu instigated the Message to the World (20 October 1962), on the grounds that the Council should display from the outset that the Church is concerned not only with herself but principally with the destiny of the world. He had a good deal to do with the

---

[7]   Created by the Congregation of the Inquisition in 1557 to control literature contrary to faith or morals; abandoned in 1966.
[8]   Thomas Philippe (1905–93) later became chaplain to an institution for men with disabilities, which subsequently inspired Jean Vanier to found L'Arche, an international network of such communities.
[9]   For this shameful story see François Leprieur, *Quand Rome condamne: Dominicains et prêtres-ouvriers* (Paris: Plon/Cerf 1989).

'optimism' of the constitution *Gaudium et Spes*, the document on 'The Church and the Modern World'.

In the aftermath, Chenu was more dismayed by the failure to implement the reforms that he expected, rather than by the surrender to the attractions of secularism that distressed many others in his generation. He died in Paris on 11 February 1990, receiving a splendid funeral in Notre-Dame, with many bishops in attendance.

Baroque Scholasticism

Chenu, then, completed the full seven years of mandatory Thomistic philosophy and theology at one of the leading institutions in Rome. The worst excesses of the anti-modernist campaign were curbed when Pius X died and was succeeded in September 1914 by Benedict XV.[10] Louis Billot SJ, recently retired from his chair at the Gregorian University, was by far the most authoritative theological presence in town.[11] The Anti-modernist Oath and the Twenty-four Thomistic Theses had recently been imposed (in 1910 and 1914 respectively). Years later, Chenu would admit to remaining marked by the Twenty-four Theses. The imposition of the Theses on all doctorate candidates he saw as one of the worst abuses of papal authority, distorting the practice of Catholic theology. Primarily a historian, and never a metaphysician, he would always have developed a different reading of Thomas Aquinas from that elaborated by Garrigou-Lagrange. His approach, one may say, a little summarily, was very much a reaction against the project (as it seemed to him) of extracting metaphysical theorems from Aquinas's work, taking them out of theological as well as historical context, creating (as he used to say) a 'sacred metaphysics'.

Chenu used to say that he profited from Garrigou-Lagrange's lectures. However, he regarded him as a divided mind: a master of spirituality, versed particularly in St John of the Cross, the Spanish Carmelite mystic, and yet an inflexible Aristotelian in philosophy, determined to keep spirituality and

---

[10] Giacomo Della Chiesa (1854–1922), a patrician and career diplomat, was said to have found a secret file denouncing his own 'modernist' heresies when he sat down at the papal desk.

[11] According to Chenu, Billot's theology is ideology; completely ignorant and careless of the historicity of the Christian economy, with no interest in biblical sources, indifferent to the pastoral experience of the Church and of the Christian people: 'a theology of the faith entirely defined by conceptual and juridical authority, with no methodological guidance from the mystery which is nevertheless its object', see *Jacques Duquesne interroge le Père Chenu: Un théologien en liberté* (Paris: Centurion 1975): 31.

speculative theology completely separate. For Chenu, by contrast, Catholic Christian theology could not be practised except with continuous reference to the historical economy of the mystery of God incarnate – which meant, as a matter of course, that theological activity was grounded in the liturgical life and contemplative asceticism with which he had fallen in love as a youngster. Chenu was no more interested than Garrigou-Lagrange was in historical scholarship for its own sake (whatever that might be). He saw the revitalization of Catholic study of Scripture by the application of the historical critical methods of biblical scholars, his fellow Dominican Marie-Joseph Lagrange in particular.[12] The same approach, with appropriate differences, would open up the theology of the medievals and especially that of Aquinas, so Chenu believed, far more fruitfully than neoscholastic Thomism could ever achieve. Aquinas's vision of the Christian revelation of God was, in a way, incarnate in his writing. To ignore the historical context, the genesis and texture, of this writing was to miss the vision.

Chenu wrote as follows:

> Those who enclose themselves in a scholastic Thomism hardened by generations of textbooks and manuals (and marginalized by the intrusion of a massive dose of Baroque scholasticism) oblige themselves thereby to summary condemnations of positions of which they are largely ignorant. This would certainly not be the path for disciples of Thomas Aquinas. And less helpful is the way of those who, colluding strangely with anti-modernism, hand the memory of the medieval doctor over to a positivist intellectualism, keeping for themselves a Thomism which is only a paragon of their own pseudo-religious integrist position. But this exploitation of Thomism (which some naively view to be salutary) cannot hide the real intentions of others, penetrated with the spirit of Thomas and with the highest requirements of scientific or theological work. They meet honestly the problems legitimately posed by the philosophy of religion, biblical exegesis, and the history of dogma. Illumined by the experience of their teacher they know how to discern in new terrain the relationships of reason and faith. Precisely this is the intellectual regime of Catholicism.[13]

Chenu's contribution is all there, already, in 1931. For Garrigou-Lagrange, however, and many who shared his view, Chenu's project risked forfeiting

---

[12] Marie-Joseph Lagrange (1855–1938) founded a centre of biblical studies in Jerusalem in 1890 and was the greatest Catholic biblical scholar. Attacked by colleagues for his support of modernism, he turned from Old to New Testament studies, less liable (then) to raise suspicions.
[13] 'Le sens et les leçons d'une crise religieuse', *La Vie intellectuelle* 13 (1931): 380 translated in Thomas F. O'Meara OP, *Thomas Aquinas Theologian* (Notre Dame, IN, and London: University of Notre Dame Press 1999: 182.

the objectivity of speculative theology as a quasi-scientific discipline in favour (as they feared) of a morass of piety, subjective experience and fideism.

Le Saulchoir: A School of Theology?

To what extent Le Saulchoir ever was, even in 1937, '*une* école', as if all the Dominicans on the teaching staff at the time had a single vision, is disputable. Some of his colleagues, at least, were infuriated by Chenu's magisterial exposition of what they stood for, collectively.

Moreover, in retrospect, *Une école de théologie* was needlessly polemical. For example, Chenu derided the curricula at seminaries and colleges (no doubt including the Angelicum): neoscholastic philosophy and theology textbooks were pervaded by 'Wolffian rationalism'. He peppered his text with insults. Natural theology as practised in Catholic institutions had no more religious character than eighteenth-century Deism. The Augustinian sap and the Dionysian mysticism had been allowed to leak away from Aquinas's theology. Catholic theology needed to be disinfected of 'baroque Scholasticism': 'the philosophy of clerical functionaries at the court of Joseph II'.[14] The 'Thomist orthodoxy' of Cardinal Zigliara, the greatest of the nineteenth-century Dominican Thomists in Rome, was 'contaminated by Wolffianism'; it suppresses the 'Platonic' interpretation of (say) Lepidi.[15] Chenu would prefer Pierre Rousselot's book, *L'Intellectualisme de Saint Thomas*, 'despite its faults'.[16] Esoteric as these *boutades* now sound, they could not but anger most Catholic theologians at the time, Garrigou-Lagrange above all.

In short, so Chenu's charge ran, neoscholastics paid no attention to 'the problems of existence, action, the individual, becoming, and time', preferring 'a philosophy of essences, in which what counts is the non-contingent, the universal, ideal and immutable relations – fine matters for definitions'.

---

[14] Joseph II (1741–90), Habsburg Emperor, and leader of the Catholic Enlightenment, subjected the Church to the state: one of the spectres haunting the Vatican at Vatican I – quite an arcane insult!
[15] Tomasso Maria Zigliara OP (1833–93) taught in Rome from 1870 to 1893 and was the chief exponent of Aristotelian Thomism. Alberto Lepidi OP (1838–1925), by contrast, who taught in France and Belgium, stressed the Augustinian strand in Aquinas. Zigliara and Lepidi represented radically divergent traditions even within the Dominican Order.
[16] Chenu, a Dominican, recommending a book by a Jesuit, was of course being provocative. Pierre Rousselot SJ (1878–1915) rediscovered a participationist philosophy of knowledge and love in the work of Aquinas, making Aristotelian Thomism irrelevant; see his 1908 Sorbonne thesis, translated as *The Intellectualism of St Thomas* (London: Sheed and Ward 1935).

Provocatively, as he must have realized, the second chapter of Chenu's manifesto begins with a quotation from a letter from George Tyrrell (whose name he misspelled) to Friedrich von Hügel written in 1904, in which he remarks that it is not on this or that article of the Creed that they differ from their adversaries, they differ over the word *credo*, on the meaning of the word 'true' as applied to dogma. This remark Chenu takes to show that there could be no doubt about 'the intellectual and religious crisis that cut across Christianity at that time'. Nevertheless, he immediately says, much has been achieved, in Catholic scholarship. He reels off the famous names: Duchesne, Batiffol, Lagrange, Mercier, and Blondel – 'the fruits of this extremely fecund activity, presided over by Pope Leo XIII'.[17] All in all, as this litany was meant to demonstrate, there was a half-century of Catholic scholarship to celebrate (always a booster, Chenu, never a knocker) – whatever 'controversies and incidents' there had been.

Interestingly, Chenu makes no attempt to discuss the concept of truth, which Tyrrell assumes that he and von Hügel share, over against the concept held by their critics. Tyrrell is making the crucial point that, philosophically, his conception of truth is quite different from that in neoscholastic theology. Chenu does not endorse Tyrell's remark, nor on the other hand does he seem to see any reason to question it.

The message of Chenu's manifesto lies, most provocatively, in the layout: the chapter on philosophy comes after the one on theology. In effect, Thomas Aquinas is to be read as a theologian from the outset. There is no need to be able to defend the Twenty-four Theses before one is allowed to pass into theological studies. It is far more important to reconstruct Aquinas's historical context than to master the metaphysical theorems that supposedly lie at the basis of his theology.

The key passage runs as follows:

> Theological systems are only the expression of spiritualities. . . . The greatness and the truth of Bonaventuran or Scotist Augustinianism are entirely in the spiritual experience of Saint Francis which became the soul in his sons; the grandeur and the truth of Molinism are in the spiritual experience of Saint Ignatius's *Exercises*. . . . A theology worthy of the name is a spirituality, which finds the rational instruments adequate to its religious experience. It is not the luck of history that Saint Thomas entered the Order of Saint Dominic; and it is not by some desultory grace that the Order of Saint Dominic received Saint Thomas Aquinas. The institution and the doctrine are closely allied with one another, in the inspiration that carried the one and the other into a new age,

---

[17]   *Le Saulchoir: Une école de théologie* (Paris: Cerf 1937): 115.

and in the contemplation, which, goal of both, guarantees the fervour, the method, the purity, and the freedom of their spirit.[18]

This is, obviously, exactly what Garrigou-Lagrange rejected. For a theologian, Chenu goes on, contemplation is not a practice in which he may engage from time to time, 'a burst of fervour, beyond his studying, as if an escape from its object and its method'. Rather, contemplation is the theologian's everyday environment, without which theology would be arid and pointless. Garrigou-Lagrange would not have dissented. Behind what Chenu is saying, however, there lies a longstanding dispute about how to divide up the day: does a theologian spend an hour on his knees without a book of any kind and then go to the library to study or to the aula to lecture; or is the hour's meditation dependent on a text and the research and teaching always contemplatively practised? Chenu, it seemed to his critics, failed to make the proper distinction between study and prayer, and was thus, unsurprisingly, liable to confuse theology and spirituality.

In the chapter on philosophy Chenu raises the perennially difficult question of the status of philosophy within Christianity. This is a practical as well as a theoretical question. As standard seminary pedagogy required, should philosophical studies precede entry into theology? Neoscholastic apologetics, the crown of the philosophy course, mistakenly regarded as 'traditional', completely misrepresents the relationship between reason and faith, 'as if it was a matter of two worlds outside one another, for which happy concordances had to be found'. No doubt this seemed to make sense, as a reaction to the deism of the Enlightenment. But it is a mistake: 'A Christian doing philosophy does not cease to be a Christian; a Christian philosopher does not cease to be a philosopher'.[19]

Chenu is sceptical about the notion of a 'perennial philosophy'. The phrase itself – *philosophia perennis* – was invented by a certain A. Steuchus, Chenu informs us, in a characteristic display of self-mocking erudition– 'this Renaissance philosopher who wanted, with this phrase, to reconcile the Paduan theism with medieval scholasticism'.[20] The problem with the phrase, however, is that it suggests that philosophy is a set of 'characterless and shapeless principles', *énoncés dépersonnalisés et avachis*, the least common denominator, so to speak, of philosophical projects which (however) actually

[18] Ibid: 148–9.
[19] Ibid: 153.
[20] Agostino Steuco (1496–1549) was a Canon Regular of the Lateran and ran the Vatican Library. His works include *Philosophia Perennis* (written 1540) which sees all religions as manifestations of a perennial philosophy that is one and eternal; the phrase was to be picked up by Leibniz.

differ considerably, 'in intuition and in systematization'. In brief, neo-scholastic philosophy – 'under the patronage of Leibniz' – adopted a false 'ideal of intelligibility'.[21]

Chenu on Thomas Aquinas on Faith

Chenu had ambitious plans to study Thomas Aquinas in historical context in such a way as to cast light on current theological matters. Perhaps the outbreak of war in 1939 would have interrupted him anyway, but ecclesiastical sanctions did not help. His first publication, back in 1923, shows the kind of work he wanted to do.

In this article Chenu offers a reading of Aquinas's consideration in his *Summa Theologiæ* of the object of faith.[22] The question is whether the object of faith is something composite, *per modum enuntiabilis*, in the form of a proposition, or first truth itself, *veritas prima*, that is to say: God, who is in no way composed of parts. Is faith in propositions or in God?

According to Chenu, the interest of this has been missed, because commentators did not place it in historical context. If we re-create the controversy, we can see the permanent importance of the position Aquinas takes. The controversy originates in the question of the identity of faith between Old and New Testaments: the immutability of faith through its development. For Aquinas, there was continuity between Christian and Jewish faith. Some of his predecessors held that, since faith is a kind of knowledge, it must have propositions as its object. He is happy to agree, since this allows him to insist on the human conditions of the act of faith: 'the way of knowing truth proper to the human mind is by an act of combining and separating'. For Chenu, this should legitimate our modern interest in the psychological conditions of faith. It should also remind writers about spirituality – 'against all illuminism' – that even the gifts of the Holy Spirit do not exempt the Christian from the regime of gradual, unending and expanding enlightenment. Faith does not short-circuit intelligence; on the contrary, it incarnates the divine truth in the very substance of our minds.

However, others held that the object of faith was God, absolutely. They are of course correct, so Aquinas argues: the reality known, according to his

---

[21] Le Chenu, *Le Saulchoir*: 154–5.
[22] 'Contribution à l'histoire du traité de la foi. Commentaire historique de IIa IIae, q.1, a.2', *Mélanges thomistes* (Le Saulchoir: Kain, 1923): 123–40; reprinted in Chenu, *La Parole de Dieu I: La Foi dans l'intelligence* (Paris: Cerf 1964): 31–50.

theory of knowledge, is the object of knowledge as it is outside the knower in its proper existence. Yet, as he goes on to say, there is no knowledge of the reality except through what there is of this reality in the knower. Analogously, the divine reality obviously exists independently of us; but our minds receive it in our own way, that is to say by combining and dividing, by way (then) of propositions.

As a historian Chenu delightedly re-creates the controversy, identifying the disputants whom Aquinas never names. Clearly, however, his motivation is to demonstrate a method of reading Aquinas which, far from losing speculative theology in the dust of historical research, or (worse) in a morass of relativism, actually enables Aquinas's solution of the thirteenth-century dispute to bear on modern disputes. We do not have to choose between saying that our faith is in propositions and saying that it is in the reality of the divine Word. In the 1920s, as now, there were disputes over whether our minds are confined within language or capable of transcending directly to reality. Catholics believed in propositions while Protestants had faith in a person, so it was often claimed. For Chenu, Aquinas dissolved this putative dilemma long ago, in a paradigmatic way. Here, less than three years since leaving Rome, Chenu was demonstrating a way of studying the text of Aquinas quite different (he does not need to say) from the way practised by Garrigou-Lagrange. This is the kind of historical theology, Chenu cheekily adds, dreamed of by Denifle.[23]

Introduction to Thomas Aquinas

Bizarrely, it required some ecclesiastical manoeuvring for Chenu to be allowed to publish his introduction to the study of Thomas Aquinas.[24] 'Higher authorities' sought to block it since, after all, his little manifesto remained on the Index of Prohibited Books.

Chenu contends, in what remains one of the best introductions, half a century later, that we cannot understand Aquinas without detailed study of the historical context to which he belonged, and of the historical conditions under which he worked: the Dominican Order, the University of Paris, the academic institutions and literary forms of the day, the legacy of Augustine,

---

[23] Heinrich Seuse Denifle OP (1844–1905), path-breaking medievalist (though he predates the Catholic appreciation of Luther), was the greatest Dominican historian of the day.

[24] *Introduction à l'étude de S. Thomas d'Aquin* (Paris: Vrin 1950, second edition 1954), translated by A.-M. Landry and D. Hughes as *Towards Understanding Saint Thomas* with authorized corrections and bibliographical additions (Chicago: Henry Regnery 1964).

Denys, and the neoplatonic tradition, and so on, as well as Aquinas's critical engagement with the recently discovered works of Aristotle. He highlights the diversity of Aquinas's work: commentaries on Aristotle, on Scripture, disputations, more than one *summa*, and so on, each genre with its own logic and relevance for spirituality. Thought and text, expression and truth, go together. Above all, however, Aquinas worked his thoughts out, most characteristically, in the classical form of the *quæstio*: considering every issue as raising questions. It was just not the same thought, Chenu means, when Aquinas's solution to the question is reformulated as a 'thesis', as if the objections that he considers to his view could be left aside.

Chenu's was the first major effort to highlight the dramatic history, so to speak, within which Aquinas's work could disclose its riches. The *Summa Theologiæ* could no longer be treated, credibly, as a self-standing system transcending all history and time. On the contrary, like any classic, we may say, it is precisely as belonging to the setting in which it is composed that it continues to disclose how permanently vital and valuable it is. We need not fear that, the deeper we get into the genesis and composition of a text, the more slippery will be the slope to relativism – just the opposite. 'The truth is no less true for being inscribed in time'.[25]

Chenu combats the then standard division of labour in expounding the *Summa Theologiæ*. Far from reflecting a decision to complete what may be demonstrated about God by reason before considering what may be said solely in virtue of revelation, the fact that Aquinas deals with the questions *de Deo uno* and then with those *de Deo trino*, 'results from an option characteristic of Latin theology, which implies a spiritual itinerary towards the God of revelation'.[26] However pervaded with metaphysics (he admits), the questions *de Deo uno* deal with the God of the Book of Genesis, not the god of Aristotle's *Physics*: the God of Abraham, Isaac and Jacob, who points us towards Christ. We have to retain the religious character of this text, Chenu insists, never reducing it to a 'deist' theodicy. He refers us to a classic (though neglected) article by his colleague René Motte.[27]

The link between the questions on God and the theology of creation, thus between the divine mystery and the world of space and time, is made by the key question on the 'missions' of the Son and of the Spirit (*Summa Theologiæ* 1.43). Throughout the first part of the *Summa*, Aquinas keeps incorporating biblical material about creation – which, Chenu notes, was

[25] *Introduction à l'étude de S. Thomas d'Aquin*: 6, my translation.
[26] Ibid: 275.
[27] R.A. Motte, 'Théodicée et théologie chez S. Thomas d'Aquin', *Revue des Sciences Philosophiques et Théologiques* 21 (1937): 5–26.

generally omitted in expositions in class of the doctrine. Chenu invites us to notice how considering religion, devotion and piety, and so on, in the context of the moral virtue of justice, perhaps points our conception of spirituality in an unusual direction.

In short, in a list of examples, Chenu opens up a quite different approach to reading the *Summa Theologiæ* from the one inculcated by the lecture courses and textbooks supposedly composed *ad mentem Sancti Thomæ*. Failure to allow for the context which he took for granted – the Christian mystery, liturgically performed, lived in disciplined contemplation – leaves the *Summa Theologiæ* as arid an exercise as most seminarians found it. Far from reducing the rigorously intellectual achievement of the *Summa*, Chenu was out to demonstrate that we miss the achievement altogether unless we get to know the mind the fruits of whose contemplation are set down – incarnated, so to speak – in the texts which we have inherited.

For all the importance of Aristotle, Chenu insists, Aquinas should not be read as if he repudiated his inheritance from Augustine. Though references to the *platonici* are usually critical, this should not occlude how much he takes for granted from the neo-Platonic tradition. He cites Denys as much as Aristotle. We need to remember the twelfth-century Renaissance, the presence of Islamic culture, the evangelism of the Friars, and much else that students of Thomas Aquinas now regard as an essential part of understanding his work.

It is salutary to remember that the approach which Chenu pioneered 50 years ago was then regarded as a threat to the standard neoscholastic exposition of Thomism and thus to the maintenance of orthodoxy in Catholic theology.

Wolffianism at Vatican II

In 1973, reflecting on what was achieved at Vatican II, Chenu returned to the charge that neoscholastic theology was pervaded by 'Wolffianism'. The unexpected rejection by the majority of the bishops, in November 1962, of draft texts in which he detected signs of 'Wolffian metaphysics', was the final defeat of the neoscholastic Thomism to which he was subjected in Rome in his youth. Once and for all, the spirit of eighteenth-century rationalism was expelled from Catholic theology.[28] This was an irreversible shift in theological sensibility, with immensely important implications, however long it might take to work it all out.

---

[28] M.-D. Chenu, 'Vérité évangélique et métaphysique wolfienne à Vatican II', *Revue des Sciences Philosophiques et Théologiques* 57 (1973): 632–40.

It is not clear how much of the prolific works of the German Lutheran theologian Christian Wolff (1679–1754) Chenu ever read. No doubt he knew that Wolff wanted to ground theological truths on evidence of quasi-mathematical certitude. Notoriously, Wolff's Pietist Lutheran colleagues were enraged by a lecture which he gave in 1721, instancing the moral precepts of Confucius as evidence of the power of human reason to attain by its own efforts to moral truth.

Wolff invented the courses on logic, ontology, rational psychology, natural theology, moral philosophy, and so on, which shaped Catholic seminary training into the 1960s, as well as university philosophy faculties everywhere. This division of labour fragmented philosophy in the sense of a sapiential exercise, a 'love of wisdom', and gave rise to the specialisms with which we are familiar in professional philosophy.

For many years Gilson had been claiming that 'Wolffianism' had infiltrated the work of Garrigou-Lagrange, an outrageous suggestion as many thought. This is, as Peddicord says, 'preposterous'.[29] The basis for Gilson's claim seems to be that, in his first major book *Le Sens commun* (1908), Garrigou-Lagrange declares a debt to Afrikan Alexandrovich Spir (1837–90), whose book *Denken und Wirklichkeit: Versuch einer Erneuerung der kritischen Philosophie* (1873) he read in French translation, the conduit through which, supposedly, he imbibed Wolffian rationalism. The genuine Thomist understanding of being – being as existence, not essence – was lost around 1729, the year when Wolff's *Ontologia* appeared. The act of being as such – *ipsum esse subsistens* – which is so central to Aquinas's metaphysics, disappears from modern philosophy, so Gilson's often rehearsed story goes. It would take us too far to untangle all this here – the point is only that Garrigou-Lagrange was being dismissed as a rationalist, as a self-styled Thomist who failed to grasp the fundamental Thomist intuition.

True enough, Garrigou-Lagrange attached great importance to the principle of sufficient reason: 'Everything which is, has a sufficient reason for existing'. That no doubt sounds Leibnizian, though Garrigou-Lagrange always held that we did not need Leibniz to formulate this principle. This is the principle, in the Thomistic Theses, on which the proofs for the existence of God are based.

Anyway, doing little more than Gilson to document the claim, Chenu contends that the version of Thomism to which he was exposed at the Angelicum from 1914 until 1920 was infiltrated by this Enlightenment

---

[29] Richard Peddicord, *The Sacred Monster of Thomism: An Introduction to the Life and Legacy of Réginald Garrigou-Lagrange* OP (South Bend, IN: St Austin's Press 2005): 103 footnote 70.

rationalism. Indeed, this explains the acrimonious controversies in the decade 1940 to 1950, when French Dominicans and Jesuits, contesting the neoscholastic theology which put would-be 'scientific' deductivism against the *ressourcement* of theology to be found in the study of the history and economy of salvation, and so in the pastoral and missionary presence of the word of God in the Church, were persecuted by the ecclesiastical authorities, removed from teaching posts and prevented from publishing. The phrase 'new theology' was applied, abusively, by Garrigou-Lagrange and his cohort in Rome to those (like Chenu and Henri de Lubac) who questioned the neoscholastic rationalism, which cut Catholic theologians off from their inheritance – the 'traditional theology' which the so-called 'new theologians' were actually retrieving.

Theology without Philosophy?

Chenu invites us to examine the text of the chapter *De cognitione veritatis* in the *De deposito fidei pure custodiendo* drafted for Vatican II. Here we find, in this would-be key text on 'keeping the treasure of faith authentically', a certain theory of 'knowledge of truth' (epistemology) at work: truth is allied with immutability, necessity, universal rationality, and suchlike. Moreover, the philosophy of being is contrasted favourably with a philosophy of becoming. The dimensions of time and history, in knowledge of truth, are totally absent. In short, the wholesale rejection of these drafts by the Council fathers opened the way to a renewal of Catholic theology, 'beyond the aporias of neoscholasticism, of which Wolffian rationalism was not the least avatar'.[30] At last, once and for all, Chenu contends, at Vatican II, the Catholic Church rejected the rationalism that prevented authentic understanding of Thomas Aquinas, as well as all theological engagement with the problems of modern life.

Consider, however, what Chenu then says. The truth of biblical revelation cannot be reduced to the formal truth of the propositions that state it. God is revealed in actions and events as well as in words. These events are not brute facts, illustrating divine ideas (as who might have thought?). They are God's actions in history. It's not good enough 'to study the abstract conditions of the possibility of a revelation, deductively', as Garrigou-Lagrange did, so Chenu says, 'in the framework of a metaphysical conception of truth'.[31] 'This analysis connects neither with the historical condition of man

---

[30] Chenu, 'Vérité évangélique': 636.
[31] Ibid.: 637.

nor with saving truth'. It is the 'purely extrinsic method of a certain fundamental theology, rendered obsolete by the Council'.[32]

What we want, Chenu goes on, is a conception of 'biblical truth, *evangelical* truth, according to the Hebrew mind' – it 'connects directly not with
what is but with what comes about, with that of which one has experience'.[33] 'Greek thought developed by reflecting on the substance of beings,
and issues into a philosophy of immutability and permanence. It left out the
proper characteristic of biblical thought: time, the fragility of things and
persons. Biblical thought is turned not to essences but to destinies; it questions itself about the feeblenesses and the promises of life'.[34]

True, he allows, it would be giving in to a pernicious and historically
controversial dualism to oppose the historical and concrete truth of the
Gospel to the abstract truth of Greco-Latin philosophy, defined as this latter
is by *adequatio rei et intellectus*, in a judgement which relates a statement with
the truth of being as being. . . . And he goes on in this strain, playing off a
supposedly evangelical concept of truth against the concept of truth inherited from ancient Greek philosophy. Admittedly, 30 years ago, the difference
between Hebrew and Greek ways of thinking, and between biblical and
metaphysical concepts of truth, was something of a commonplace, even
among Catholic theologians. No doubt it was high time that the grip of
neoscholastic rationalism was broken. But opting for a biblical notion of
truth over against a metaphysical concept was a move that would have
excited Garrigou-Lagrange's suspicions, not altogether unjustifiably.

Conclusion

Chenu's lasting achievement was to challenge from inside the standard
reading of the *Summa Theologiæ*. Unbelievable as it may seem to theologians
in other church traditions, as well as to Catholic theologians of the post-
Vatican II era, fears that his approach led to relativism, and so to modernism,
were so prevalent among his fellow Dominicans that he was dismissed from
teaching in any Dominican institution simply for insisting that Thomas
Aquinas's exposition of the truth of Christian faith becomes all the more
enlightening as we read him in historical context.

The best access to Chenu's distinctive approach to Aquinas is to be found
in a recently translated book, in which, by reconstructing the historical

---

[32] Ibid.
[33] Ibid.
[34] Ibid.: 637–8.

context, he brings out Aquinas's evangelical intention and its actuality for today.[35] As for Chenu's legacy, it may now be traced in the work of many theologians, such as Jean-Pierre Torrell, Gilles Emery, Gregory P. Rocca, and Matthew Levering, who take it for granted that Aquinas needs to be studied in historical context – which does not mean he has nothing to say that bears on matters of great theological interest today – just the opposite.[36] The second volume of Torrell's *magnum opus* presents Aquinas as 'spiritual master' – his theology as clearly oriented towards contemplation as his spirituality expresses itself in his theology. Though he obviously owes far more to Chenu's example, perhaps Chenu's and Garrigou-Lagrange's versions of Thomism reach a degree of reconciliation in Torrell's book.

Then, given the place of neo-Aristotelian 'virtue ethics', at the cutting edge of English-language moral philosophy, as well as in Christian ethics, the best testimony to Chenu's advocacy of historical-contextualist studies as the way to retrieve and appropriate Aquinas's thought most creatively may be found in the work of the Belgian Dominican Servais Pinckaers.[37] His doctoral dissertation – 'The Virtue of Hope from Peter Lombard to Thomas Aquinas' – was supervised by Garrigou-Lagrange – and he invited Chenu to write the preface to his first major book, *Le Renouveau de la morale* (1964).

Most Catholic theologians, however, do not find it attractive, or even necessary, to study Aquinas in Chenu's or anyone else's way. Outside the English-speaking world, especially, recourse to Aquinas seems mere antiquarianism, a failure to face up to the unavoidable implications of postmodernism. In the most influential movement currently in Catholic theology, the Song of Songs and the patristic and medieval commentaries thereon play a much more significant role than Thomas Aquinas's work.

---

[35] Originally published in 1959, recently translated with an introduction by Paul J. Philibert OP; see *Aquinas and His Role in Theology* (Collegeville, MN: The Liturgical Press 2002).

[36] Jean-Pierre Torrell OP, *Saint Thomas Aquinas*, vol. 2 *Spiritual Master* (Washington DC: Catholic University of America Press 2003); Gilles Emery OP, *Trinity in Aquinas* (Ypsilanti, MI: Sapientia Press 2002); Gregory P. Rocca OP, *Speaking the Incomprehensible God: Thomas Aquinas on the Interplay of Positive and Negative Theology* (Washington DC: Catholic University of America Press 2004); Matthew Levering, *Christ's Fulfillment of Torah and Temple* (Notre Dame, IN: University of Notre Dame Press 2002), and *Scripture and Metaphysics: Aquinas and the Renewal of Trinitarian Theology* (Oxford: Blackwell 2004).

[37] Born in 1925 in Belgium, Servais Pinckaers joined the Dominicans in 1945, taught at the University of Fribourg, Switzerland, from 1973: his influence is only now reaching the English-language world, see *The Sources of Christian Ethics* (Washington, DC: Catholic University of America Press 1995); and especially John Berkman and Craig Steven Titus (eds.) *The Pinckaers Reader: Renewing Thomistic Moral Theology* (Washington, DC: Catholic University of America Press 2005).

Chapter Three

YVES CONGAR

According to the American Jesuit theologian Avery Dulles, in an obituary, 'Vatican II could almost be called Congar's Council'.[1]

Yves Congar was born on 13 April 1904, at Sedan, in the Ardennes region of north-east France, a few miles from the frontier with Belgium.[2] His father Georges Congar was a bank manager. His very devout mother Lucie read *The Imitation of Christ* to the children and on Saturday evenings the next day's gospel text. They had Jewish friends as well as Protestant neighbours, unusual for Catholics in France in those days. Back in the sixteenth century the local princes were Protestant. Even in the early twentieth, when the princes were of course long gone, there were Protestants and Catholics and even a few Jews living peaceably together in the town. Right in the path of the German army in 1914, the town was besieged, and the Catholic church burned down. The Catholics were allowed by the Reformed pastor to use the local Protestant church for Sunday worship. Congar's father was among the men deported by the Germans to Lithuania, occupied by the German army in September 1915.

Encouraged by a local priest, Congar entered the diocesan seminary. In 1921 he moved to Paris, to study philosophy. He attended courses by Jacques Maritain, the lay man who was soon to become one of the leaders of the renaissance of Thomism.[3] He went to retreats conducted near Paris by Réginald Garrigou-Lagrange. They were all drawn to Action Française, a

---

[1]   Avery Dulles SJ, 'Yves Congar: In Appreciation', *America* 173 (15 July 1995): 6–7.
[2]   For details see Aidan Nichols OP, *Yves Congar* (London: Geoffrey Chapman 1989); and Elizabeth Teresa Groppe, *Yves Congar's Theology of the Holy Spirit* (Oxford: Oxford University Press 2004).
[3]   Jacques Maritain (1882–1973), a French Thomist philosopher, held chairs at Paris, Toronto and Princeton. He applied Thomist principles to metaphysics, moral, social and political philosophy, the philosophy of education, history, culture and art.

political movement attractive to Catholics who deplored the anti-clericalism of the socialist politicians of the Third Republic and sometimes even wanted to restore the monarchy, as well as the influence of the Catholic Church.[4] The Dominicans at Le Saulchoir, however, they regarded as treating the study of Thomas Aquinas more as an exercise in historical scholarship intended to impress the medievalists at the Sorbonne, rather than the timeless system of speculative theology which most Dominicans at the time took it to be.

Congar's year of mandatory military service (1924–5) was spent in the Rhineland. He forsook the diocesan clergy in order to enter the Dominican Order, where in a year or two he fell under Chenu's spell.[5] His first publications suggest he was destined for a future as a medievalist. It soon became clear to him, however, that his vocation lay in working for Christian reunion. His first book *Chrétiens désunis* appeared in 1938, the first volume in the series he founded under the name *Unam Sanctam* – a series he saw as contributing to Christian reunion, principally, in the beginning anyway, by retrieving forgotten themes of Catholic tradition.[6] An anonymous article in *L'Osservatore Romano* attacked the book; and the Provincial of the Paris Dominicans was summoned to Rome to explain why the book had been permitted to appear.

As a reservist Congar was mobilized in September 1939. He was captured in May 1940, when France surrendered. The next five years he spent in high-security prisons, twice at Colditz. Back from the war, he was impatient to continue his interest in promoting Christian reunion. Few Catholics in the English-speaking world understand the traumatic effects in the ancient Catholic countries of western Europe of the serial catastrophes of Nazism, military occupation, collaboration, the round-up of Jews, the invasion and the bombing, and so on. In 1945 the Christian faith, and especially the Catholic Church, was rising from the dead, returning from hell to new life. In 1950 Congar published *Vraie et fausse réforme dans l'Église*.[7] This went

---

[4] Action Française was founded in 1898 at the height of the Dreyfus affair and was hostile to the Third Republic which was extremely anti-Catholic. The best-known leader Charles Maurras (1868–1952), journalist, philosopher, monarchist, militant atheist and anti-Semite, only became a Catholic in his last years. In 1926 Pope Pius XI forbade Catholics to support the movement because of its extreme nationalism and misappropriation of Catholic doctrine. His action provoked a grave crisis of conscience for many clergy and faithful.
[5] As a novice he was given the name Marie-Joseph, eventually dropped; his early publications are attributed to M.-J. Congar.
[6] *Chrétiens désunis: Principes d'un 'oecuménisme' catholique* (Paris: Cerf 1937), translated as *Divided Christendom: A Catholic Study of the Problem of Reunion* (London: Centenary Press 1939).
[7] *Vraie et fausse réforme dans l'Église* (Paris: Cerf 1950); never translated into English; second, revised edition 1969.

too far – the very idea of 'reform', whether true or false, in the Catholic Church, was a provocation. The papal nuncio in Paris, Archbishop Angelo Roncalli, inscribed in his own copy the question 'A reform of the Church – is it possible?' Less than ten years later, when he had become Pope John XXIII, the idea that the Catholic Church could be reformed – renewed, anyway – was firmly on the agenda. In 1953, as if anticipating that renewal, Congar brought out *Jalons pour une théologie du laïcat.*[8]

Dated now, of course, these three books nevertheless laid out what would, quite unexpectedly, dominate the agenda for Vatican II: a form of ecumenism acceptable to Catholics; acceptance of the truth that the Church was always in need of reform (*ecclesia semper reformanda*); and recovery of a sense of the Church as the people of God, clergy and laity together. At last the Catholic Church would concede that Christians outside her visible membership were at least worth talking to, their 'churches' had elements of 'true Church' in them.

If Congar was already under suspicion in 1938 for his ecumenical interests, worse was to come in 1953 when he became interested in the worker-priest movement. Its members were priests who sought to evangelize the deeply anti-clerical industrial workers by becoming workers themselves, in the hope of breaking down the barrier. The movement worried many of the French bishops. Some bishops feared that these priests were losing their priestly status, accepting election as trades union officials, and so on. An article he published in September 1953 on the future of the movement led to Congar's being dismissed from teaching at Le Saulchoir, and forbidden to set foot in any study house of the Dominican Order. This was only an excuse: suspicion of his interest in Christian reunion was the true reason for the treatment to which the Order subjected him, perhaps under pressure from Vatican authorities. Nothing Congar published was ever censured by the Holy Office, or placed on the Index of Prohibited Books, nor was he ever summoned to defend his ideas in Rome. He was kept hanging about, mostly in Rome, while no one, none of his fellow Dominican friars, could or would tell him why he was forbidden to teach or preach or publish or live in the same house as friars in formation. Congar's misery culminated in February 1956 when he was sent by the Master of the Order to the English Dominican house in Cambridge, for an indefinite period, forbidden to lecture or preach. This proved the unhappiest six months of his life, worse than being in Colditz. In December 1956 the bishop of Strasbourg rescued him, quite as arbitrarily, enabling him to resume a (limited) ministry. In

---

[8] *Jalons pour une théologie du laïcat* (Paris: Cerf 1953), translated as *Lay People in the Church: A Study for the Theology of the Laity* (Westminster, MD: Newman Press 1965).

1958 Congar was allowed to publish his book *Le Mystère du temple* – a study of the history of the presence of God in the world from Genesis to the Apocalypse – the product of some months of exile in Jerusalem. There was no possibility of republishing, even with revisions he wanted to make, any of the three great books.

Then, to everyone's amazement and many people's dismay, Pope John XXIII announced in January 1959 that he was convoking a full-scale council, the Second Vatican Council – to reform the Church explicitly in order to bring about reunion among Christians. In July 1960 Congar was among the first appointed by John XXIII to draft texts for the bishops to consider. Initially Congar was sceptical about any good the Council might do, assuming, as many others did, that there could only be a wave of condemnations of Communism, of the 'new theology', of 'ecumenism', and of much else, or, on the positive side, a dogmatic definition of the Blessed Virgin Mary as Mediatrix of All Graces.[9]

On 20 November 1962, after days of bitter exchanges in the aula, the majority of the Council fathers voted against the draft text *de fontibus revelationis*, on 'the sources' of Christian revelation, the work of a team of (mostly) Roman university theologians, presided over by Cardinal Ottaviani and Sebastian Tromp sj. The vote – 1368 to 822 with 19 null – did not reach the two-thirds required by the rules to reject a text – though it was nonetheless an affront to those who regarded themselves, and were widely regarded, as the custodians of Catholic doctrine. John XXIII exercised his authority on the side of the majority, naming a new commission to compose a fresh text. This was the turning point, not only the defeat of the Holy Office theologians; but, as many saw at the time, incredulously, with delight or dismay, the close of an age – in principle, at least. Congar's doubts about John XXIII and the Council were settled. By early 1963 he was playing a major part in drafting the new texts which eventually became the documents of Vatican II.

During the Council Congar published two volumes on the theology of Sacred Tradition (1960 and 1963): the reform or renewal of the Catholic Church that he envisaged was to be on the basis of a retrieval of the fullness of the Catholic tradition that he believed had been lost as Catholics reacted against Protestantism in the so-called Counter-Reformation, and against

---

[9]   For decades many Catholics have wanted Mary declared Mediatrix of All Graces or Co-Redemptrix: as Mother of God (*Theotokos*: God-bearer) she has for ever a maternal-mediating role in God's self-communication to the faithful (entirely subordinate and speaking analogously); as the one who gave her consent at the Annunciation she has a co-operative role in the history of redemption (again, of course, subordinate and analogously).

the ancient churches of the East when they rejected papal authority as conceived and practised in the early Middle Ages.

In the aftermath Congar published much, documenting how traditional Vatican II's understanding of the Church actually was. Finally, in 1979–80, he published a major work on the doctrine of the Holy Spirit – elementary in the way it summarizes the history of how the presence of the Holy Spirit has been perceived down through the ages and across the various conflicting ecclesiastical traditions – the ultimate aim, however, being to prepare the way for reunion between Eastern and Western Christianity.

Gradually incapacitated by the neurological disease first detected in 1935, Congar was moved in 1984 to Les Invalides, the military hospital for heroes of the Republic, where he died on 22 June 1995, having been named a Cardinal by Pope John Paul II the previous year – an honour which Congar accepted although, in his view, the status by the eleventh century of the Cardinals in Rome had all but destroyed the authority of the episcopate.[10]

Ecumenism

Preparing for ordination to priesthood, in 1930, Congar meditated on chapter 17 of the fourth gospel – 'that all shall be one'. Then – unheard of at the time, for a Catholic theologian – he wanted to meet Christians of other traditions. He visited Germany, to meet Lutheran pastors and professors. Never having heard of the legend of the Grand Inquisitor (in Dostoevsky's *Brothers Karamazov*) he was shocked to learn that, for his new Lutheran friends, this was their picture of the Catholic Church: 'Catholics are the subjects of the Pope and prisoners in a hierarchical ecclesiastical system where consciences are enslaved, the relations of souls with God are at second-hand and stereotyped – religion in fact by proxy for the benefit of the clergy, an ecclesiastical kingdom of which the Pope is the autocrat.'[11] Whatever else ministry in the service of Christian reunion would mean, so Congar realized, the first and most urgent requirement was to engage in discussion with Lutherans in order to liberate them from their prejudices about what Catholics actually did and thought – and he would not get very far without doing his best to learn what Protestants actually did and thought – to overcome his own prejudices.

---

[10] In 1059, no doubt under the influence of Hildebrand, the future Pope Gregory VII, Pope Nicholas II ruled that the cardinal bishops alone should elect the pope (in the hope of excluding simony).

[11] *Divided Christendom*: 34

In 1937 Congar visited England, as a guest of A.M. Ramsey, who much later became Archbishop of Canterbury and a friend of Pope Paul VI. He fell in love with Anglicanism, at least with the beauty of the liturgy in a great cathedral like Lincoln, where he stayed with Ramsey.[12]

Amazing as this all now seems, talking theology and praying, with Lutherans, Anglicans and Orthodox, was widely regarded as inappropriate for Catholics. There were, of course, suspicions on both sides – the Orthodox, even today, are often suspicious of overtures from Rome, greeting them as new ways to trap the Orthodox into submission to Rome's longstanding desire for control, as the Orthodox see it, not altogether unjustifiably.

Divided Christendom

In *Divided Christendom* Congar outlines the historical origins of the division between Eastern and Western Christianity and, secondly, the split in the West at the Reformation. The former Congar attributes to political and cultural factors, much exacerbated by the advance of Islam. The gulf between Protestants and Catholics is 'practically impassable': indeed, we should speak of 'two different Christianities'. Protestant opposition to Catholicism is (however) quite understandable: in theology and piety, there was 'a great emphasis on man's own moral activity and a less-marked sense of the supreme theocentricism of the great tradition'; and such stress on the juridico-social aspect of the Church that by mid-nineteenth century the Church was 'as much like a fortress as a temple'.[13]

The doctrine of the unity of the Church is grounded in God as Trinity; historically given in Christ; the Church his Mystical Body, the People of God, a fellowship, a great sacrament, and so on. Chapter 3, on the Catholicity of the Church, insists that the 'great diversity of religious experience – of ways of feeling or living the Christian life and of interpreting the religious objectivity – is not only legitimate but desirable in the Church' (110).

Chapter 4 offers a fairly severe critique of the theories underlying the Ecumenical Movement, first as manifested in the Stockholm Conference in 1925 – which 'emanated from a pragmatist and chiefly English-speaking

---

[12] Arthur Michael Ramsey (1904–88) was appointed subwarden of Lincoln theological college in 1930; canon-professor at Durham in 1940; Bishop of Durham in 1952, Archbishop of York in 1956, and was Archbishop of Canterbury from 1961 to 1974; see his *The Gospel and the Catholic Church* (1936), which Congar much admired.

[13] *Divided Christendom*: 33, 35. Subsequent page references for quotations are given in the text.

milieu under the aegis of a Protestant modernist'; and then at Lausanne (1927): 'a characteristic product of the Anglican outlook' – concluding that Catholic co-operation should take the form of 'theological assistance', 'certainly not the form of official membership'.

Chapter 5 outlines Anglican doctrine of the Church, as Congar understands it, quite sympathetically, concluding however that, as to 'non-Roman Catholicism', if that is what Anglicans believe they represent, then 'there is no such thing' (197).

Orthodoxy, it turns out in chapter 6, has an 'incomplete' ecclesiology; nonetheless Congar breaks with the then prevalent Catholic view that Christians who were not in communion with Rome and thus under the authority of the Holy See are *ipso facto* 'heretics'. Indeed, so Congar contends, Catholics have much to learn from the Russian Church ('to know and experience a more interior and mystical outlook', 220). About Greek Orthodoxy, oddly, he says nothing.

Chapter 7 invites Catholics to see other Christians as 'brethren' – 'separated' yes; but as 'Christians who already possess in greater or lesser degree what we desire to see fulfilled in them, and who themselves secretly look for such a consummation' (247). Though 'born into an erroneous form of Christianity', non-Roman-Catholic Christians are 'very rarely real heretics'.

In the concluding chapter, an outline for a practical programme, Congar allows that 'some day we shall have complete reunion', namely with the Eastern Church. For any chance of reunion with Protestants, however, 'vast changes' would be required – 'the specifically Protestant mind is gradually destructive of the objects of its own belief, and of what survives of the heritage of historic Christianity' (274).

That last remark could have been made by any anti-modernist. It is difficult to imagine why colleagues and the authorities in Rome were so worried about Congar's principles of Catholic ecumenism. He sees no chance of reunion with Protestant churches – and perhaps the possibility – remote – of reunion with the Anglican Church. The ecclesiology of the Orthodox is defective, yet, so he thinks, they are definitely not heretics – perhaps that was a shocking thought in 1938. More shocking, however, was no doubt the assertion that non-Roman-Catholic churches have 'in greater or lesser degree' true elements of what the Church really is – other Christians, that is to say, are members of churches which are, sacramentally and in other ways, not completely and totally null and void.

Intégrisme

Vraie et fausse réforme dans l'Église runs to 650 pages. In the first part Congar deals with sin in the Church (chapter 1); how reform should take place (chapter 2); and the part played by reforming prophets (chapter 3). The second part lays out four conditions for reform without schism: acknowledging the primacy of charity; remaining in communion with the whole Church; patience; and renewal by *ressourcement*, return to the sources. The third part deals with the Reformation, principally with Luther, contending that the mediatory role of the visible Church falls away into oblivion. In the conclusion Congar admits understandable reservations and hesitancies but argues that the time is ripe, especially in France: there is nothing 'modernist' or 'revolutionary' to fear; the bishops are welcoming, the would-be reformers are loyal Catholics; the reform required obviously issues out of pastoral concern.

Nevertheless Congar acknowledges the problem of a split – *une scission spirituelle* – among Catholics, between one country and another, between France and (say) Flanders, Quebec, the Netherlands, Ireland; and also between Catholics in the same country!

Accordingly, the book ends with 18 pages on *intégrisme* in France. Modernism, as it existed from 1895 to 1910, Congar says, was indeed a heresy. He happily quotes Pope Pius X against it. *Intégristes*, on the other hand, maximize orthodoxy so much that this also becomes a way out of Catholicism. He adapts Newman, writing to W.G. Ward:

> Pardon me if I say that you are making a Church within a Church, as the Novatians of old did within the Catholic pale, and, as outside the Catholic pale, the Evangelicals of the Establishment . . . you are doing your best to make a party in the Catholic Church, and in St Paul's words are dividing Christ by exalting your opinions into dogma . . . I protest then again, not against your tenets, but against what I must call your schismatical spirit.[14]

This sectarian tendency to maximize whatever is settled by authority slips into condemning all openness, research, and questioning of received ideas. A Catholic's orthodoxy becomes measurable by the degree of hatred that he shows for those he suspects of heterodoxy. The problem with *intégrisme* is, finally, Congar thinks, that it has too little confidence in the truth, insufficient love of the truth – 'Lord enlarge my soul, as Catherine of Siena prayed.'

---

[14] 9 May 1867, quoting W. Ward, *The Life of J.H. Cardinal Newman* (1913), vol. 2: 233; now *The Letters and Diaries of John Henry Newman*, vol. XXIII (Oxford: Clarendon Press 1973): 216–17.

Lay People in the Church

Lay People in the Church is a classic. For decades, especially under the influence of Pius XI and Pius XII, there were tremendous developments in the lay apostolate. It was time for reflection and an attempt to recapitulate the place of lay people, structured on the doctrine of their participation in the Church's three-fold priestly, regal/pastoral and prophetical function. The theology of laity really demanded a total ecclesiology.

The Church is the collectivity of the faithful, the *congregatio fidelium* in a phrase that Congar likes to quote from Thomas Aquinas. The faithful, one has to remember, include the clergy! For generations, in understandable but one-sided reactions to 'spiritual' sects, conciliarism, Gallicanism, the Reformation, and so on, Congar says, ecclesiology gradually became 'hierarchology'. The lay apostolate has outmoded this. Clergy and laity participate equally in Christ's messianic mission, yet in different ways: the clergy, by celebrating the sacraments, constitute the faithful people; whereas the laity, by their graced activities, consecrate the world, making of all things a sacrifice of praise and temple of God. We need to retrieve the doctrine of the priesthood of the laity, which Congar develops entirely on the basis of quotations from Aquinas.

The regal or pastoral function extends to the laity's participation in running the Church. Congar recalls how much lay people have done, historically, in administrative and legal matters. He includes a paragraph on the possibility of a lay man's being elected pope, as Benedict VIII in 1012 and John XIX in 1024 were, he tells us. A small piece of forgotten history destabilizes a long-held assumption.[15]

As for the prophetical function, Congar insists that, in doctrinal development, there is co-operation, in the conservation and development of the deposit of faith, between laity and clergy. In the Church, all are animated by the Holy Spirit, according to their place and part: the bishops to teach, the laity to believe; but believing is an active appropriation, not mere passivity.

Congar introduces the Russian Orthodox idea of *sobornost'*, suggesting that the translation as 'conciliarity' should give way to what the Western

---

[15] He doesn't go far enough: Benedict VIII (pope 1012–24) and John XIX (1024–32) were brothers, succeeded by their nephew, Benedict IX (1032–45), also a lay man. He, in turn, abdicated in favour of his godfather Gregory VI (1045–6), who was deposed by a synod called and presided over by the Holy Roman Emperor, who then had 'elected' the first of the four German popes he imposed: not a glorious period in papal history, but showing that three popes were lay men when elected, while one was deposed and four imposed, by a keen young lay man determined to reform the Church, or anyway to get the papacy out of one Roman family's clutches.

canonical and theological tradition means by 'collegiality'.[16] It was a fact of life for centuries. The term 'collegiality' needs to be allowed to retrieve its meaning in the cluster of allied concepts related to Christian life in fellowship and community. It is a Trinitarian concept: the sublime mystery of the Holy Trinity is 'a sort of concelebration'[17] – which is the law of the whole economy of grace. As Paul says (1 Corinthians 11, Ephesians 5), hierarchy and people are like husband and wife (*sic!*). This involves 'much deep doctrine'.[18] What happens in the Church is on analogy with 'the happiness of communing with as well as communicating to, of giving itself a fellow as partner and helper, with whom a dialogue and co-operation are set up, then a sharing, and finally a communion',[19] namely, in the triune Godhead. These remarks, more provisional than the summary makes them sound, anticipate the doctrine of nuptiality which, as we shall find, came to dominate Catholic theology by the end of the twentieth century.

This leads to the *sensus fidelium*: 'The Church loving and believing, that is, the body of the faithful, is infallible in the living possession of its faith'. This 'infallibility' is 'not simply a submissive deference to the hierarchy, a moral act of docility or obedience, but it is of a vital, moral nature, connected with righteous living'.[20]

Finally, Congar trawls through history for evidence of lay participation in teaching the Christian faith, by poets and artists, by many lay movements, and by lay theologians – back to Justin, Tertullian and suchlike. He returns, at length – 150 pages – to Catholic Action, lay people taking part in the Church's mission; lay holiness; sanctification in the world, the existing reality on which his book is only a reflection.

Vatican II

On the eve of the Council, in 1962, Yves Congar's help was not wanted, either by the French bishops or by the Master of the Dominican Order, despite his having taken part in the preparatory drafting. In August 1962 he

---

[16]   The Russian word *sobornost'* (catholicity) means that the catholicity of the Church is found in the unity in Christ which exists in the event of the worshipping congregation especially in the eucharist; taught by Russian theologians such as Georges Florovsky (1893–1979) and Alexei Khomiakov (1804–60), it perhaps has not such prominence in Orthodox tradition as Congar seems to think.

[17]   *Lay People in the Church*: 271.

[18]   Ibid.: 272.

[19]   Ibid.: 271.

[20]   Ibid.: 275.

offered his services to the bishop of Strasbourg who at first refused – not, however, because of reluctance to employ the still suspected theologian, only because he feared he would have to pay Congar's expenses in Rome. However, he was among the 200 'experts' appointed by Pope John XXIII. In the event, though Congar was not the principal begetter of the Vatican II document on the Church, the layout – the Church as mystery, as people of God, as clergy and laity, and so on – obviously displays his sense of priorities in expounding the doctrine.

While the idea of a chapter on 'the people of God' seems to have been suggested by Albert Prignon, then Rector of the Belgian College in Rome, Congar drafted it. In his journal, for 2 October 1963, Congar records the speech by the Master of the Dominican Order, attacking the idea of the Church as the people of God, warning of the risk of falling into exaggerated *democratismus*. He records the very fair presentation (as he thinks) of the idea of episcopal collegiality by Cardinal Michael Browne, spokesman for the doctrine commission; making it clear however that he (Browne) rejected the doctrine himself: to say the bishops formed a college would be to say they were all equal – which could not be right, since bishops have no juris-diction outside their own diocese; if they share in governing the Church it is by favour of the pope, he alone is the source of their authority.[21]

Back in 1953, as we saw, Congar put the word 'collegiality' into circula-tion. The idea of the Apostles as a college, in parallel with the bishops as an order, was already to be found in the draft constitution *de ecclesia* prepared for discussion in 1870. Few knew these texts, in which it was noted, for example, that ancient conciliar practice shows it to be a dogma of faith that the bishops share in governing and teaching the universal Church. In 1963, however, this talk of episcopal collegiality seemed new – a newly introduced word to express an essential dimension of the Church's life all along, as Congar believed; a new word to smuggle in an attack on papal supremacy, as the likes of Browne and Fernandez feared. For Congar, the balance was being restored between papal primacy and episcopal collegiality – essential if there was ever to be reconciliation with the Orthodox. But this was only one of the most intractable questions at Vatican II. From the ultramontanist minority, fearful of the implications of the very idea of episcopal collegiality, to the much larger number who voted against including the text on the Virgin Mary in the document on the Church, through to the stubborn resistance to successive drafts of the text on religious liberty, the speeches on the floor exposed the deep rift between two very different versions of Catholic theology and sensibility.

---

[21] *Mon Journal du Concile* I (Paris: Cerf 2002): 426, 380.

In October 1963 a large majority of the Council fathers voted in favour of the doctrine of collegiality – that supreme authority in the Church lay with the bishops as a whole, of course including the pope. However, over 408 were against the doctrine. After much redrafting, in response to the bishops' written suggestions, when the text was resubmitted in September 1964 there were still 322 out of 2,000 against the doctrine – and this minority included many powerful figures. More than four decades on, while they are no doubt all dead, the fact remains that there has not been anything like the decentralization, the return of authority to local bishops, that the text promulgated in 1964 envisages. The power of the papal Curia that the majority of the bishops expected to be balanced by new or revitalized instruments of collective episcopal authority seems, if anything, only to have become more secure, as we enter the twenty-first century.

Religious Liberty

Yves Congar had a hand in half of the Vatican II texts, at some stage. The Decree on Ecumenism contains his dearest themes: recognition of the elements of truth and grace in non-Catholic Christian communities; the importance of 'dialogue'; of 'spiritual ecumenism'; and of 'reform'. He worked closely with his young colleague Joseph Ratzinger on rewriting the rather miserable draft on Missions – producing what is acknowledged to be one of the finest texts.

But nothing is more revealing about Congar's character, as well as his ecumenical approach, than his involvement in drafting *Dignitatis Humanæ*, the Declaration on Religious Liberty. The history of the production of this text displays radically conflicting visions of Catholicism. Congar tried hard to make it a much stronger text, more scriptural and more theological, grounding it in the New Testament doctrine of our freedom in Christ, and so on. Eventually he gave up, deciding that any further substantial modifications to the text-in-progress would likely end in there being no text at all.

After the Nazi German and Soviet Russian attempts to exterminate the Church, as well as the introduction of anti-Catholic laws in France, Mexico and elsewhere, something about the freedom of the Church from state control had to be on the agenda. In any case, it was a major issue inherited from the First Vatican Council. It was even *the* major issue: the point of Vatican I's doctrine of papal supremacy was, in its own way, equivalent to the Oxford Movement's resistance to erastianism in the Church of England, and to the Disruption of 1843 in the Church of Scotland, and parallel movements elsewhere. Certainly, the Roman university theologians who (mostly) drafted the document wanted a clear statement, asserting the right of the Church to exercise her mission, free of civil interference, including practical matters like freedom to run schools, own property, and so on, preferably in harmony with, and indeed with the support of, the state, and so (tacitly) including tax relief and other such benefits.

Controversy heated up when the bishops of the United States of America entered the debate. Of course they sought freedom of action for the Church over against the state – but they wanted also freedom of conscience for individuals. They wanted a clear admission that the Catholic Church officially recognized the rights of members of other religions to practise their faith. This was an essential step for engagement in the ecumenical movement, in a religiously pluralist society like that of the United States, so they insisted. (The first Catholic President was elected in 1961.)

The conflicting views were so intractable, as the Council speeches show, that a decision to vote on the text was repeatedly postponed. In September 1964, at the third session, the US cardinals took the floor, accepting the text as it stood at that date. They did not want it sent back for further rewriting, perhaps fearing that it would disappear for ever. Further amendments, if any were needed, should strengthen the Church's commitment to religious freedom, a natural right of every person, one of the aspects of natural human freedom, and so on, but the text should stand. What they sought, it seemed, was something like the First Amendment to the Constitution of the United States (1791): 'Congress shall make no law respecting an establishment of religion, or prohibiting the free exercise thereof'. No Church – however 'true' – would ever be granted privileged status by the state; no religious body – however bizarre – was to be prevented by the state from worshipping God or propagating its teachings in whatever way it chose.

Many Europeans could not stomach this. For one thing, they did not see why what Catholics believe should be tempered in any way to relieve anxieties on the part of others. As regards freedom to practise one's religion itself, Cardinal Ottaviani, in effect speaking for the Holy Office, of which he was still the Prefect, argued that the text would be saying nothing new – no one is to be coerced in religious matters, as the Catholic Church has always recognized. Nonetheless there needed to be an explicit affirmation of the primary right to religious freedom, in the proper sense of 'right', which belongs, objectively, to those who are members of the one true revealed religion. Moreover, the rights of the true religion are based, he argued, not on merely natural rights, but on the rights which flow from revelation.

Two eminent Spanish bishops were much less sympathetic: the text was totally unacceptable, it appeared to favour union with the separated brethren, it endorsed the 'liberalism' which the Church had so often condemned, it denied the fact that, objectively speaking, no other religion but the Roman Catholic Church had the right to propagate its doctrine; and so on.

The leading Dominicans at the Council weighed in against the text. According to Cardinal Michael Browne, it could not be approved as it stood, since it asserted that religious freedom is founded on the rights of conscience, which is simply *not true*. Aniceto Fernandez, his successor as Master of the Order, wanted a good deal of revision, arguing that the text was too *naturalistic*. Both of these critics, obviously, feared that the Catholic Church was being manoeuvred into adopting some version of Thomas Jefferson's belief in the absolute freedom of private judgement and his assumption that creeds were the bane and ruin of Christianity.[22]

The text as it stood, at this stage, so Congar thought, was 'premature'. The Catholic Church's previous position about freedom in religious matters – 'error has no rights' – was embedded in a history, Christendom, Catholic states, and suchlike, and should certainly be abandoned. Yet, he thought, the draft replaced what had been believed for centuries, much too abruptly, whereas there needed to be more sense of continuity. The statement should not be allowed to give the impression of being a total reversal of previous teaching.

Much revised, the text (now in its fourth draft) returned to the bishops for debate in November 1964. So much revision had taken place that some wanted time to reconsider it. Accordingly, the praesidium decreed that discussion would be deferred until the fourth (and everyone hoped final) session of the Council. At this, the US bishops were outraged – the confidence of the entire Christian and non-Christian world in the Catholic Church would be forfeit, if there were any further delay over what seemed to the Americans a perfectly straightforward and simple matter: do Catholics believe in freedom of conscience or not? Pandemonium broke out on the Council floor; Paul VI, watching on closed-circuit television, telephoned the secretary general to come to him at once, the Americans started to gather signatures for a petition – in vain: the pope decided to leave the decision until the fourth session, guaranteeing it would be first on the agenda. For this reason, among others, the third session concluded, on 21 November 1964, with a grim-faced Paul VI being carried on the *sedia gestatoria* out of the basilica through tiers of stony-faced bishops, whose lack of enthusiasm, so uncharacteristic of such events, testified to the seriousness of the impasse over several issues, at this point in the history of Vatican II.

---

[22] *Mon Journal du Concile* II (Paris: Cerf 2002): 157, 162.

The reason for deferring the vote once again was simply that the pope and the inner circle of his advisors feared that there would be as many as 800 votes against the text, out of 2,300, much too significant a minority. What would it look like, to the outside world, if the Catholic Church were to endorse religious liberty but with one in three of the bishops against it? More anguishing for Paul VI, what would it feel like, for ordinary Catholics the world over, to discover how divided the Church was? He sought as much consensus as possible, but, like other observers at the time, he had no illusions about the deep and bitter conflict between two radically different versions of Catholic Christianity.

In February 1965, while working on the text to be presented at the final session, Congar regarded the draft as simply too optimistic – the drafting committee lacked the benefit of having opponents among them who would oblige them to compromise, instead of just celebrating what he calls their 'euphoric unanimity'.[23] He even wished that Cardinal Michael Browne, and two other stalwart adversaries of everything he wanted from the Council had been on the commission. In May 1965 he confided to his journal that while the Declaration would reduce fears of the Catholic Church, yet it would also very likely encourage indifferentism in religious matters among Catholics. Indeed, he predicted, it was likely to encourage the idea that the norms of morality, standards in ethical conduct, and so on, reside in people's being sincere and having good intentions, rather than in anything objective.[24]

In the end, when they voted on 19 November 1965, of the 2,216 Council members present, 1,954 voted in favour, 249 against, and 13 votes were invalid – which was, of course, a decision by far more than the required two-thirds majority. Nonetheless a hard core of opponents remained.

The history of the production of the document on freedom of religion convinced Yves Congar that the achievement of the Council could never have been completely satisfactory, in the sense of satisfying everyone. He saw the deep and bitter differences within Catholic theology, and piety, and sensibility.

In 1965 he listed problems that were never seriously engaged with at all. There was a gap between biblical scholars and theologians; no one should be awarded a higher degree in Catholic theology, he suggested, unless they have published some worthwhile work on the Bible, a pretty daunting requirement. Integrating modern biblical studies with doctrine would be one of the major problems to come. Second, while Vatican II admitted the

<hr />

[23]   *Journal* II: 329.
[24]   Ibid.: 370.

concepts of development and historicity, the long-resisted obvious fact that institutions change over time and that interpretations of events and texts also change, the implications for the Church, and for Scripture, were still to be faced. Third, major ethical and practical issues were not decided, and in some cases not even discussed. These issues included contraception, mixed marriages, penitential discipline, and indulgences.[25] ministries other than presbyteral; the place of women in the Church; how priests are paid; how bishops are appointed; the reform of the papal Curia and of titles and pomp – a somewhat heterogeneous agenda of unfinished business. Yet, he had no doubt, flawed and compromised as Vatican II's 'reform' of the Church was, it was much greater than he or anyone else could have imagined in the dark days of the 1950s.

Reception and Re-reception

In 1972 Congar published a landmark essay on the theological concept of 'reception': the way in which the Gospel is received and understood by the Church.[26]

The term is not to be found in the relevant volume of the *Dictionnaire théologique catholique*, the principal French authority, unsurprisingly since it came out in 1951. The *Oxford Dictionary of the Christian Church* (1957) has no entry either; whereas in the 1997 edition, the term receives a dozen lines, with no bibliography: Anglicans and Orthodox have emphasized 'reception' in recent times, we are told, but the definition of papal authority led to its being comparatively neglected by Catholics.[27]

---

[25] Visitors to churches in certain Catholic countries are often surprised to find that indulgences, the practice by which the Church remits the temporal penalty due to forgiven sin in virtue of the merits of Christ and the saints, remains in operation; the latest edition of the Enchiridion *Indulgentiarum* includes a new plenary indulgence granted for participation in the Week of Prayer for Christian Unity.

[26] 'La "réception" comme réalité ecclésiologique', *Revue des Sciences Philosophiques et Théologiques* 56 (1972): 369–403.

[27] The Faith and Order Consultation at Louvain in 1971 spoke of reception as 'the process by which the local churches accept the decision of a council and thereby recognize its authority. This process is a multiplex one and may last for centuries . . . the process of reception continues in some way or other as long as the churches are involved in self-examination on the basis of whether a particular council has been received and appropriated properly and with justification. In this sense . . . in the ecumenical movement the churches find themselves in a process of continuing reception or re-reception of the councils', see *The Dictionary of the Ecumenical Movement*, edited by Nicholas Lossky et al. (Geneva: World Council of Churches 1991), s.v. 'Reception'.

Congar means the whole process by which the Church accepts and integrates into her life this or that doctrinal decision, liturgical reform, or whatever. The Church is inherently receptive: she exists only in virtue of receiving the Holy Spirit (John 20:22; Acts 1:8). The Church teaches what she has received, not what is invented or discovered (1 Cor. 11:23; 15:3). Even if the faith 'has been delivered to the saints once and for all' (Jude 3), reception does not cease: the Spirit keeps leading the Church more deeply 'into the truth' (John 16:13).

The reception of this or that doctrinal decision, then, needs to be situated in the context of this ongoing reception of the Gospel. The Church as a whole receives the truth, not this or that element in the Church, such as the bishops (say). Thus the reception of the doctrine of the Council of Chalcedon (451), for example, is to be found not only in the teaching of the subsequent councils but in hymnody, prayers, icons, a whole spirituality. Reception of doctrine, in this sense, is an 'ecclesiological reality', as Congar calls it: a reality which goes far beyond accepting certain propositions.

Moreover, historically, the reception or assimilation of a doctrine defined at a Council has not always been immediate or unanimous. After Nicaea (325) it took decades for the Church to receive the doctrine defined then. Indeed, formulations have been rejected, as Chalcedon was by much of the Eastern Church – hence the existence of the Oriental Orthodox Churches.

Furthermore, a doctrine is never received once and for all. Absorbed into the existing body of doctrine, it necessarily affects all the rest. Reception is a permanent process. We might speak of 're-reception', Congar says. For example, in the light of Vatican II on collegiality, there cannot but be a re-reception of Vatican I on papal primacy. This does not mean abandonment of the dogma, as if it were now redundant; nor does it mean revision, as if it were mistaken. Rather, a doctrine long held simply begins to look different in the context of a newly promulgated doctrine – that is what Congar means.

The term 'reception' is making its way slowly. In the Anglican–Roman Catholic Agreed Statement *Authority in the Church* (1977),[28] the way is prepared in phrases such as the Christian community's being 'enabled by the Holy Spirit to live out the gospel and so to be led into all truth'; its being 'given the capacity to assess its faith and life' (§2); its having to 'respond to and assess the insights and teachings of the ordained ministers'; in a 'continuing process of discernment and response' (§6); to 'the recognition and reception of conciliar decisions and disciplinary decisions', 'a substantial part

---

[28] *Authority in the Church: An Agreed Statement by the Anglican–Roman Catholic International Commission* (London: Catholic Truth Society 1977).

in the process of reception' being played by 'the response of the faithful' (§16) – which implants the concept of reception, very much in Congar's terms. In an important text (though of course not authoritative in either the Anglican Communion or the Catholic Church), *The Gift of Authority*, the Agreed Statement by ARCIC (1999), we even hear of 're-reception':

> Even though promised the assistance of the Holy Spirit, the churches from time to time lose sight of aspects of the apostolic Tradition, failing to discern the full vision of the kingdom of God in the light of which we seek to follow Christ. . . . Fresh recourse to Tradition in a new situation is the means by which God's revelation in Christ is recalled. The insights of biblical scholars and theologians and the wisdom of holy persons assist this. Thus, there may be a rediscovery of elements that were neglected and a fresh remembrance of the promises of God, leading to renewal of the Church's 'Amen'. There may also be a sifting of what has been received because some of the formulations of the Tradition are seen to be inadequate or even misleading in a new context. This whole process may be term *re-reception*.[29]

Conclusion

Much that Yves Congar stood for, and suffered for, passed into Catholic doctrine at Vatican II. That does not mean, however, that all his theological ideas are now history. With the concept of reception – and of re-reception – Congar opened questions and possibilities, which we have barely begun to confront.[30]

[29] *The Gift of Authority (Authority in the Church III): An Agreed Statement by the Anglican–Roman Catholic International Commission* (London: Catholic Truth Society 1999): (§25).
[30] See *Yves Congar: Theologian of the Church*, edited by Gabriel Flynn (Louvain: Peeters 2005), with good bibliography.

Chapter Four

EDWARD SCHILLEBEECKX

While he regarded himself as a theologian in the historico-contextualist school of his older Dominican colleagues Chenu and Congar, Edward Schillebeeckx was always far more sensitive to philosophical questions than either of them. The Dominican priory at Louvain, by his day, was no longer an enclave of pure Thomistic philosophy.[1] Young Schillebeeckx was taught by Dominicus De Petter,[2] who was by then working out a synthesis of Thomas Aquinas and contemporary phenomenological and personalist philosophy, maintaining that in our experiential knowledge of entities we have an immediate intuition of being. He was particularly interested in phenomenology, Husserl and problems of the intentionality of consciousness. From the outset, this directed Schillebeeckx away from anything that Garrigou-Lagrange could have recognized as Thomism.

Edward[3] Cornelis Florent Alfons Schillebeeckx was born on 12 November 1914, sixth of what would be 14 children, in a devout middle-class Flemish family.[4] He grew up in Kortenberg, an old town in Brabant. His father worked as an accountant for the Belgian government. His early years

---

[1]   As it no doubt was, in the heyday of the legendary Antoninus – M. Dummermuth (1841–1918), inflexibly anti-Jesuit defender of the Thomist doctrine of physical premotion, and the equally memorable Marcolinus – M. Tuyaerts (1878–1948), who believed most 'solutions' to questions adopted by Thomas Aquinas could be turned into defined dogmas of the Church.

[2]   Dominicus De Petter (1905–71) trained at the Institut Supérieur de Philosophie at Louvain founded by Cardinal Mercier.

[3]   If Edward, spelled thus, seems an unusual name for a Belgian it goes back to the Middle Ages when English influence was strong in Flanders.

[4]   For detail see Erik Borgman, *Edward Schillebeeckx: A Theologian in His History*, vol. I: *A Catholic Theology of Culture (1914–1965)* (London and New York: Continuum 2003); Philip Kennedy OP, *Schillebeeckx* (London: Geoffrey Chapman 1993); *The Schillebeeckx Reader*, edited by Robert J. Schreiter (New York: Crossroad 1984); and Edward Schillebeeckx, *I Am a Happy Theologian: Conversations with Francesco Strazzari* (London: SCP Press 1994).

were overshadowed by the German occupation of Belgium. He received a classical education at a Jesuit school, for which he had to learn to speak French. (Flemish was not permitted in Belgian schools and universities.) His decision not to follow an older brother into the Society of Jesus was made after he read Humbert Clérissac's *L'Esprit de Saint Dominique* (1924). He entered the Dominican Order in 1934. He read the mystics, taking the standard Dominican line: mysticism is the life of virtue and devotion directed towards God, which the Holy Spirit grants to all believers, quite distinct from episodic religious 'experiences', or anything essentially 'abnormal'. As a novice he added the name of Henricus to the four he already had, in honour of Henry Suso (c. 1295–1366), the German Dominican spiritual writer. Like Congar, Schillebeeckx eventually dropped his religious name.[5]

Like all Belgian seminarians, Schillebeeckx did military service, in a barracks reserved for student priests, rabbis and pastors, passing the year reading Husserl, Heidegger and Merleau-Ponty. Recalled to the army in October 1939 he was never involved in fighting. When the Belgian government capitulated in May 1940 he returned to Louvain where he pursued his four years of theological studies, virtually undisturbed by the war.

In 1942, however, De Petter was replaced as Regent, part of the wider campaign by the Dominican authorities in Rome to eradicate 'modernism'. De Petter's talk of 'intuition of being' seemed to turn Thomist realism into some form of subjectivist idealism. This crisis affected Schillebeeckx all the more because he discovered sympathies with Nazi ideology in some of Karl Adam's early work. Put on to reading Adam by De Petter, precisely as an alternative to 'rationalist' neothomist fears of the place of 'experience' in Catholic theology, he found that Adam's Tübingen School emphasis on 'life', 'community', 'das Volk', and so on, exposed him to the charms of Nazism. In 'Nature and Supernature', Schillebeeckx developed his own understanding of the orientation of human nature towards God, against Karl Adam's use of the supposedly Thomistic theorem 'grace perfects nature' to justify Catholic Christian collaboration (up to a point) with Nazism.[6]

As soon as the war ended, Schillebeeckx went to Paris to work on a doctoral dissertation on faith and culture, effectively a variant of the grace/nature theme, at the pontifical faculties of Le Saulchoir. As so often happens in Dominican life, however, he was soon recalled to Louvain to teach dogmatic theology, long before he was properly qualified to do so. In his year in Paris, Schillebeeckx took courses at Le Saulchoir (Yves Congar among

---

[5]   In his first publications, as *De sacramentele Heilseconomie* (1952) he appears as Henricus Schillebeeckx.
[6]   Summarized by Borgman, *Schillebeeckx*: 56–9.

others), at the Sorbonne (René Le Senne, Louis Lavelle, Jean Wahl), the École des Hautes Études (Chenu) and the Collège de France (Gilson).[7] The dissertation came to nothing.

In 1952, however, he published *De sacramentele heilseconomie*, 'theological reflection on St Thomas's doctrine of the sacraments in the light of tradition and of modern problems about the sacraments', the first volume of an extensive investigation of the tradition that was to form the basis of a synthesis, never completed, expounding the sacraments as celebrations, expressions, of the Christian faith in all its fullness. This massive book – 700 pages – was the product of two lecture courses on the sacraments. The historical-contextualist approach to Thomas Aquinas, characteristic of Chenu, and the trawling through patristic and medieval scholastic literature as practised by Congar, are very evident – while the interest in phenomenological philosophy already indicates the conditions for Schillebeeckx to develop his own distinctive approach. This book earned him the doctorate at Le Saulchoir.

From 1946 to 1957 Schillebeeckx taught dogmatic theology to young friars in the Dominican study house at Louvain. As a member of a religious order, he could not have had a chair at the Catholic University of Louvain. In 1958 he was sounded out about a chair at the University of Nijmegen. The Flemish Dominicans, at first refusing to let him go, withdrew their objections when, with his connivance, appeal was made to the Master of the Order, Michael Browne, who decreed that he should take up the offer of this prestigious chair. Ironically, three or four years later, Browne was one of the leaders of the minority (as they turned out to be, much to their surprise) at Vatican II, pitted against Schillebeeckx, by then the 'progressive' in-house theologian of the Dutch bishops.

When he got to Nijmegen, Schillebeeckx found Catholic theology in the Netherlands 'almost non-existent': that is to say, adhering to the non-historical approach in neoscholastic Thomism and avoiding dialogue with current philosophy. Never an official *peritus* at Vatican II, blocked by the Holy Office, though the Cardinal Archbishop of Utrecht (Alfrink) asked twice that he be appointed, Schillebeeckx, since he was not bound by the oath of confidentiality required of 'experts', was free to influence opinion as the bishops from all over the world found their feet. He lectured attractively in English, he alluded to ideas in the secret drafts, criticizing them and sketching alternatives. Advised principally by Schillebeeckx, the bishops of the Netherlands had a united and often decisive voice at the Council. The

---

[7]   Ibid.: 103: Schillebeeckx found Congar 'closed, withdrawn and impatient': 'When lecturing, Congar seemed distant, tired, dull' (this in 1945–6); whereas Chenu was 'a natural talent with a delight in life'.

clash behind the scenes between Schillebeeckx, the Flemish Dominican, and the Dutch Jesuit Sebastian Tromp (1889–1975), famous in the Netherlands for his role in enforcing the dismissal in the mid-1950s of seminary professors sympathetic to the so-called 'new theology', signalled the move from a deeply traditional, ultramontane Catholicism to the 'progressive liberalism' with which Dutch Catholics were to become identified in the immediately post-Vatican II years. (This conflict between Catholic sensibilities and convictions in the Netherlands has never been resolved.) Immediately after Vatican II Schillebeeckx devoted a great deal of energy to spreading his ideas about the Council's achievement. Increasingly, however, he broke new ground, in rethinking classical Christology in the light of historical-critical biblical studies. He retired in 1983 to work on the sacraments.

Delations

Lecture tours, especially in the United States, stimulated Schillebeeckx's thinking in many respects. John Robinson's *Honest to God*, the so-called 'God-is-dead' theologians, and suchlike, confronted Christian theology with very fundamental questions, he believed, with which he sought to grapple by drawing on 'critical theory' (the Frankfurt School, Jürgen Habermas), hermeneutical philosophy (Paul Ricoeur, Hans Georg Gadamer) and to some extent anglophone linguistic philosophy. While certainly seeing Vatican II as a breakthrough, he predicted, in 1964, that the Council's decisions would rapidly become outdated for Catholics in the Netherlands, being far too ambiguous and anodyne to speak to the adversaries in the stormy conflicts already occurring. After 1970, as the mutual hostility between the Vatican and many Dutch Catholics over liturgy, ministry and church organization, mired down into an impasse, and the 'progressive' bishops were gradually replaced by loyal ultramontanists, Schillebeeckx turned away into an entirely unprecedented project for a Catholic theologian: classical Christology needed to be rethought in the light of 'scientific' historical criticism of Scripture. Schillebeeckx immersed himself in the secondary literature in German, French and English. His research issued in a trilogy, *Jezus, het verhaal van een levende* (1974), *Gerechtigheid en Liefde* (1977) and *Mensen als verhaal van God* (1989).[8]

The first volume was delated to Rome by fellow theologians who no

---

[8]   *Jesus: An Experiment in Christology* (London: Collins 1979); *Christ: The Christian Experience in the Modern World* (London: SCM Press 1980); *Church: The Human Story of God* (London: SCM Press 1990).

doubt believed that he was too close to the Dutch bishops for them to curb his work. Though never forced out of teaching or forbidden to publish, he had several colloquies with officials at the Congregation for the Doctrine of the Faith.[9]

Influential figures in the Vatican had been angered for years, especially by Schillebeeckx's influence at the Council. As everyone knew, the brochure published by the Dutch bishops in 1961 – *The Bishops of the Netherlands on the Council* – was drafted by Schillebeeckx. The text speaks, most unsettlingly for anyone of ultramontanist inclinations, of 'papal infallibility [as] also involved in the ministerial infallibility of the world episcopate' (bad enough!), then goes on to maintain that 'the ministerial infallibility of the world episcopate' in its turn is 'also borne up by the infallible faith of the whole of the community of faith'. Each bishop was going to the Council as 'the voice of the whole community of faith for which he is responsible'. This, and much else in the brochure, looked like an attempt to revise the dogma of papal infallibility by locating infallibility in the faith of the whole community. Such ideas sounded uncannily like the heresies eliminated at Vatican I, not to mention what George Tyrrell was suggesting in his reply to Cardinal Mercier.

In 1967 the little book Schillebeeckx published, no doubt to prepare people for the expected abandonment of the requirement of celibacy for clergy in the Latin rite (*Clerical Celibacy under Fire: A Critical Appraisal* 1968), was delated to the Vatican by a well-known Dominican scholar.

In 1968, Karl Rahner telephoned Schillebeeckx to say that he had been appointed to defend him before the officials of the Congregation for the Doctrine of the Faith. He mailed the dossier: copies of interviews given to newspapers in the United States. The issue was Schillebeeckx's statement about 'secularization' (it was thought at the time that religion was on the wane). On 24 September 1968 *Le Monde* disclosed that the Congregation was investigating Schillebeeckx 'on suspicion of heresy'. Since he himself was supposed to know nothing of the investigation, and all other parties were sworn to silence, the Congregation officials were infuriated. Rahner was summoned to the Vatican, interrogated for three hours by Archbishop Paul Philippe OP (1905–84), on behalf of the Congregation. Rahner repeatedly denied telling Schillebeeckx – and eventually Philippe apologized. Rahner believed that he had to speak to the accused, whatever the Congregation rules prescribed – the oath of secrecy which he had sworn when

[9]   See *The Schillebeeckx Case: Official Exchange of Letters and Documents in the Investigation of Fr Edward Schillebeeckx OP by the Sacred Congregation for the Doctrine of the Faith 1976–1980*, ed. Ted Schoof OP (New York: Paulist, 1984).

appointed was required by church law, but the justice required by natural law took priority. 'My conscience told me to make a mental reservation', Rahner told Schillebeeckx.[10]

Delated as soon as it appeared, Schillebeeckx's *Jesus* raised quite serious problems. By this time the Congregation rules were changed, enabling the accused to defend himself. He replied in writing to one request from the Congregation to clarify (1) the preference for certain schools of biblical exegesis; (2) the implications for the history of Jesus and particularly for his resurrection; and (3) the implications for the doctrines of the Incarnation, the Trinity, the virginal conception of Jesus and the foundation of the Church. Eventually, in December 1979, in Rome, over two and a half days, Schillebeeckx answered questions put to him by three Congregation theologians: Albert Descamps, a distinguished biblical scholar from Louvain, an old friend ('I am here as an exegete and not as a dogmatic theologian'), who had already reviewed the book, critically but respectfully; Albert Patfoort OP, the epitome of mainstream Dominican Thomism, then lecturing at the Angelicum, innocent of any other theology or philosophy apart from Aquinas's (he asked Schillebeeckx to explain hermeneutics); and Jean Galot SJ, another Belgian, Louvain trained, lecturing at the Gregorianum, and already an internationally known dogmatic theologian on the distinctly 'conservative' wing (unfortunately he chose to display a newspaper photograph of Schillebeeckx preaching at the marriage of a priest in a Dutch parish, and had to be brought to order by the neutral chairman for this irrelevance). The colloquium was mounted, as the rules said, in an 'ecclesial spirit of respect and mutual trust'; certainly every effort seems to have been made to assemble theologians familiar with the Low Countries. (Patfoort was a Fleming from Lille.) In the event, on 20 November 1980, Schillebeeckx received a letter from the Congregation inviting him to clarify some points and remove some ambiguities – stating, however, that while some questions remained open on matters which are not in accord with the doctrine of the Church, they were in accord with the faith. There was no 'condemnation'.

Thomism Revised

For three years Schillebeeckx attended courses on Thomistic philosophy, including by De Petter, without actually reading texts of Thomas Aquinas.

---

[10] For the whole story see Schillebeeckx, *I Am a Happy Theologian*: 32–4. Karl Lehmann, then Rahner's assistant, now Cardinal Archbishop of Mainz, had the task of reading the dossier and drafting Rahner's speech.

In the four years of theology, he and his companions did read Aquinas, though completely unhistorically. They read nothing apart from the *Summa Theologiæ*, paying little attention to the historical or narrative context of whichever section they had before them.

In 1937–8 Schillebeeckx undertook a project under De Petter's supervision to consider whether knowledge is conceptual or includes a non-conceptual element. The question was about how God comes to be known – conceptually, intuitively, or experientially. Against neoscholastic philosophy, which evidently favoured an ahistorical system of concepts, so it was thought, this was opening the possibility of a certain non-conceptual element. During his military service he read the newly published *Geist in Welt* by Karl Rahner. As we shall see, Balthasar, with his book on truth, and Lonergan, with his book *Insight*, also felt the need to surmount the neoscholastic theory of knowledge that they inherited. With many of their contemporaries in Reformed and Anglican theology, though in almost total ignorance of their work, this generation of Catholic theologians felt compelled to deal with questions in religious epistemology, and in particular to challenge what they took to be a merely conceptualist approach.

From the outset, when he expounded Aquinas's theology to young Dominican friars in Louvain, Schillebeeckx insisted on contextualizing concepts in their genesis, offering a historical reading, taking into consideration the patristic sources and the twelfth-century 'Masters'. He believed that the most important decisions in the history of theology were made in the twelfth and not in the thirteenth century – an insight no doubt from Chenu. When he went to Nijmegen his predecessor Gerard Kreling advised him to begin with the *de Deo uno*, the course on God's existence, nature and attributes then assumed to be the dogmatician's favourite topic. Kreling was a great theologian, Schillebeeckx recalled, authentically Thomist, but in the sense of 'pure scholasticism without the historical dimension'. He was infuriated when Schillebeeckx began with eschatology. (For the 10 years remaining to Kreling he lived in increasing isolation in a small parish – sidelined; one should not forget the pain suffered by his generation.)

Before Vatican II, then, Schillebeeckx had broken with neoscholastic theology. Then, in 1965, another shift occurred when he discovered hermeneutics. 'This changed the way I did theology.' A principle often enunciated by Thomas Aquinas – 'omnia quæ recipiuntur recepta sunt secundum modum recipientis' (everything that is received is received according to the mode of the one who receives) – legitimized taking account always of the social and historical conditions under which any knowledge takes place. Neothomistic theology was never related properly or sufficiently to experience:

concepts were treated as if they were eternal; as if they had no history. This is very much Chenu's critique of Garrigou-Lagrange's approach.

In *Jesus* Schillebeeckx explicitly breaks with the religious epistemology taught by De Petter. He now rejects the whole idea of implicit intuitive participation in being, the whole of meaning, allegedly, manifest or anyway intuitively discoverable in every particular experience of meaning. This was a brilliant development of Thomas Aquinas, he allows. In Aquinas's day, moreover, when it was a self-evident truth that human beings had a single destiny – the beatific vision – and there was a range of 'appropriate plausibility-structures' in place to sustain it, Aquinas's theology was in place, incontestably. For us, now, however, in a society in which divergent ideologies and outlooks compete in the market of world history, so Schillebeeckx contends, the idea of our participation in a simply given structure of being has no purchase whatsoever. Where we have to start is with the idea of anticipating a total meaning in the history we are always still making.

The *Jesus* Book

Hitherto, Catholic expositions of Christology began from the doctrines defined at the Council of Chalcedon in 451 ('two natures in one person'). The celebration in 1951 of the centenary of the Council spurred Karl Rahner, among other Catholic theologians, to contemplate the possibility of a renewal of Catholic Christology, but the fears articulated by Pope Pius XII, however, in the same year, in his encyclical *Humani Generis*, damped enthusiasm for radically new developments. By 1970, however, for Schillebeeckx among many others, it no longer seemed possible to expound Christology solely on the basis of the classical creeds and conciliar definitions. A half-century of historical research, by Catholic scholars as well as others, needed to be incorporated. Christology could begin, not from the doctrine of the Incarnation, as Thomas Aquinas does, but from the New Testament narratives, the story of how the man Jesus is discovered as Lord, scrutinized in the light of the best modern critical exegesis.

As he made clear at the outset, Schillebeeckx sought to reconstruct Christology beginning with the apparently diverse Christologies to be found in the three synoptic gospels, according to the exegetes by whose work he was most attracted. He took Mark as the first gospel, already a controversial decision in the eyes of most traditional Catholic theologians, but helping to substantiate the claim that a version of the story of Jesus existed with no account of his birth and infancy, and no account of his resurrection either (Mark being assumed to conclude with the women leaving the empty tomb). Schillebeeckx accepted the existence of the so-called 'Q' document: the hypothetical source of the material shared by Matthew and Luke and absent in Mark.[11] He takes the 'Q' material as the interweaving by Matthew and Luke into their narratives of a text that was originally the creed of one of the first Christian communities (*Jesus* 410–12). This creed says nothing about the suffering, death and resurrection of Christ. He was even attracted by the thought that we can detect developments within the history of this supposed Q-community, with its distinctive 'Christology' existing without any interest in the Incarnation, Passion or Resurrection.

That he always planned to move from the supposedly diverse Christologies in the first three gospels to the Christologies developed in the fourth gospel, in the letters of the apostle Paul, and in the rest of the New Testament, was always clear. This is, of course, what he did in the second volume, another masterly engagement with a vast amount of secondary literature. By then, however, so much anxiety had been raised that he responded with the *Interim Report*, explaining and to some extent modifying the claims that seemed so contentious.[12]

Obviously, coming late in the day and largely self taught, Schillebeeckx was bound to make mistakes. He always goes for the most exciting theory. On the other hand, as an experienced professor of systematic theology, he came to the results of biblical scholarship with much greater awareness of the implications for Christian doctrine than biblical scholars commonly display.

At one level, the *Jesus* book is a vast compendium of the most recent biblical research. The aim, however, is to reconstruct the history of the development of the New Testament literature, beginning with the synoptic gospels, so as to reveal how faith in Jesus emerged: 'With the aid of *Formgeschichte* [the study of the historicity of biblical writings by studying their literary form] our aim is, among other things, to penetrate to the earliest layer of the pre-canonical tradition, in order thus to open the way to Jesus of Nazareth' (744).

The assumption is that the text as we have it can be pressed to disclose the elements out of which it was created. Schillebeeckx burrows into what he calls the 'incubatory history' of the texts, with methods analogous to those of an art restorer who strips off one level to exhibit an underlying sketch. If Christianity is neither to become 'an historical relic' nor to appeal to 'supernatural hocus-pocus', its message must be reconstructed historically

---

[11] Known as 'Q' since the 1890s (German *Quelle* = source); see J. Kloppenborg, *The Formation of Q* (Philadelphia, PA: Fortress 1987).

[12] *Interim Report on the Books 'Jesus' and 'Christ'* (London: SCM Press 1980).

by a critical study of the New Testament texts and then submitted to reinterpretation.

This kind of project is at least as old as nineteenth-century liberal Protestant exegetes. Rudolf Bultmann's effort to 'demythologize' the New Testament with the aid of Heidegger's existential categories seems to engage Schillebeeckx's interest more. He simply reverses Bultmann's strategy. Whereas Bultmann maintained that hardly anything could be known about Jesus as a historical figure, with the result that the whole Christian phenomenon is to be found in the *kerygma*, in the proclamation of the Christ of faith ('Jesus rose into the kerygma', as Bultmann put it), Schillebeeckx asserts that the New Testament, properly studied, with the tools of modern critical-historical research, delivers substantial, verifiable information about Jesus of Nazareth. Indeed, this history 'can then show us what exactly it was that very early Christianity understood by the affirmation: he is the Christ, the son of man, the Son of God, the Lord' (pp. 437, 440; cf. pp. 71 and 515).

This quasi-archaeological excavation of the synoptic gospels lays bare five levels.

1   Jesus's own experience of God and of his mission – Jesus's 'Abba experience': highlighting these references takes us to the historical Jesus, in his historically unique way of addressing God as 'Abba'.

2   The experience of Peter and the Twelve: some weeks or months after Jesus's death, Peter had an experience of being forgiven for his faithlessness, gathered the disciples, in a setting of doubt and debate, recalled with them the life and 'Abba' experience of Jesus, then 'They all of a sudden "saw" it' (391) – Jesus crucified, has been definitively vindicated by God and is alive with his Father.

3   The Q-community tradition: faith that Jesus was the expected latter-day prophet and messianic judge who was 'exalted' to God.

4   The early Palestinian Christians: following Jewish custom, they started a practice of venerating the tomb of Jesus at Jerusalem, which gave rise to the story of women finding the 'empty tomb' 'on the third day'; 'an aetiological cult-legend, intended to shed light on the (at least) annual visit of the Jerusalem church to the tomb in order to honor the risen [exalted] One' (336); and from this practice, in the 'first few generations', the language of a bodily resurrection from the dead began to take precedence over the language of 'exaltation' to the right hand of the Father (396).

5   From a 'theology of Jesus' to a 'Christology': from interpretations of the meaning of Jesus concerned not with who or what Jesus was but with what he was meant to do, thus 'first-order' 'functional' descriptions, to

the 'second-order' 'ontological' claims about the identity of Jesus, already there in Paul and John.

The claim, then, putting it too simply, is that, by re-creating the history of how faith in Jesus of Nazareth arose, it becomes possible to arouse faith in him in people not hitherto Christian believers, who would not find ready access to him through the doctrines of the Church – Incarnation, Passion, Resurrection, and so on.

Few Christians, certainly no Catholics before Vatican II, ever depended on doctrines apart from a great deal of *experience*. No doubt theologians, and even ordinary Catholics, shied away from the word, it was too much associated with modernism. Yet, in practice, in the liturgy, in personal asceticism (regular confession, acts of penance, continence in marriage, and so on), in acquaintance with men and especially women living under vows of poverty, chastity and obedience (monks, nuns, sisters), and much else, 'cradle' Catholics were born and brought up in a whole culture, empirically habituating them to 'the Christian thing' (as G.K. Chesterton called it) – such that there was plenty of 'experience', a richly textured background, carrying and completing the doctrines. In effect, the Christ whom most Catholics encountered principally at Mass, with all that penumbra of religious experience, Schillebeeckx was suggesting, could now also be found in reconstructing and appropriating the history of the initial encounter with the Jesus of the New Testament.

The Easter Experience

Obviously, the very idea of rethinking Christology on the basis of 'scientific' historico-critical exegesis of Scripture rather than in terms of the dogmas of the Church was always going to shock most Catholic theologians, neoscholastic or otherwise – let alone pastors charged with protecting the beliefs of 'the simple faithful'. For one thing, there was always the danger of genetic fallacy: discovering its origins does not guarantee getting nearer the truth of a claim. On the other hand, Schillebeeckx took risks, sometimes with a handful of extremely sensitive topics, which distracted readers from learning from the immense bibliography digested for them by his omnivorous reading.

One problem, of course, is that of the virginal conception of Jesus. As a result of the 'Easter experience', reflection eventually shifted to Jesus's baptism by John and thus to the emergence and actual constitution of his being man – in other words, to the conclusion that Jesus owes his human existence, his very being, solely to the Holy Spirit. In due course this Christological reflection assumed a historical form – 'one that is indeed concrete, albeit not empirically ascertainable, but to be approached and evaluated only within a context of faith – in a Virgin Birth' (*Jesus* 555–6). In other words, so it seemed to most readers, what has been taken as an account of something that happened – the conception and birth of Jesus, his mother remaining a virgin – is actually a representation as a piece of history of the prior and independent belief in Jesus's unique origin in the Holy Spirit.

Then again, what did the disciples 'see', when they encountered the risen Lord Jesus? According to Schillebeeckx, it seems, in the literal sense of vision they saw nothing – nothing happened that might have been experienced physically, or photographed. They simply 'saw', on reflection together, that Jesus is 'the living One'. His resurrection from the dead should not be understood 'objectively', as an empirically verifiable, historical event – that is what fundamentalists believe. On the other hand, the resurrection of Jesus should not be understood as something that took place entirely in the heads of his followers, as a subjective renewal of their faith – as Bultmann and others hold, so Schillebeeckx says. He wants a middle path. He locates the original Easter experience in a conversion process (subjective), in which the disciples 'saw', or came to believe, that Jesus was alive with God (objective).

Most Christians, if they believe in the resurrection of Jesus from the dead at all, literally understood, suppose that this belief is based on the evidence of the tomb's being found empty and of the physical encounters with Jesus after his death. Schillebeeckx argues, however, that the language of 'resurrection', the concept of 'being raised from the dead', far from being the original interpretation of what happened, is second order, supplementary, and the product of later reflection. Originally, the Christian faith was, not that Jesus was raised from the dead, but that he was 'exalted into heaven', 'sitting at the right hand of the Father' – obviously analogical and metaphorical language. In fact, the figurative language that we are no doubt inclined to regard as secondary and optional (exaltation) is, on the contrary, what is basic and original.

Thus, the 'Easter experience', historically, was always independent of the 'tradition' of the appearance stories, and equally so of the 'tradition' of the empty tomb (397). The problem here, with how the empty tomb stories grew up, is that the evidence for there being veneration of anybody's tomb at the time is scanty – never mind the leap from visiting Jesus's tomb to claiming it was empty. 'The vital context', namely for the story in Mark of the women's visit to the tomb, 'is a tomb where a liturgical service is conducted' – which 'is something grounded deep in human nature' (336). In the extensive, and valuable, bibliography to the analysis of the empty tomb stories there is really nothing bearing this out except a reference to five pages in Joachim Jeremias's book on popular pilgrimages to sacred tombs in the early Christian environment.[13]

The reference to 'the third day' – as it were the Sunday three days after Good Friday – says nothing about the date on which Jesus was raised from the dead – rather, it is code for the definitive, eschatological saving action of God as regards the crucified Jesus (532). On the third day Joseph releases his brothers from prison (Gen. 42:18); God makes a covenant with his people (Exod. 19:11, 16); God gives life to his people and raises them up (Hos. 6:2–3); and so on. That 'the third day' has all this previous biblical significance is, of course, a valuable insight. Why this insight makes it redundant to think that Jesus actually rose on the third day, as Schillebeeckx seems to suggest, rather than making what really happened that more deeply significant, is the kind of question that goes beyond the parameters of biblical criticism.

The fears of those including fellow Dominicans who delated him to the Congregation for the Doctrine of the Faith are, of course, that Schillebeeckx's emphasis on 'experience' undermines belief in the teaching office of the Church as the norm of truth. In *Interim Report* – essentially his reply to critics of the first two volumes on Christology – Schillebeeckx insists that he should not be dismissed as a 'neo-liberal'. He refuses to concede that he devalues the tradition of the Christian community. He insists that he never offered more than prolegomena to a future Christology – his project should therefore not be attacked for what it is not. He discusses many other issues, in what is in some ways his most interesting contribution to theological methodology. From the point of view of those concerned with his notion of 'experience' he takes us back to the literature referenced in the *Christ* book, though highlighting the work of Karl Popper, T.S. Kuhn, Imre Lakatos, Paul Feyerabend and the Erlangen School (Paul Lorenzen). The point he wants to make is that his conception of the interrelationship of the concepts of revelation, experience and interpretation would indeed be misleading if we supposed that every experience is accompanied by conceptual or metaphorical articulations. Since Kant, and particularly in the philosophers he mentions, it has been recognized that theory or model has a certain primacy over experience, in the sense that there can be no experience without at least an implicit theory. On the other hand, theories cannot be derived from experiences straight off, as if by induction; they are the product of creative initiative on our part.

---

[13] Joachim Jeremias, *Heiligengräber in Jesu Umwelt* (Göttingen: Vandenhoeck and Ruprecht 1958).

For Schillebeeckx, then, the point is that biblical and ecclesiastical expressions of faith are never purely and simply articulations of supposedly 'immediate religious experiences', such as experiences of Jesus that his disciples may be said to have had. These expressions are always already theory-laden. He allows that this needed much more discussion, in the two books on Jesus. It needs much more than he takes space to discuss in *Interim Report*. However, it is enough to insist that even expressions of faith are never straight presentations of religious experience – they necessarily include an element of theory. Experience is always already interpretative. To deny this, he suggests, is to fall into a form of neo-empiricism – and it is surely clear that what he means is that some of his critics at any rate rely on a 'naïve confidence in so-called direct experiences'.[14]

Conclusion

Totally committed to renewal of the Church, Schillebeeckx never played down the many crises and conflicts at the Council, as we see in the accounts he wrote.[15] On the whole, he rejoiced in what he saw as the new relationship between Church and world, which the Council established. The pastoral constitution on the Church in the Modern World, *Gaudium et Spes*, opened the way (he expected) to bring Catholicism into fruitful interaction with secular culture. The Council was a 'compromise', he recognized. It lifted the shadow of *Humani Generis* and ended the climate of intimidation in which Catholic theologians worked since the modernist crisis. Indeed, 'it was the theology of theologians who had been condemned, removed from teaching posts, sent into exile, that triumphed at the Council'[16] – however, as he noted, the neoscholastics were defeated only temporarily, and there would be a return of the repressed, such that a kind of restoration was unavoidable.[17] Without much need of hindsight, we do better to say that, while on some extremely important issues the anti-modernist ultramontanist minority were outvoted, the conflicting versions of Catholicism on show on the floor of the Council reflect the division within the Church then – and prefigure the division that there is still.

---

[14] *Interim Report*: 18.
[15] *Vatican II: The Struggle of Minds and Other Essays* (Dublin: M.H. Gill 1963) and *Vatican II: The Real Achievement* (London: Sheed and Ward 1967).
[16] *I Am a Happy Theologian*: 15.
[17] Daniel Speed Thompson, *The Language of Dissent: Edward Schillebeeckx on the Crisis of Authority in the Catholic Church* (Notre Dame, IN: University of Notre Dame Press 2003).

The debate in philosophy, analytic and hermeneutic, has of course moved on in the past 25 years. Perhaps Schillebeeckx does not explain himself perfectly, or even all that skilfully, philosophically. The position that he wants to occupy, in theological epistemology, namely, somewhere between naïve empiricism and subjectivism, is anyway controversial. What remains impressive, in his generation of Catholic theologians, is his readiness to engage with the central philosophical issue of the relationship between experience and interpretation. Moreover, he has not had many successors as yet in the field of Catholic theology who dare, or are even competent, to rework the doctrines of the faith as defined by the early Councils and expounded in the classical theology of the Fathers and the Scholastics, in the light of serious study of Scripture and related literature. The gulf between professors of doctrine and biblical scholars is as wide as ever.

Chapter Five

HENRI DE LUBAC

Thomas Aquinas was, of course, a Dominican friar. At their chapter in Paris in 1286, 12 years after his death, the Dominicans decreed that every friar should promote his teaching and if anyone taught the contrary he was to be suspended *ipso facto* from whatever office he held until he thought better. For all that, the reception of Aquinas within his own Order has a chequered history.[1] Then, even when they were all professing Thomists, Dominicans such as Chenu, Congar and Schillebeeckx, could, as we have seen, clash with confrères like Garrigou-Lagrange, in radically different and effectively incommensurable interpretations of Aquinas even within the confines of the Dominican Order.

When we turn to such eminent Jesuit theologians as Henri de Lubac, Karl Rahner, Bernard Lonergan and Hans Urs von Balthasar, however, it turns out, according to their recollections, that, as far as their years of mandatory Thomist philosophy were concerned, they were taught what they came to recognize as 'Suárezianism'.[2]

In any case, de Lubac's early years as a Jesuit were so disrupted by the Great War that he seems to have been left largely to get on with his own reading, undisturbed by lecture courses. His superiors seem not to have regarded him as a future professor, either of philosophy or of theology. He often expresses gratitude to scholars of the previous generation, nearly all of whom were his fellow Jesuits; but effectively he was self-taught.

---

[1]   Newman, on his way to Rome in autumn 1846, as yet undecided which religious order if any he should join, was shocked to learn of the Dominicans in Florence manufacturing scented water, possessing a cellar of good wines, and with no interest in Thomas Aquinas, which decided him against them, *The Letters and Diaries of John Henry Newman*, vol. XI (London: Thomas Nelson and Sons 1961): 260, 263.
[2]   See chapter 8 for Balthasar's account of Suárezianism.

Henri Joseph Sonier de[3] Lubac was born on 20 February 1896, at Cambrai, in north-east France.[4] The family returned in 1898 to the Lyons district. His father, a banker, originally from Ardèche (where, in the local dialect, *l'ubac* means the shady side of a mountain), admired the Catholic social renewal project inspired by Albert de Mun.[5] His maternal grandparents were old-fashioned royalists, adhering to the elder branch of the Bourbon dynasty. Schooled by Jesuits in Lyons, Henri studied law for a year, before entering the Lyons province of the Society of Jesus, then in exile at St Leonards on the south coast of England. His noviciate was interrupted when he was drafted in 1914, into the French army. He saw action in Flanders, receiving the serious head wound at Les Eparges, in 1916, which afflicted him for the rest of his life.

Demobilized, he returned to the Jesuits, at Canterbury, then on Jersey. Years later, he reported that 'a certain Suárezian and Molinist orthodoxy' was required of the professors, claiming that on Jersey two were 'savage Suárezians' – whereas by 1950, ironically, 'against the abusive dominance of a "Thomist" school that was then in power', there were Jesuits seeking freedom to 'follow the Suárezian interpretation of Saint Thomas'.[6] Clearly, he distances himself from both. On his own, he studied Thomas Aquinas, in the light (however) of Etienne Gilson's 'fundamental book', which, he notes, again with some irony, was 'in the bookcase of light reading that was generously unlocked for us during holidays', together with Rousselot's thesis at the Sorbonne on Aquinas's intellectualism.[7] Colleagues mocked him as a 'Thomist' (as his colleagues laughed at George Tyrrell). As regards his philosophical culture, de Lubac read Maurice Blondel, with enthusiasm.[8] Evidently unaffected by lecture courses, he owed a great deal to discussions with contemporaries, some of whom were to be friends for life, including

---

[3]   The nobiliary particle, correctly used only with the *prénom* or initial, but, even in French, we find him often referred to as de Lubac, the standard practice in English.

[4]   For biographical details see Jean-Pierre Wagner, *Henri de Lubac* (Paris: Cerf 2001) and Henri de Lubac, *At the Service of the Church* (San Francisco: Ignatius Press 1993), his selective memoirs.

[5]   Albert de Mun (1841–1914), leader of the liberal Catholics in France, founded Catholic workers' circles and was a prolific writer.

[6]   *Letters of Etienne Gilson to Henri de Lubac* (San Francisco: Ignatius Press 1988): 188.

[7]   Ibid.: 7–8; the second 1922 edition of *Le Thomisme*, 'less dependent on modern Thomists', it 'contained a more penetrating analysis of the actual text of Saint Thomas'; *L'Iintellectualisme de saint Thomas* (1908, English translation 1935), by the French Jesuit Pierre Rousselot, killed in action at Les Eparges in 1915 aged 36.

[8]   Maurice Blondel (1861–1949), lay Catholic, philosopher, highlighted the pre-reflective desire of human beings for vision of God: *L'Action: Essai d'une critique de la vie et d'une science de la pratique* (1893), translated by Oliva Blanchette (Notre Dame, IN: University of Notre Dame Press 1984). A devout Catholic, he lived for years in terror of having his work placed on the Index of Prohibited Books, and was harassed especially by the Dominicans.

Pierre Teilhard de Chardin.[9] Mainly, however, he had already begun working his way through the Greek and Latin patrologies and the medieval Scholastics, gathering the quotations out of which he would weave his books. As his younger colleague and friend Hans Urs von Balthasar would note, de Lubac preferred 'to let a voice from the great ecclesial tradition express what he intends rather than raising his own voice' – yet, unmistakably, his views 'can be easily discerned in the web of quotations, especially when one pays close attention to the critiques and corrections of the passages cited'.[10] This means, of course, that de Lubac's views are easily missed by hasty readers, impatient to locate a position to challenge or to adopt – he is too elusive for that; yet, as one becomes accustomed to the procedure of multiplying references, de Lubac's theological options soon reveal themselves.

In a way de Lubac re-created a whole pre-modern Catholic sensibility which he wanted to inhabit. Much later, about 1960, looking back on the results of his decades of research in patristic and medieval-scholastic theologies, de Lubac would say that, for him, the 'great century' of the Middle Ages began around the year 1100, with 'the Bayeux tapestry, the murals at Saint-Savin, the sculptures at Toulouse and Moissac, the Heavenly Jerusalem at San Pietro al Monte (Civate), the basilicas of Cluny and Vézelay, the first mosaics at San Marco'.[11] This was the age of Rupert of Deutz (c. 1075–1129/1130), of William of St-Thierry (1075/80–1148), and of Bernard of Clairvaux (1090–1153), 'the last of the Fathers . . . the first of the great moderns'.[12] What is remarkable about William, of course, is his wide knowledge of Eastern as well as of Western patristic literature. In referring to him, de Lubac is reminding us that the Greek fathers remained in the memory of the Latin Church well into the twelfth century. Rupert, on the other hand, is best remembered for supposedly holding the doctrine later known as impanation.[13] He also wrote a commentary on the Song of Songs, in which he interprets the beloved as the Virgin Mary, and was among the

---

[9] Marie-Joseph Pierre Teilhard de Chardin (1881–1955), mobilized in December 1914 as a stretcher-bearer, received several citations for valour. He was professor of geology in Paris 1920–5, mostly in China 1923–46 studying early human remains, in New York 1951–5 with the Viking (Wenner-Gren) Foundation. From 1925 he was required to submit religious writings to such rigorous censorship that little appeared, but his work has been immensely popular posthumously. As a Jesuit student at Hastings he participated in the 'discovery' of Piltdown Man.

[10] Hans Urs von Balthasar, *The Theology of Henri de Lubac: An Overview* (San Francisco: Ignatius Press 1991): 26–7.

[11] *Exégèse mediévale: les quatre sens de l'Ecriture*, Collection Théologie 41 (I and II), 42 (III0, 50 (IV) (Paris: Aubier 1959, 1961, 1964). Here, II: 232.

[12] Ibid. III: 426–7.

[13] The Body of Christ is 'impanated', 'im-breaded', so to speak, at the eucharistic consecration, on analogy with the Word's becoming incarnate, 'enfleshed'.

earliest to do so. What no doubt attracted de Lubac is that Rupert, on several occasions under suspicion by ecclesiastical authorities, is one of the many misunderstood characters in the history of theology whom he seems to have made a deliberate choice to highlight. Against the 'devastating con-tractions of [modern Catholic] theology', as Balthasar noted, de Lubac chose to write, not about Bonaventure, Nicholas of Cusa, Pascal, Möhler, Newman, and so on, whom one would have regarded as his 'allies' in the history of Catholic theology; but on 'other representatives of universal thought, namely, the great among the vanquished who have fallen because of the machinations of smaller minds or of a narrow Catholicism that is politically rather than spiritually minded', from Origen to Teilhard de Chardin.[14] It was also, as we shall see, important that Rupert contributed to the tradition of commenting on the Song of Songs. Finally, in this little cameo, de Lubac signals that the 'great century', for him, in Western Chris-tianity, was not the thirteenth, with Thomas Aquinas, as most neoscholastic theologians would have claimed.[15]

Key Books in Modern Catholicism

In 1929, after the Jesuits returned to France, de Lubac began lecturing on fundamental theology at the Theology Faculty of Lyons, the required doc-torate having been conferred by the Gregorian University in Rome at the behest of the Father General of the Society of Jesus, without de Lubac's setting foot there or ever submitting a dissertation.[16] For better or worse, like many of the eminent Catholic theologians of his generation, de Lubac was never subjected to the discipline of doctoral research in which their Protestant contemporaries, especially in Germany, began their careers. He never taught any of the main theological courses to Jesuit students or anyone else.

The books that he wove out of his reading, which he usually passed off as 'occasional', and put together at someone else's urging, soon began to appear. Three were to become major texts in modern Catholic theology. The first, *Catholicisme: Les Aspects sociaux du dogme*, appeared in 1938 though the outbreak of the Second World War meant that it reached the wider readership only in the expanded edition of 1947. It appeared in English as

---

[14] Balthasar, *The Theology of Henri de Lubac*: 30–1.
[15] For that matter, Chenu's best work, some might say, is to be found in his book *La Théologie au douzième siècle* (Paris: Vrin 1957).
[16] *At the Service of the Church*: 143.

Catholicism in 1950.[17] Many, including Congar, Balthasar, Wojtyla and Ratzinger, regarded it as the key book of twentieth-century Catholic theology, the one indispensable text. Against the background of the liberal-capitalist and totalitarian ideologies of the 1930s, de Lubac sought to show that, in Catholic Christianity, the claims of person and of society are equally respected. Very much a tract for those times, primarily directed against the overly individualistic and introspective spirituality of his youth, as he saw it, the book is nevertheless as relevant a therapy for those who might now be inclined to over-emphasize the communal structure of Catholic piety. In a substantial appendix, de Lubac offers 55 extracts, mainly from patristic and medieval sources, often neglected and little known, but including Newman, Friedrich von Hügel, and Teilhard de Chardin, taking us from the Christian anthropology of Gregory of Nyssa to a vision of the Cosmic Tree misattributed to John Chrysostom. Here, already, de Lubac notes that, until late in the Middle Ages, the expression 'corpus mysticum' referred to Christ's eucharistic body, rather than to the body of Christ in the sense of the Church. Already, much more contentiously, de Lubac, insisting that the whole of Catholic Christian dogma is a series of paradoxes, declares that the greatest paradox of all is that, while the vision of God enjoyed by the blessed is a free gift, unanticipated, unmerited, never owed to them, yet the desire for it is, naturally and constitutively, in every human soul.

These two themes are spelled out in the next two books. De Lubac's life was, of course, interrupted by the German occupation of France. After the capitulation, many Catholics were content with the Vichy government: it seemed the restoration of the traditional Catholic France that the anti-clericalism of the Third Republic (and its hated atheist and Jewish deputies) had repressed. De Lubac was one of the minority who resisted, against the will of his Jesuit superiors in Rome.[18] He went into hiding, but his Jesuit colleague and friend Yves de Montcheuil, arrested among the Maquis at Vercors, was executed by the Gestapo at Grenoble in August 1944.[19]

Ready for publication by 1939, *Corpus Mysticum: Essai sur l'Eucharistie et l'Eglise au Moyen Age*, appeared in 1944. This 'naïve book', as he called it, retrieved the doctrine, put pithily, that 'the church makes the eucharist and the eucharist makes the church'. Leafing through volumes of Migne's

---

[17] Originally published under the title *Catholicism* (London: Longman Green 1950) it was reissued in 1988 as *Catholicism: Christ and the Common Destiny of Man* (San Francisco: Ignatius Press).

[18] Henri de Lubac, *Christian Resistance to Anti-Semitism: Memoirs from 1940–1944* (San Francisco: Ignatius Press 1990).

[19] For his memoir of his colleague see Henri de Lubac, *Three Jesuits Speak* (San Francisco: Ignatius Press 1987).

Patrologia Latina, he hit on the phrase 'corpus mysticum' in the work of Florus of Lyons (who died around 860).[20] This started him off on the trail. In modern times, and especially since Pope Pius XII's encyclical *Mystici Corporis Christi* (1943), the Church was referred to, in seminary courses, primarily as the 'mystical Body' of Christ. As he pursued his research in medieval and patristic authors, however, de Lubac concluded that the phrase *corpus mysticum* referred initially to Christ's *eucharistic* body, and *not* to the visible Church as an institution. For de Lubac, discovering this shift in reference marked a breakthrough: according to the pre-modern understanding Christ should be regarded as mystically present and at work where and when the eucharist was being celebrated. In effect, de Lubac's book inaugurated the eucharistic ecclesiology rehabilitated – or invented? – at Vatican II.[21]

The third of de Lubac's decisive interventions in twentieth-century theology, *Surnaturel: Etudes historiques*, the most controversial, which he had started at Hastings in his student days, again presented as no more than 'historical studies', appeared in 1946. According to the standard Thomist reading, by Renaissance commentators like Cajetan as well as by de Lubac's contemporaries, Jesuit and Dominican, Aquinas taught that human beings have a natural end or destiny, as well as the supernatural end conferred by divine grace. On the contrary, so de Lubac affirmed, Aquinas subscribed to the teaching of the Fathers of the undivided Church, namely, that the human creature desires by nature a fulfilment, which can only come 'supernaturally', as a gift by sheer divine grace. The decisive point, however, is that, on de Lubac's reading, Aquinas did not believe in any destiny for human beings, now that the Incarnation has happened, other than the supernatural end envisaged and promised in the New Testament dispensation. In short, for Aquinas, there is no destiny for human beings apart from Christ – and, if there are texts in which he seems to suggest the contrary, then Aquinas would only be playing with the thought experiment of a world, a human nature and fulfilment, as if the history of God's intervention in Christ could be bracketed out.

This book gave rise to the most acrimonious controversy in twentieth-century Catholic theology – an outbreak of *rabies theologica*. This 'merely historical' study, as de Lubac disingenuously calls it, was a direct challenge

---

[20] Joseph-Paul Migne (1800–75), a parish priest with no claims to great scholarship, founded a printing-house in Paris to bring out *Patrologia Latina* (221 volumes) and *Patrologia Græca* (162 volumes), still the standard means of reference and citation, the basis of the twentieth-century revival of patristic theology. His workshops and stereotype moulds were destroyed by fire in 1868.

[21] For de Lubac's ecclesiology see Paul McPartlan, *The Eucharist Makes the Church: Henri de Lubac and John Zizioulas in Dialogue* (Edinburgh: T&T Clark 1993).

to the standard neoscholastic theology of grace and nature. The book is peppered with barely coded insults directed at august Thomist commentators past and present. However, it was not only that, according to de Lubac, they more or less all misinterpreted Aquinas – a shocking enough contention, of course – they did so, he claimed, because of their ignorance of traditional patristic and medieval Catholic doctrine. In particular, they denied or occluded the doctrine of natural desire for God. According to traditional Catholicism, human beings were destined by *nature* to enjoy by divine *grace* everlasting bliss with God. Since the sixteenth century, however, allowing themselves to be shaped by opposition to Lutheranism, Catholic theologians made so much of the distinction between nature and grace that they lost all sense of the 'finality' of nature for grace – of the way in which the human and the natural has always already been embraced within the supernatural.

For neoscholastic Thomists, following Cajetan, so de Lubac claims, it was axiomatic that Aquinas did not just entertain the concept of 'pure nature', as a thought experiment, but held it as an indispensable doctrine. However, as de Lubac wrote in a letter to Maurice Blondel, as early as 3 April 1932: 'This concept of a pure nature runs into great difficulties, the principal one of which seems to me to be the following: how can a conscious spirit be anything other than an absolute desire for God?'[22] For his neoscholastic opponents, this was – unfairly, albeit not totally without justification – tantamount to saying that God could not deny the supernaturally given destiny of everlasting life in communion with the Trinity to creatures with the kind of nature which human beings possess.

The controversy was never purely academic. It needs to be placed against the background of the bitter struggle that dominated politics in France in the early twentieth century between supporters of the Third Republic with their anti-clerical 'laicism', as it was called, and adherents of traditional Catholicism with their monarchist nostalgia and papalist-ultramontanist inclinations. The conflict centred on the education system, with one side fearing that Church schools were not forming children in loyalty to the ideals of the Republic (and thus of 'liberty, fraternity and equality'), while the other side regarded state schools as seedbeds of socialism and militant atheism. In wider theological terms, the problem was how to respect the autonomy of the secular without abandoning the sacred to the realm of the purely private. In this light, Catholicism was out to correct what seemed to de Lubac an extremely individualistic and privatized religious sensibility by

---

[22] Cited by Lawrence Feingold, *The Natural Desire to See God according to St. Thomas and His Interpreters* (Rome: Apollinare Studi 2001): 628.

reminding Catholics of the inherently social nature of Christianity. He saw a double failure. On the one hand, Catholics were too often satisfied with a purely conventional religion, which was little more than the socially useful 'religion for the people' – religious practice as social control. On the other hand, inside and outside the Church, Christianity seemed to be a religion devoted to saving one's soul. To counter these apparently antithetical deviations, de Lubac sought to show that 'Catholicism' means that the Church addresses all aspects of human life, the social and historical as well as the personal and spiritual.

The central thesis of *Surnaturel*, then, is that, neither in patristic nor in medieval theology, and certainly not in Thomas Aquinas, was the hypothesis ever entertained of a purely natural destiny for human beings, something other than the supernatural and eschatological vision of God. There is only this world, the world in which our nature has been created for a supernatural destiny. Historically, there never was a graceless nature, or a world outside the Christian dispensation. This traditional conception of human nature as always destined for grace-given union with God fell apart between attempts, on the one hand, to secure the sheer gratuitousness of the economy of grace over against the naturalist anthropologies of Renaissance humanism and, on the other hand, resistance to what was perceived by Counter-Reformation Catholics as the Protestant doctrine of the total corruption of human nature by original sin. The Catholic theologians, who sought to protect the supernatural by separating it conceptually from the natural, facilitated the development of the humanism which flowered at the Enlightenment into deism, agnosticism and ultimately atheism. The conception of the autonomous individual for which the philosophers of the Age of Reason were most bitterly criticized by devout Catholics was, de Lubac suggested, invented by Catholic theologians. The philosophies which broke free of Christianity, to develop their own naturalist and deist theologies, had their roots in the anti-Protestant and anti-Renaissance Catholic Scholasticism of the late sixteenth and early seventeenth centuries.

The loss of the patristic-medieval sense of the internal relationship between the order of creation and the dispensation of grace led to a conception of grace as something so totally extraneous and alien to human nature that anything and everything natural and human was downgraded and demeaned. In particular, when questions about politics or sexuality (say) were detached from the traditional unitary theology of grace as fulfilling nature, it was not surprising if politics was treated with cynicism and sexuality with suspicion. When the dispensation of divine grace was no longer assumed to have resonance and even roots in some kind of natural desire for God, human nature – and that means reason, feeling, and the body –

became temptingly easy to denigrate. On the other hand, so de Lubac claimed, the idea of a 'purely natural' human domain, perhaps once only a thought experiment, eventually gave rise to the space of the secular, free of religion and indeed of God.

In effect, de Lubac undermines neoscholastic dogmatic theology as radically as he destroys standard natural theology. Doctrine remains 'extrinsic', just a set of abstract propositions, perhaps imposed by ecclesiastical authority, yet lifeless, barely relevant, practically unintelligible, unless connected to, and resonating with, the 'intrinsic' desire on the part of the given human nature of the one accepting or teaching the doctrine. Thus, philosophy, we may say, requires the supplement of theology, yet theology equally requires the foundation of philosophy – which cannot be had. De Lubac's paradox, as neothomist critics understandably objected, looks more like an irresolvable *aporia*. Indeed, as John Milbank highlights, we find Balthasar describing de Lubac's writing as occupying a problematic 'suspended middle' – 'De Lubac soon realised that his position moved into a suspended middle in which he could not practice any philosophy without its transcendence into theology, but also any theology without its essential inner structure of philosophy'.[23]

If grace did not fulfil the deepest longing of our nature, of our ethical, contemplative and (even) naturally mystical impulses, then it would be external, alien, and irrelevant. The life of the Spirit, instead of its being real (ontological) participation in the divine nature ('divinization') would become a purely nominal change in the believer's status by the decree of an alien God operating by the external institutions of the Church. So at least the story goes.[24]

Under Suspicion

In 1950, his Jesuit superiors in Rome, fearing that he was among the theologians anonymously censured in the encyclical *Humani Generis* – among those, that is to say, who 'destroy the gratuity of the supernatural order, since God, they say, cannot create intellectual beings without ordering and calling them to the beatific vision' – asked de Lubac to stop teaching Jesuit students

---

[23] Balthasar, *The Theology of Henri de Lubac*, 15; cf. John Milbank, 'The Suspended Middle: Henri de Lubac and the Debate concerning the Supernatural' in David Ford (ed.) with Rachel Muers, *The Modern Theologians* (Oxford: Blackwell 2005), and the expanded version, *The Suspended Middle: Henri de Lubac and the Debate concerning the Supernatural* (London: SCM Press 2005), a path-breaking study, on which I gratefully rely.

[24] The best summary of the issues as he saw them is in de Lubac's A *Brief Catechesis on Nature and Grace* (San Francisco: Ignatius Press 1984).

(which he had not been doing anyway).[25] Never summoned to defend his views in Rome, he always denied being targeted in the encyclical. Nevertheless, his books were removed from Jesuit libraries and withdrawn from sale. He was ostracized for a decade, his views frequently traduced, as the leader of *la Nouvelle Théologie*.[26]

However, never forbidden to publish (as Congar was), de Lubac continued to bring out books on a range of subjects: a study of Origen's biblical exegesis (1950), three books on Buddhism (1951–5) and, above all, *Méditation sur l'Eglise* (1953). The last of these, not intended as a full-blown treatise on the Church, and not at all 'scholarly', as he insisted, merely the result of conversation with fellow-priests at days of recollection and suchlike, was only an 'echo' of 'essential texts of Tradition', as the introduction tells us. The nine chapters, taking us from 'The Church as Mystery' through to 'The Church and Our Lady', seem to anticipate much that appeared, a decade later – in retrospect, it looks like laying out the structure of *Lumen Gentium*, the Council document on the nature of the Church; but of course de Lubac never imagined that he would be involved in drafting such a text. For the immediately pre-Vatican II generation of seminarians and lay people, this was a widely read and much treasured book – a reminder of just how rich pre-Vatican II ecclesiology was.[27]

Teilhard de Chardin died in 1955, which freed his lay friends to start publishing the books hitherto held back by his being obliged as a priest to have ecclesiastical approval. At the behest of his Jesuit superiors in France, de Lubac set about clearing Teilhard's name of longstanding suspicions of unorthodoxy, and even trying to establish him (implausibly as it seems to me) as a major Catholic thinker.[28] He continued to browse through patristic and medieval theology, the results of which were published between 1959 and 1964, a massive attempt at retrieval of precritical biblical hermeneutics.[29] By then, however, de Lubac was among the first summoned by Pope John XXIII to help draft the texts for Vatican II. He learnt of this when casually reading a newspaper in a convent parlour. Much of the experience

---

[25] *Humani Generis*: §26.

[26] See Joseph A. Komonchak, 'Theology and Culture at Mid-century: The Example of Henri de Lubac', *Theological Studies* 51 (1990): 579–602; Aidan J. Nichols OP, 'Thomism and the *nouvelle théologie*', *The Thomist* 64 (2000): 1–19.

[27] Translated as *The Splendour of the Church* (New York: Sheed and Ward 1956; San Francisco: Ignatius Press 1986); not a good title.

[28] *La Pensée religieuse du Père Teilhard de Chardin* (1962, English 1967); *La Prière du Père Teilhard de Chardin* (1964, English 1965); *Teilhard, missionaire et apologiste* (1966); *L'Eternel féminin* (1968, English 1971), and an edition of Teilhard's correspondence with Blondel (1965, English 1967).

[29] Susan K. Wood, *Spiritual Exegesis and the Church in the Theology of Henri de Lubac* (Edinburgh: T&T Clark 1998) with good bibliography.

he found quite comic, beginning with the oath of secrecy the theologians took on the first day, on their knees between two candles, before Cardinal Ottaviani, then Prefect of the Holy Office. In the event, de Lubac had a hand in composing the major documents, *Dei Verbum*, *Lumen Gentium* and *Gaudium et Spes*. Before the Council concluded, however, he saw signs of a growing 'paraconciliar agitation', demanding reforms in the Church quite different from what was envisaged.

In the 1970s de Lubac became increasingly distressed as he saw the achievement of Vatican II undermined, as he believed, principally by 'progressive' clergy, with their craze for liturgical 'experiment' and preference for Marxist sociology rather than traditional theological study. The Catholicism, which he had struggled to free from the 'separist' conception, as he labelled it, which kept nature and grace apart, was now allowing the economy of grace to collapse into humanistic naturalism. In his last two major works, *Pic de la Mirandole* (1974, untranslated)[30] and *La Postérité spirituelle de Joachim de Flore*,[31] he continued his rehabilitation of marginalized figures. In 1983, when he was nearly 87, he accepted Pope John Paul II's decision to make him a cardinal, reluctantly, on condition that he not be ordained a bishop. He died on 4 September 1991.

Knowledge of God

De Lubac denied being a philosopher. *De la Connaissance de Dieu*, revised under pressure and retitled *Sur les chemins de Dieu* (1956), another very influential book, was offered as an exercise in Christian apologetics, but, explicitly, as in no way a substitute for neoscholastic theodicy.[32]

---

[30] Giovanni Pico della Mirandola (1463–94), Italian philosopher and scholar, based his views chiefly on Plato, in opposition to Aristotle. He is famous for his *Conclusiones philosophicæ, cabalasticæ et theologicæ* (Rome, 1486), including 13 theses identified as 'heretical' (out of 900), and he defended Christianity against Jews, Mohammedans and astrologers. Many editions of his works appeared in the sixteenth century and he is a symbol of the Renaissance blend of the Christian and Platonic traditions.

[31] Two vols., 1983. Joachim of Fiore (c. 1135–1202), a monk, was an exponent of a Trinitarian theology of history, in three ages: the age of the Father, 'the order of the married', the dispensation of the Old Testament; the age of the Son, 'the order of the clergy', the New Testament; and the age of the Spirit, 'the order of monks or contemplatives', when new monastic orders would arise to convert the whole world and usher in the 'Ecclesia Spiritualis' – some Franciscans believed they were the ones.

[32] Published in English as *The Discovery of God* (London: Darton, Longman and Todd 1960), translated from *Sur les chemins de Dieu* (Paris: Aubier 1956). Subsequent page references are given in the text.

The second chapter opens with Aquinas's axiom: 'All knowers know God implicitly in all they know'. We are referred immediately to Hans Urs von Balthasar's essay in Thomistic philosophy (*Wahrheit der Welt*, see chapter eight). However, the next reference is to Blondel, in support of the thesis that every human act, whether of mind or will, 'rests secretly upon God', in the sense that 'nothing can be thought without positing the Absolute in relating it to that Absolute; nothing can be willed without tending toward the Absolute, nor valued unless weighed in terms of the Absolute' (*Discovery* 40). This does not mean, de Lubac hastens to say, that reasoning in order to prove the existence of God is superfluous. He does not want to be accused of anti-intellectualist modernism. Nonetheless, the status of the argument is not what most exponents of Thomistic natural theology would have supposed – 'our affirmation of God is not the conclusion of an argument'. For them, the proposition that God exists was indeed the conclusion of causal or cosmological proofs. For de Lubac, however, unless we already had a certain idea of God – 'not objectified, not conscious, yet present to consciousness, and in fine, *not conceived*' – indeed, 'previous to all our concepts and always present in all of them' – then 'the purification to which we subject [our concepts] in order to think God correctly' would have no point (42). He cites Chenu, to the effect that, for Thomas Aquinas too, 'the analyses in which negation triumphs, less favourable to illusion than superlatives, unfold in an atmosphere of mystery'. 'God is known better by being not known', *Deus qui scitur melius nesciendo* – which is 'a classical form of Thomism', de Lubac insists (43).

The idea of God 'is mysteriously present in us from the beginning, prior to our concepts, although beyond our grasp without their help, and prior to all our argumentation, in spite of being logically unjustifiable without them' – 'it is the inspiration, the motive power and justification of them all' (43). The idea of God, which is not a concept, is a reality: 'the very soul of the soul; a spiritual image of the Divinity, an *eikon*' (44). In a crucial footnote, de Lubac refers us to 'the tremendous importance of the notion of the image of God imprinted in man', something noted at Vatican I. The existence of God is not obvious from the word 'go'. There is no question of 'a natural intuition of God as an original apanage of the human mind' (48). On the other hand, the thought that the existence of God is 'probable' we should reject ('You might as well say our own existence is probable.'). 'God does not form part of our common experience' (50). We do better to say that 'the life of the spirit rests on a belief, and at its root is a certain kind of confidence' (50). Better still, citing Clement of Alexandria, our minds rest on a certain 'anticipation', *prolepsis*. 'God must be present to the mind before any explicit reasoning or objective concept is possible . . . he must be secretly affirmed and thought' (58). In short, before God can be 'identified' by a conscious act, there must exist a certain 'habit of God' in the mind (59).

This is what Thomas Aquinas held, de Lubac contends, citing Chenu again: Thomas calls in question the existence of God in order to prove his existence rationally, starting from the faith which he already has – which, however, does not mean that the rational demonstration depends on the act of faith and which, moreover, is not an exercise of methodical doubt as in Descartes (59).

Thus, if there is a truth which is lived before it is known, perceived with certainty before being subjected to the discipline of proofs and the control of concepts – because it is connatural to us – then this is, without a doubt, properly described as *knowledge of God* (59).

In the end, de Lubac places his natural theology in the context of the doctrine of the image of God: '*intelligence* is the *faculty* of being because *spirit* is the *capacity* for God' (75, his italics).

The philosophical problems here seem considerable. That people might be in a better position to talk sense about God if they had already acquired (let us say) habits of reverence and wonder may be an acceptable thesis. It is another matter to claim that there has to be a certain 'habit of God' in the mind before God can be 'identified' – not in words, only in some kind of mental act. It is difficult to understand how God can be 'secretly affirmed and thought', prior to there being any of the judgement or concept forma-tion which we normally mean by affirming and thinking. How does one 'affirm' God – even 'secretly' – prior to one's thinking about God in some way that is in principle communicable to others? What affirming God can there be prior to being able to say something intelligible? Above all, what is this 'idea' that we have of God, 'mysteriously present in us from the begin-ning', which is antecedent to all our concepts? What is an 'idea', which is beyond our grasp *without the help of concepts*? An idea which is 'prior to all our argumentation, in spite of being logically unjustifiable without them [our concepts]?' This preconceptual idea that we have of God, which is 'not a natural intuition of God', yet which is 'the inspiration, the motive power and justification', it seems, of all our concepts, turns out to be the imprint on the soul traditionally referred to in terms of our being made in the image of God. *The Discovery of God* is an immensely rich text, still well worth reading – philosophically, however, quite puzzling, particularly for students familiar with the kind of philosophical problems that Garrigou-Lagrange surveys. The idea of a concept – of God or of anything else – prior to the network of concepts we inherit as we are initiated into language, needs a good deal of discussion.

Retrieving Origen

The most surprising development in twentieth-century Catholic theology –
for neoscholastic theologians and especially for Thomists[33] – was the
retrieval of Origen.[34]

Inaugurated in 1948 by Jean Daniélou,[35] this revival was soon confirmed
by de Lubac's path-breaking study of Origen's biblical exegesis (1950), Hans
Urs von Balthasar's anthology of texts (1950) and, even more significantly,
the translation of Origen's Homilies on the Song of Songs, by Olivier
Rousseau (1953 and 1966). By the mid-1950s, in the heyday of neoscholasticism, when Pope Pius XII seemed to preside over an inviolably monolithic
Catholicism, Origen had returned, from neglect and longstanding denigra-
tion as a near-heretic, to centre stage. The themes, developed by de Lubac
and others from Origen's fertile speculations, are, to say the least, somewhat
audacious, and would have astonished most of us engaged in neoscholastic
studies back then, had we known anything much about them.

For instance, Origen was first to develop the theme of the five spiritual
senses: the possibility for spiritual persons who have attained the supreme
virtue, wisdom, of experiencing, by intimate personal communion, or by
connaturality, the supernatural realities – articulating all this in terms of figurative or allegorized biblical expressions and from neo-Platonist imagery.

Much more significantly, however, Origen is the source of the nuptial
theology, taken up by de Lubac, again by Hans Urs von Balthasar (chapter
eight), by Pope John Paul II (chapter ten) and in an important document
issued by the Congregation for the Defence of the Faith over Cardinal
Ratzinger's signature (chapter eleven), as we shall see – becoming, perhaps

---

[33] Origen is cited by Karl Barth as a precursor of Molinism: not a happy thought for strict
Thomists; for a lucid, entertaining account of the conflict between Molinists and Thomists
over the relationship between human free will and divine grace see *Church Dogmatics* II/1
(Edinburgh: T&T Clark 1957): 568–73.

[34] Origen (c. 185-c. 254) was born in Egypt, probably at Alexandria, and brought up as a
Christian. His father Leonides was martyred. According to Eusebius, Origen took Matthew
19: 12 literally. He was well versed in Middle Platonism. Ordained priest in 230, he established a school at Caesarea. He was tortured during the persecution of Decius and was a
confessor of the faith. He was buried at Tyre. A highly controversial figure, he was denounced
as a heretic by the late fourth century and has been suspected ever since. See Henri Crouzel,
Origen (Edinburgh: T&T Clark 1989).

[35] Jean Daniélou (1905–74), entered the Jesuit Order in 1929. His Sorbonne doctorate *Pla-
tonisme et théologie mystique* (published 1944) deals with the spiritual theology of St Gregory of
Nyssa. He contributed greatly to the revival of patristic theology and hence to the sidelining
of neoscholasticism. He was a backstage operator at Vatican II and was made a cardinal in
1967. He died while exercising a ministry to fallen women.

disconcertingly, the dominant theme in papally endorsed and papally inspired Catholic theology at the end of the twentieth century.

The Epithalamic Tradition

The interpretation of the creature's relationship with God on the analogy of marriage is, of course, biblically grounded. In Hosea, particularly, the covenant between the Lord God and the people of Israel is represented as a marriage, memorably introduced by Hosea's being commanded by God to marry Gomer, in full knowledge of her sexual promiscuity, thus allowing her to become the central symbol of the idolatrous people who forsake the Lord (Hos. 1:2: 'Go, take unto thee a wife of whoredoms and children of whoredoms: for the land hath committed great whoredom, departing from the Lord', and so on). In the Song of Songs, the virgin who comes in search of the king as her sexual companion is understood as the soul in search of the lover who is God. In Isaiah 61 the soul, no doubt here of a man, exults because the Lord God has 'covered him as a bridegroom decks himself with a garland and as a bride adorns herself with her jewels'; 'as a young man marries a virgin, so the Lord God's sons marry the land, and as the bridegroom rejoices over the bride so shall the Lord God rejoice over the singer's soul (Is. 61:10–62:2).

The imagery carries over into the New Testament. In response to the coming and calling of the Lord Jesus Christ, every human soul is feminine: bridal, spousal. In the vision with which the New Testament closes, the holy city, the new Jerusalem, appears as beautiful as a bride prepared to meet her husband (Apoc. 21:2).

In his major paper on mysticism, de Lubac mentions the symbolism of 'spiritual marriage', *pneumatikos gamos*, 'the theme of pursuit-union', in Origen, and from there to Bernard of Clairvaux, in the twelfth century.[36] We find it very eloquently, in Augustine: 'The Bridegroom's bed chamber was the Virgin's womb', because 'in that virginal womb were joined the two, the Bridegroom the Word, and the bride the flesh' – as Isaiah 61:10 prefigures: 'He hath set a mitre upon me as upon a Bridegroom, and adorned me with an ornament as a Bride'. In effect, Christ in the Incarnation makes himself at once Bridegroom and Bride.[37]

As de Lubac notes, the Dominican mystical writers Meister Eckhart

---

[36] 'Mysticism and Mystery' in *Theological Fragments* (San Francisco: Ignatius Press 1989): 35–69, 60.
[37] Augustine, *On the Epistle of John to the Parthians* 1, 2 (PG 36, 1979).

(c. 1260–c. 1328) and John Tauler (d. 1361), for all their exoticism in other ways, seem rather reticent about this 'epithalamic tradition'. Despite the long tradition of writing commentaries on the Song of Songs, we have none from the hand of Thomas Aquinas. The early catalogues list a *Super Cantica*; his young confrere William of Tocco reports that he dictated a brief commentary on his deathbed; to date, however, no commentary has been found, and the two commentaries printed in the Parma and Vivès editions of Aquinas's work are now known to be by others (Hymo of Auxerre and Giles of Rome).

The Song probably dates from the third century BC. In the Talmud, dating from the fifth century AD though including older material, the Song is regarded as an allegory of the Lord God's dealings with his people. In the Christian tradition, from Origen onwards, the relation between the lover and his beloved has been seen as a description of God's relation with the Church (his bride), or with the individual soul (his spouse). While there is no strong tradition of nuptial exposition of the Song in Eastern Orthodox and Byzantine theology, the theme has come to the fore in recent times, with *The Bride of the Lamb* (recently translated, posthumously published in Russian in 1945) by the Russian theologian Sergius Bulgakov (1871–1944), and more recently still *Variations of The Song of Songs* by the Greek Orthodox theologian Christos Yannaras, highlighting the poetry that invites us to see sexuality and spirituality as complementary to each other.[38]

The Latin tradition is well documented. Until the twelfth century the Song was treated principally as an allegory for the relationship between Christ and the Church. While this theme is present in Origen, it is only in Bernard of Clairvaux that the relationship between Christ and the soul, central in Origen, comes to the fore.[39]

The theme survived the Reformation. The Scottish Presbyterian theologian Samuel Rutherford (c. 1600–61), in particular, in his *Letters*, published in 1664, articulates the Christian soul's intercourse with God entirely in erotic metaphors from the Song. Frequently reprinted, most recently in 1984, *Joshua Redivivus or Mr Rutherfoord's Letters* was the most widely read devotional classic in Scottish Presbyterian homes until (it seems) embarrassment with the raw eroticism of Rutherford's picture of Christ as lover developed.[40] While he applies the Song to Christ and the Church as well,

---

[38] I owe this point to Fr Andrew Louth.

[39] Cf. the indispensable account: E.A. Matter, *The Voice of My Beloved: The Song of Songs in Western Medieval Christianity* (Philadelphia: University of Pennsylvania Press 1990).

[40] My attention was drawn to Rutherford's 'nuptial mysticism' by Professor David Fergusson. Cf. John Coffey, *Politics, Religion and the British Revolutions: The Mind of Samuel Rutherford* (Cambridge: Cambridge University Press 1997), situating Rutherford in the context of both Catholic and Puritan trends in seventeenth-century Europe, a superb book.

his emphasis is very much on the believer's longing for union with God, which he describes in frankly sensual terms ('Christ, Christ, nothing but Christ can cool our love's burning languor', and so on). While as a radical Presbyterian he did not celebrate the communion service very frequently, Rutherford's deeply sacramentalist piety is very like Counter-Reformation Catholic eucharistic devotion. He clearly believed that, taken in faith, Holy Communion brought substantial union with Christ. He was familiar with Catholic controversies at the time, indeed he followed Thomas Aquinas and other Dominicans against Molinist doctrine ('the Pelagian way, sacrilegiously robbing the grace of God'). He refers on several occasions in the *Letters* to Bernard's Homilies on the Song.

While the standard neoscholastic theology course was dealing with the relationship between creature and Creator in terms of primary and secondary causality and the like, Henri de Lubac was already reintroducing this high theology of the epithalamic relationship between the believer and Christ which would flower in the writings of Hans Urs von Balthasar and Pope John Paul II.

Church as Mother

A theme that attracted Henri de Lubac even more is that of the Church as 'mother' – *mater ecclesia*.[41] Of course he cites a large number of texts. Among the best known come from Cyprian (d. 258), bishop of Carthage: 'it is impiety to abandon the mother' – meaning the Church: 'We are born from her womb, nourished by her milk, animated by her spirit'; 'The Spouse of Christ brings forth sons spiritually for God . . . He alone can have God as his Father who first has the Church as his mother'.[42] But he returns us to Origen, independently saying much the same thing: 'He who does not have the Church for mother cannot have God for father'.[43]

This repertoire of maternal imagery for the Church de Lubac happily traces back to the cult of the Great Mother – *magna mater* – that dominated Hellenistic paganism, assuring us that this is a legitimate transposition, indeed 'a typical example of the boldness of Christian thought which was strong enough to seize, without contamination, everything which could serve to express it' (54). In pagan religion the Earth was enclosed in the

---

[41] See *The Motherhood of the Church*, French original 1971 (San Francisco: Ignatius Press 1982). Subsequent page references for quotations are given in the text.
[42] Cyprian, Epistle 44.3; *De Ecclesiæ catholicæ unitate* 4, Epistle 74.7.
[43] Origen, *In Leviticum* 11.3.

earth mother; all living creatures issued from her womb and returned to it. Analogously, the new creation, the redeemed world, is 'included' in the Church. In short, the doctrine of creation is contained within the doctrine of the Church.

However, equally numerous, in patristic texts, we hear of the Church as *virgin* mother, for example as early as Eusebius (c. 260-c. 340).[44] Neglected in recent centuries, de Lubac observes, this image has been taken up by Paul Claudel, Pierre Teilhard de Chardin, Jules Monchanin and Hans Urs von Balthasar, among others. Again, however, 'the voice of the great Origen is here the voice of all Catholic tradition' (65) – the church father with the best account of the Church as virgin mother.

Moreover, Origen provides the analogy between Church and soul: each Christian soul is virginal and maternal, receptive to the seed of the Word, bearing the Word it has received. As de Lubac documents, this theme of the birth of the Word in the womb of the Christian soul may be traced in the twelfth-century Cistercians, in the Rhineland mystics, among others (79).

However, the mothering role of every human soul, of the faithful people as a whole, and of the Church, cannot exist except in conjunction with a certain paternity. The bishop is father of one's soul, and father of the Church entrusted to him. We must not set pastors against people, de Lubac insists, coming down to brass tacks as one might say. Every member of the *ecclesia mater* exercises, or should exercise, the maternal function – but there is also necessarily a paternal role.

Karl Barth is right, de Lubac observes: the Marian doctrines are indeed central to Catholicism. There is, however, no reason to be embarrassed about this. De Lubac seems not to have read much of Barth's work. He knows, at least, that, for Barth, Mariology is precisely what makes it impossible for him to regard Catholicism as truly Christian. To this de Lubac responds with page after page, dense with citations, from the ancient Marian prayer 'Sub tuum praesidium' (discovered in 1938 on a third-century papyrus) to the poetry of Paul Claudel. He draws on medieval litanies and sequences, and much else. He keeps returning to commentaries on the Song and especially to that of Origen, 'one of his masterpieces' (273). The inmost nature and destiny of the Church is most fully and richly expressed in this exuberant nuptial symbolism – Church, soul and Mary all in a sense, analogously of course, *sponsa Christi*. The chapter concludes with a hymn to the Trinity, the *idiomelon* of Leo the Despot at Great Vespers in the Byzantine rite.

---

[44] Eusebius, *Historia Ecclesiastica*; 5.1.45–6.

De Lubac allows that he has reproached neoscholasticism for its abstract objectivism (164). Approvingly, he quotes Karl Rahner as explaining the decline of Marian piety by the tendency to make Christian faith an ideology, the Church regarded as a system, not as our mother, episcopal collegiality as no more than bureaucracy. He insists, however, that, for all the aridity of seminary theology, there were plenty of other creative alternatives, even in the darkest times.

Conclusion

Though always insisting on how traditional his Catholicism was, Henri de Lubac kept choosing somewhat marginal figures to celebrate. In *Pic de la Mirandole* he contents himself with expounding the often eccentric views of Pico (1463–94), never expressing his own theological views. However, he did not write these 400 pages with no motive other than vindicating a much-maligned figure and bringing him back to the great Christian tradition (119). It turns out that Pico – not any of the greatly admired Thomists, he silently implies – was the one who understood the ontological difference in Thomas Aquinas and in his *De Ente et Uno* pitted Aquinas's doctrine that *esse* is the supreme reality against the newly revived pagan neo-Platonic view that the 'One' takes priority over 'Being'.[45] For Pico, this metaphysics was ultimately theological. If we have to allow that, compared with Aquinas, Pico collapses philosophical and theological discourses into each other, then this (for de Lubac) is not a sign of an incipient humanist naturalism, but rather a return to the ancient patristic understanding of philosophy as implicitly 'Christian', and a rejection in advance of any doctrine of 'pure nature' – which is (he would think) the ultimate – neoscholastic! – source of atheistic secularism.

The importance of de Lubac's *Surnaturel* thesis, then, would lie in revealing that the space for the emergence of Enlightenment modernity was created by a neoscholastic theology, which forgot that we have by nature a desire for God. For de Lubac, the truly 'new theology', far from being the retrieval of patristic tradition in which he and his maligned companions were engaged, was the neoscholasticism, to be found in the work of their enemies in Rome, such as Garrigou-Lagrange and his allies.

Often picking august names in the neoscholastic tradition to mock, and, with Origen, Amalarius of Metz, Joachim of Fiore, Pico della Mirandola

---

[45] *Pic de la Mirandole*: 261–87.

and Teilhard de Chardin among many others, choosing to celebrate manifestly offbeat and idiosyncratic figures, Henri de Lubac seems a somewhat paradoxical 'man of the Church', *vir ecclesiasticus*, yet that is how he regarded himself. That so many others have come to regard him in the same way says a good deal about the transformation of Catholicism, which he helped to bring about. It is hard to believe that he did not plan his books in order to destroy neoscholastic theology. That was the effect, for better or worse, as we can see; yet he seems never to have seen, let alone intended, it that way.

Chapter Six

KARL RAHNER

Karl Rahner was born on 5 March 1904 at Freiburg im Breisgau, of a middle-class family, 'Catholic but not bigoted'.[1] He recalled his enthusiastic patriotism, as a schoolboy, during the First World War, in which an older brother was seriously wounded. In the generation of young Catholics inspired by Romano Guardini at Burg Rothenfels, he joined his brother Hugo in the Society of Jesus in 1922.[2] He followed the standard neoscholastic courses in philosophy and theology, from 1924 until 1933, with lectures and examinations all in Latin. He taught Latin, which he spoke fluently, to younger colleagues, including Alfred Delp.[3]

Never thinking of being anything but a pastor, he was surprised by being designated to teach philosophy. In 1934, pursuing doctoral research at Freiburg im Breisgau, he attended lectures by Martin Heidegger though, as a black-clad Jesuit, he felt anxious about the 'brown shirts' attracted by

[1] Karl Rahner, *I Remember: An Autobiographical Interview with Meinold Krauss* (London: SCM Press 1985); Herbert Vorgrimler, *Understanding Karl Rahner: An Introduction to His Life and Thought* (London: SCM Press 1986) and William V. Dych SJ, *Karl Rahner* (London: Geoffrey Chapman 1992).

[2] Hugo Rahner (1900–68), church historian and patristic scholar, not as prolific as his brother but *Greek Myths and Christian Mystery* (New York: Harper and Row, English translation 1963) and especially *Man at Play* (New York: Herder and Herder, English translation 1967), long out of print, deserve not to be forgotten. His untranslated *Maria und die Kirche* (Innsbruck: Marianischer Verlag 1951) documents how Mariology was first thought out by the Fathers as ecclesiology, the Church anticipated and personified by the Virgin Mother, and *vice versa*. It is a key text in modern Catholic self-understanding.

[3] Alfred Delp (1907–45), entered the Jesuit Order in 1926. *Tragische Existenzen* (1935) builds on Heidegger to develop a 'theonomous humanism' for a social order after the collapse of the National Socialist regime. He was surprised by the 20 July 1944 attempt to kill Hitler, but, since he had been in contact with the Kreisauer Kreis, round Helmuth James Graf von Moltke, he was arrested and executed for treason on 2 February 1945 in Berlin-Plötzensee.

Heidegger's Nazi sympathies. For supervision Rahner went to Martin Honecker,[4] who, in the end, failed the dissertation: a study of Thomas Aquinas's account of knowledge.

Rahner's second attempt at a doctorate succeeded, with the Jesuits at Innsbrück: the typological interpretation of John 19:34 ('One of the soldiers pierced his side with a spear, and at once blood and water came out') in patristic literature, the Church as second Eve issuing from the wounded side of Christ the new Adam. Then assigned to teach dogmatic theology, beginning with the doctrine of grace, he broke away from the metaphysical style of neoscholastic *de gratia* courses, by focusing on biblical and patristic material, under the heading of grace as 'God's self communication to human beings'. This resulted in his first publications, on the concept of the 'supernatural' in Clement of Alexandria, on Augustine and semi-Pelagianism, and suchlike. He drew on these purely historical studies in his first famous speculative essay, on the concept of uncreated grace (1939), reprinted in the first volume of his *Schriften* (1954).[5] While staying within the then familiar neoscholastic mode of discourse, the essay radically revised the theology of grace, reaffirming the priority of God's self-gift rather than concentrating on subtle discussions of the effects on creatures.

By this time Rahner wanted to reconstruct the standard neoscholastic curriculum quite radically. With Hans Urs von Balthasar he outlined how to go about it: the plan, in a version for which Rahner takes responsibility, appeared, 16 years later, in 1954.[6] It remains an interesting witness to how Catholic theology courses needed to be reformed, in the judgement of two young Jesuits in 1938.

In July 1938, after the *Anschluss*, the Innsbrück theological faculty was closed by the Nazi regime. The next 10 years Rahner spent as the pastor he had always wanted to be, discovering at first hand the problems lay people had with their faith, the context for much of his later writing. He worked in Vienna, returning in 1945 to Munich, a ruined city, to preach to the survivors. Like many priests of his generation, he had to help to rebuild the Christian faith of a completely demoralized population, shattered physically, exhausted spiritually, and having to come to terms with national defeat and the truth about the Nazi regime.

---

[4]   Martin Honecker (1888–1941), a distinguished historian of Renaissance ideas, Nicholas of Cusa and Ramon Lull.

[5]   'Some Implications of the Scholastic Concept of Uncreated Grace', in *Theological Investigations* I: *God, Christ, Mary and Grace*, translated with an introduction by Cornelius Ernst OP (London: Darton, Longman and Todd 1961): 319–46.

[6]   'A Scheme for a Treatise of Dogmatic Theology', ibid.: 19–37.

In 1948 he returned to Innsbrück, to teach dogmatic theology. He was never dismissed, like Chenu, Congar and de Lubac, delated for their supposed heretical inclinations. As a Jesuit, he submitted whatever he wanted to publish to anonymous peer judgement. An article published in 1949, questioning the point of each priest's saying 'his own Mass' every day (in the phrase at the time), and airing the possibility of concelebration, was attacked (obliquely) in 1954 by Pope Pius XII: Rahner was forbidden by the Holy Office to discuss the issue of concelebration ever again.[7] An article on the perpetual virginity of Mary, published in 1960, created such anxiety that, in 1962, the Holy Office required his work to be submitted to even stricter censorship.[8]

Later that year, in October, Rahner was nominated a *peritus* at the Council. In May 1963 he heard that he no longer needed any censorship beyond the normal Jesuit practice of peer review. By this time, he was among the most influential theologians at Vatican II.

In 1964 he succeeded to Romano Guardini's chair at Munich, hoping that a university post (at last) would protect him against any further Vatican harassment, and counting on more secretarial assistance than the Jesuit faculty at Innsbrück provided. However, the chair was in the philosophy faculty, and theology faculty rules did not permit him to supervise postgraduate degrees in theology. This ludicrous position ended in 1967 when, to Guardini's dismay, Rahner accepted a theology chair at the University of Münster. He retired in 1971, but continued to engage in an immense variety of theological and pastoral activities. He died in Innsbrück on 30 March 1984.

In one of his last interviews Rahner spoke of the 1980s as a 'wintry season' in the Catholic Church. By this he meant, however, not the 'disintegration' of Catholicism deplored by Louis Bouyer, Henri de Lubac and many others, but disappointment at what he regarded as reaction into a certain pre-Vatican II ultramontane authoritarianism. He was shocked in 1979 when Cardinal Ratzinger, then Archbishop of Munich, invoked the Concordat between Bavaria and the Vatican to prevent the appointment of J.B. Metz, their old friend and colleague, to the principal chair of theology at the University of Munich – against the unanimous recommendation of

---

[7] Eventually translated as *The Celebration of the Eucharist* (London: Burns and Oates 1968): concelebration, joint celebration of the eucharist by a number of priests (sometimes hundreds) was 'restored' in 1963.

[8] 'Virginitas in partu', in *Theological Investigations* IV: *More Recent Writings* (London: Darton, Longman and Todd 1966): 134–62: the doctrine that Mary's hymen remained intact during her son's birth.

the university senate.[9] One of Rahner's last acts was to write to the bishops of Peru in 1983 in support of Gustavo Gutiérrez and his version of liberation theology.[10]

Metaphysics of Finitude

The failed Freiburg dissertation appeared, in 1939, as *Geist in Welt*.[11] It takes the form of a reading of *Summa Theologiæ* 1. 84.7, where Thomas Aquinas considers whether the human intellect can have knowledge of things 'by means of the ideas it has within itself' (*per species intelligibiles quas penes se habet*) – that is to say, 'without turning to the sensibly given' (*non convertendo se ad phantasmata*). In effect, this is Rahner's refutation of the so-called 'Cartesian' picture of the self wrapped up in its own consciousness, with no direct knowledge of other minds or of the supposed external world. For Rahner, as the title of the book suggests, our minds are always already 'in the world'.

For Rahner, the phrase *conversio ad phantasmata* 'says that intellectual knowledge is possible only with a simultaneous realization of sense knowledge' – 'something is known only in a turning to the sensibly given'.[12] His main concern, evidently, is to insist that the only knowledge we have 'in this present state of life' is conditioned by our intellect's being conjoined with receptive corporeality. There is no purely intellectual intuition. Rather, from the outset, we find ourselves embedded in the world in virtue of our being embodied. This means that we are always already interacting with things in our environment, in their potential intelligibility. There is no problem about bridging the gap between mind and world. The world as known is always already the world to which we belong – world, here, is 'essentially a concept complementary to man'.[13]

---

[9] For details of this rather disgraceful episode, see John L. Allen Jr, *Pope Benedict XVI* (London: Continuum 2005): 124–6; Rahner died without a reconciliation with Ratzinger; Ratzinger attended Metz's seventieth birthday celebrations in 1998.

[10] One of the disadvantages of treating twentieth-century Catholic theology in terms of the most celebrated individuals is that significant movements, such as liberation theology especially, are short changed: see Rebecca S. Chopp and Ethna Regan, 'Latin American Liberation Theology', in David Ford (ed.) with Rachel Muers, *The Modern Theologians* (Oxford: Blackwell 2005): 469–84.

[11] *Geist in Welt: Zur Metaphysik der endlichen Erkenntnis bei Thomas von Aquin* (Innsbrück 1939); second edition revised and expanded by Johannes Baptist Metz (Munich 1957), of which the English translation is *Spirit in the World* (London: Sheed and Ward 1968) with an important introduction by Francis P. Fiorenza.

[12] *Spirit in the World*: 236–7.

[13] Ibid.: 406. The fundamental study, at least in English, is Thomas Sheehan, *Karl Rahner: The Philosophical Foundations*, preface by Karl Rahner (Athens: Ohio University Press 1987).

Now, in order to speak to us, God must address us where we already and always are. Rahner's philosophical considerations, that is to say, have an openly theological aim. Christianity, he insists, is not the idea of an absolute spirit, incarnate in history, as supposedly with Hegel. Rather, for Rahner, Christianity is Jesus of Nazareth. For Rahner, Aquinas's metaphysics of knowledge is Christian in the sense that it summons us back into the here and now of our finite world, since the Eternal has entered our world as Jesus Christ, so that we might find him and in him might find ourselves. Rahner's version of what Christianity is could not be more radically embedded in the historical existence of Jesus Christ – in the doctrine of the Incarnation.

Rahner's interpretation, in *Geist in Welt*, of Aquinas's account of knowledge in terms of the formal identity between mind and world in an act of knowing, develops, in *Hörer des Wortes*, into an account of what it is to be a human being in the world – this *body*, this open and receptive listening human body, which is thus at least capable of 'hearing the Word'.[14]

Taking these two books together, in sum, Rahner has reconstructed neoscholastic natural theology: the turn to the subject implicit in Aquinas's consideration of the soul, together with the subject as always already in the world according to his realist-metaphysical emphasis on *conversio ad phantasmata*, yields a theological anthropology in which these finite human beings which we are, are by nature open to hearing the Word – the Word who, as Christian faith maintains, has become incarnate in Jesus Christ.

Experiential Expressivism?

Rahner's theological anthropology has been heavily criticized. In his important introduction to the second English translation, Francis P. Fiorenza rejects criticisms by Cornelius Ernst ('a typical Anglo-Saxon reaction to German thought'), who allegedly misunderstood Rahner's conception of the convertibility of being and intelligibility as a form of metaphysical idealism. Fiorenza also rejects criticisms by Hans Urs von Balthasar, who accused Rahner of 'an anthropological and subjectivistic reduction of theology and Christianity', 'an un-Christian glorification of the human personality and of subjectivity, falsely concentrating on man's freedom instead of his obedience

---

[14] See Karl Rahner, *Hearer of the Word: Laying the Foundation for a Philosophy of Religion* translated from the original 1941 edition by Joseph Donceel (New York: Continuum 1994); the English translation of the second edition, *Hearers of the Word* (New York: Herder 1969) is often inaccurate.

to the cross' – Fiorenza's phrases,[15] summing up his reading of Balthasar's ferocious attack on Rahner, especially in *Cordula oder der Ernstfall* (1966).[16]

The criticisms of Rahner's theology often go back to his philosophy, and in particular to the use he made of transcendental analysis of the human subject in his theological reflections.[17]

George Lindbeck, for example, in his widely discussed book, identifies Rahner, along with Bernard Lonergan, as instances of the experiential-expressivist strategy he takes to have bedevilled modern theology.[18] Typical of this strategy, according to Lindbeck, is the concern to expound Christian doctrine by laying down a foundation in supposedly common, human religious experience before describing the forms in which this experience finds expression in this or that culture, or at one time or another. The motivation is, of course, benevolent: all human beings have, or at any rate are open to the possibility of having, a primitive experience of the sacred, logically prior to the personal and social practices by which they are related to this experience and, if and when need arises, bring it to expression. Underlying all the manifest differences that distinguish and divide the great religions, not to mention the Christian churches, there is a core experience to which they each have access, however variously they express it.

The worry about this, for Lindbeck and anyone else who accepts something like the lesson of Wittgenstein's so-called private language argument, is that the very idea of pre-conceptual experience sounds remarkably like an experience which occurs prior to being expressible. When a child is hurt he cries, that is the primitive, the natural expression of his sensation: his parents comfort him, talk to him, teach him exclamations, 'new pain-behaviour', soon including sentences.[19] That is how a human being learns the meaning of words like 'pain', 'toothache', 'headache', and so on. That is how these concepts come into the child's vocabulary. The child's natural expressions of his sensations gradually develop, in favourable circumstances, into mastery of a variety of concepts. How, on the other hand, does this work in the case of experiences which are presumably not primitive sensations? What occurs to a person experientially that he later identifies as experience of the sacred?

---

[15] *Spirit in the World*: xxxi–xxxiii.
[16] *Cordula oder der Ernstfall* (1966), translated as *The Moment of Christian Witness* (San Francisco: Ignatius Press 1994).
[17] Paul D. Murray, 'The Lasting Significance of Karl Rahner for Contemporary Catholic Theology', *Louvain Studies* 29 (2004): 8–27: a fine discussion to which the following pages are heavily indebted.
[18] George A. Lindbeck, *The Nature of Doctrine: Religion and Theology in a Postliberal Age* (London: SPCK 1984).
[19] Ludwig Wittgenstein, *Philosophical Investigations* (Oxford: Basil Blackwell 1953): §244.

It is one thing to have a sensation of pain, before having the words and so the concepts to articulate it. It seems another altogether to have an experience of the sacred independently of the language in which to recognize and realize it.

Lindbeck's critique recalls the fears that theologians such as Garrigou-Lagrange had of theologians (such as Chenu and de Lubac, not to mention Tyrrell) whom they regarded as 'modernist'. Paradoxically, the emphasis on the historical, social and linguistic nature of human experience, in mid-twentieth-century philosophy (Continental as well as analytic), only confirms the kind of criticisms that Garrigou-Lagrange made. His appeal to the authority of the Church, and especially to that of the hierarchy, as placing bounds on religious experience, private judgement and so on, is mirrored by the appeal to the priority of language, conceptuality and community, excluding the very possibility of preconceptual experience. What 'we say', as privileged by philosophers in the wake of the later Wittgenstein, is as determinative for the bounds of meaning and truth as what 'the Church teaches', in Catholic Christianity.

Theologically, the charge is that Rahner's heuristic strategy of returning us always to the self's experience of transcending finitude diverts attention from allowing God's unique self-revelation historically in Jesus Christ to shape Christian self-understanding. Moreover, following Lindbeck, Bruce Marshall, for example, argues that Rahner treats the Christ event as merely an example, albeit the supreme one, of something that happens to us all. The unique particularity of the Christ event should define for us what it means for Jesus to be who and what he is, and what he does for us, whereas on Rahner's story Christ seems to be defined as a special case of the self-transcendence to the Absolute which is happening to us all the time.[20] The encounter of the ever self-transcending human with the ever-widening horizon of being occurs completely and perfectly, in the hypostatic union, in the union of human and divine natures in Christ.

Such criticisms have given rise to the widespread belief that Rahner's theology is 'anthropocentric', whether either admirably or unacceptably so.[21]

However, other interpretations are possible. Richard Lennan, for one, sees Rahner as a thoroughly ecclesial theologian. More than half of his published work, after all, deals with themes related to ecclesiology, practical and theoretical, such that, if we have to have any one thing that constitutes the

---

[20] Bruce Marshall, *Christology in Conflict: The Identity of a Saviour in Rahner and Barth* (Oxford: Blackwell 1987).
[21] For the most recent criticism along these lines see Patrick Burke, *Reinterpreting Rahner: A Critical Study of His Major Themes* (New York: Fordham University Press 2002).

key to his theology, it would be his experience and understanding of life in the Church – not his metaphysics of self-consciousness.[22]

This is a claim Rahner would appear to support. The appropriate context for theological work, he once said, is one of 'faith and love and observance, in worship, in the ordinances and the activity of the Church'.[23] Then, as the footnotes to any of his major essays indicate, he always seeks to think with the mind of the Church, in the sense of trying to be faithful to the tradition. This does not mean uncritically repeating what has always been said. It means that, whatever revision or innovation he proposed, he wanted to expound in continuity with the neoscholasticism, *die Schultheologie*, which he so often lambasted. Self-consciously, anyway, Rahner was a theologian 'within the system', as he often said. He was never as subversive of neoscholastic theology as Chenu, Schillebeeckx or de Lubac.

Anonymous Christianity

Karl Rahner will forever be associated with the concept of 'anonymous Christianity'.[24] This brought down on him the most severe criticism, especially from his former colleague Hans Urs von Balthasar, with what justice we do not have room to discuss.[25]

The problem is, of course, that, for most of the opponents of the idea, it seems that, if human beings are all 'anonymously Christian', there is no point in trying to convert them to Christianity. When he speaks of the universal mission of the Church, so he says, Rahner includes the idea that it is incumbent on every single human being to become a Christian, and that means a Christian in an explicitly ecclesiastical form of Christianity. There is no way of being Christian without being in the Church. In the full sense, of course, being a Christian means having a conscious awareness of faith, explicitly adhering to the Creed, and so on. Yet, Rahner contends, Christianity is already present, incipiently, not yet developed so as to be expressed in its historical and social modality and visibility. After all, according to the doctrine taught by the Church, an individual can already be possessed by sanctifying grace, even before he or she has explicitly made any statement of faith or been

---

[22]   Richard Lennan, *The Ecclesiology of Karl Rahner* (Oxford: Clarendon Press 1997).

[23]   Karl Rahner, 'The Development of Doctrine', *Theological Investigations* I: 39–77 (45).

[24]   See for example 'Anonymous Christians', *Theological Investigations* VI (London: Darton, Longman and Todd 1969).

[25]   Not much, if you follow Eamon Conway, *The Anonymous Christian – A Relativised Christianity? An Evaluation of Hans Urs von Balthasar's Criticisms of Karl Rahner's Theory of the Anonymous Christian* (Frankfurt: Peter Lang, 1993).

baptized. What Rahner means by 'anonymous Christianity' is simply the fact that the interior grace that reconciles the sinner with God, forgives the repentant sinner, and grants a share in divinity, can be present before baptism.

We may ask, then, who is thus justified prior to baptism? Catechumens? Surely we are going to say that people preparing to become members of the Church, who have the desire to be baptized, are already in some sense 'Christian'? It is the traditional teaching of the Church that adults who want to be baptized are already 'converted', in the sense that their being actually baptized only manifests the justifying grace which they have been granted. What about people who believe that 'God exists and that he rewards those who seek him' – which seems a good deal less than having a desire for baptism, and so on (cf. Heb. 11:6)? Does this mean, Rahner asks, any more than believing in God as guarantor of the moral order? In any case, according to the teaching of Vatican II, whole categories of people who are not explicitly Christian, in the sense that they have not yet accepted the Gospel, are welcomed as 'related to the people of God in various ways' (cf. *Lumen Gentium* §16).

The first admitted are the Jews (not that the word appears) – 'that people to whom the covenants and promises were made, and from whom Christ was born in the flesh, a people in virtue of their election beloved for the sake of the fathers, for God never regrets his gifts or his call'. Second, among those who acknowledge God as Creator, there are the Moslems, who 'profess to hold the faith of Abraham, and together with us they adore the one, merciful God, who will judge humanity on the last day'. Here the idea is evidently that, through the faith of Abraham, the Jewish people and the Muslim community, respectively, are 'related' to the Church. Besides these, however, as Vatican II goes on to say, God is 'not remote from those who in shadows and images seek the unknown God'. People who, through no fault of their own, know nothing of the Gospel or of the Church, yet seek God with a sincere heart and, moved (of course unawares) by grace, try to do God's will as they know it according to the dictates of their conscience – these clearly 'may attain eternal salvation', and here we are directed in a footnote to the Letter of the Holy Office to the Archbishop of Boston. Moreover, God will not deny the grace necessary for salvation to people who, again through no fault of their own, have no explicit knowledge of God and who simply try to live a good life – of course, again without their being aware of this, a life that is 'not without grace'. Indeed, 'whatever of good or truth is found amongst them is considered by the church to be a preparation for the Gospel and given by him who enlightens all men and women that they may at length have life'.[26]

---

[26] *Lumen Gentium* §16.

In sum, for Rahner, the anonymous Christianity thesis can appeal for support in this text of Vatican II: there can be justifying grace apart from explicit Christianity – at least in the case of mature individuals no other limits can be set to salvation than those of grave subjective guilt.

The Boston Heresy

Thus, at *Lumen Gentium* §16, Vatican II explicitly rejected the 'Boston Heresy', asserting, in effect, that there is indeed no salvation outside the Roman Catholic Church – *extra ecclesiam nulla salus* – yet that is because, in one way or another, every human being belongs within her.[27]

This is the most significant development of Catholic doctrine, so far, due to theologians from the United States of America.

The contribution that the excommunicated Leonard Feeney made to the clarification of this doctrine was well known to Rahner.[28]

Leonard Edward Feeney (1897–1978), Boston Irish by birth and up-bringing, entered the Society of Jesus in 1914. He studied English literature at Oxford. He first became famous as a spokesman for American Catholics, in 1928, commending Governor Al Smith, defeated in his bid for the US Presidency for standing by his Catholic convictions ('If only you could have soft-pedalled the fact that you go to Mass on Sundays, if only you could have snubbed a few Catholic priests in public, or if only you could have come out with some diatribe against nuns and Religious Orders, or some-thing of that sort, nice and compromising, you could have had the White House, garage and all, for the asking.'). Engaged in campus ministry at Harvard in the 1940s, he came to believe that the decadence and cor-ruption in the Church – in the mid-1940s! – was due to neglecting this one fundamental dogma, that 'outside the Church there is no salvation'. 'Higher authorities' forced his superiors to move him to pastures 50 miles from Harvard – reluctantly, however, he put obedience to the truth before obedience to his ecclesiastical superiors, and founded his own religious congregation, to defend the doctrine.[29] Dismissed from the Jesuits in 1949,

---

[27] See Francis A. Sullivan SJ, *Salvation Outside the Church? Tracing the History of the Catholic Response* (New York: Paulist Press 1992).

[28] *Theological Investigations* XII (London: Darton, Longman and Todd 1974): 167. Rahner refers us to Catherine Goddard Clarke, *The Loyolas and the Cabots* (Boston: Saint Benedict Center 1950) (subtitled *The Story of the Crusade of Saint Benedict Center 1940–1950*, reprinted 1992) – a highly partisan account, but reliable enough, from which most of the detail above is taken.

[29] The Slaves of the Immaculate Heart of Mary, which still exists, though split in two.

excommunicated in 1953, Feeney indulged in increasingly raucous polemics against the Jesuits, seminaries depleted of students, Ronald Knox, Harvard, Newman Clubs, Communists, 'Masonic-Jewish Internationalism', and so on. In the end, in 1972, when he was probably too ill to realize quite what was going on, he joined in as the Auxiliary Bishop of Boston led the community in singing the Athanasian Creed – 'Whosoever wishes to be saved, before all things it is necessary that he hold the Catholic Faith. Which Faith except everyone do keep whole and undefiled, without doubt shall perish everlastingly' – regarding this as sufficient to end the excommunication.

Feeney's views did more than anything else to provoke the Catholic Church into determining that the meaning of the doctrine – no salvation outside the Church – is not, as he held, that unless you are a practising member of the Roman Catholic Church, you will go to hell; but rather that, if you are united to her by desire and longing, you need not be incorporated into her actually as a member in order to be saved.

On 8 August 1949, the famous letter from the Holy Office to the Archbishop of Boston stated that 'among those things which the Church has always preached and will never cease to preach is contained also that infallible statement by which we are taught that there is no salvation outside the Church.' 'However,' it continued, 'this dogma must be understood in the sense in which the Church herself understands it' – which is that 'it is not always required that [a person] be incorporated into the Church actually as a member, but it is necessary that he at least be united to her by desire and longing'.[30]

With the concept of anonymous Christianity Rahner did little more than spell out the doctrine expressed in the Boston Letter.

Mission?

What, then, of the mission of the Church to 'make disciples of all nations' (Matt. 28:19), and so on, if anonymous Christianity is universally prevalent? Surely the whole idea of mission rules out talk of people being always already somehow members of the Church?

Rahner neatly reverses the problem, asking if the task of mission is conceivable otherwise than on the assumption that anonymous Christianity is

[30] Letter of the Holy Office to the Archbishop of Boston (1949) in *The Christian Faith in the Doctrinal Documents of the Catholic Church*, revised edition edition, edited by J. Neuner SJ and J. Dupuis SJ (London: Collins 1983): 240–2.

always already present as an enabling condition for a preaching of the faith, in the person to whom the preaching is addressed.

We have as yet no worked-out theology of mission, he cautions, in his way; we can only be tentative. Let us agree, anyway, that preaching Christ presupposes the grace of faith at least as offered in your audience, since, after all, the word of God as preached can be heard and received as the word of *God* only through this already existing grace of faith. We are not talking of some psychological aid provided by God to overcome intellectual or emotional obstacles deriving from the nature of the listener, his or her culture, personal history, etc.

That seems incontestable, so far. But now, Rahner asks, surely it would be to suppose the miraculous, even to indulge in mythology, to think that this grace of faith was granted precisely at the moment one hears the Gospel proclaimed, like a bolt from the blue, an entirely arbitrary intervention. No doubt there is a moment when the grace of faith becomes actual, effective and demanding action, he goes on; but this is precisely 'in virtue of the fact that it has been present all along', 'in the same way as the natural spiritual faculties are present all along in man even though they only become actual and effective when they encounter an external object of experience which corresponds to them'.[31] In short, the preacher who seeks to impart faith as an appropriation of grace speaks to persons who already have grace as offered and perhaps even as freely accepted in an implicit way: 'The individual concerned would in this sense be an anonymous Christian' (171). Far from threatening the missionary preacher, the concept of 'anonymous Christianity' is only an explication of what missionary preaching has always taken for granted.

On the other hand, the concept of anonymous Christianity does not make explicit Christianity redundant. On the contrary, Rahner asserts, the dynamism inherent in the existence of Christ anonymously in an individual demands a certain expression – to be realized, most fully, in the visible sacramental mode and in the dimension of the Church.

There is nothing unacceptable about all this, Rahner insists. According to Thomas Aquinas, God forgives the contrite independently of any sacrament. In his view, and the tradition, it is taken for granted that when the sinner comes to the sacrament of penance he has already been justified, indeed he would not be coming at all unless he was already contrite, converted. Yet, as Aquinas saw, the sacrament of reconciliation remained meaningful and indeed necessary even if the *res sacramenti*, the reality that is being justified

---

[31] *Theological Investigations* XII: 170. Subsequent page references for quotations are given in the text.

and forgiven, justification, was already granted. There is no conflict between grace and sacrament, between what is spiritual, interior and invisible, and what is ceremonial, public and external. The grace of God has an 'incarnatory' character (176). In the individual it impels him or her to the behaviour which articulates it, embodies it, whether ethically or liturgically. Of course this dynamism of grace constitutes the Church. As missionaries go out, as Christ's redeeming work in the world continues, in them or in countless unseen ways, Christ, the Gospel, are present among all peoples in their own specific histories and cultures, thereby achieving an always new 'incarnatory' presence of Christ in the world: 'Once and for all Christianity is not intended merely to assure a salvation conceived of embryonically and almost in abstract terms for the individual in the other-worldly dimension, but is rather intended to make God's grace manifest here below in all its possible forms and in all historical spheres and contexts' (176).

It fits with all this that, for Rahner, celebrations of the eucharist are not occasional incursions of the sacred into a radically secular world but on the contrary they are manifestations of the always already graced state of the world. Liturgy is not an oasis of the holy in the otherwise completely profane world, but the visibility of the praise and intercession which are happening all the time, in the 'mysticism of ordinary life' (140).

The Hidden God

Rahner has a fine essay 'On the Hiddenness of God'.[32] The problem which he sets himself is that with *die Schultheologie*, while God is indeed held to be 'mystery', this is in virtue of the divine *incomprehensibilitas*, which 'follows from the essential infinity of God which makes it impossible for a finite created intellect to exhaust the possibilities of knowledge and truth contained in this absolute fullness of being'.[33] In effect, the thought of the incomprehensibility of God, so Rahner suggests, is the other side of a negative picture of human finitude. Moreover, the emphasis is desire for theoretical understanding, and the model of knowing is one in which the object is penetrated and mastered. The ancient Greek will to absolute

---

[32] Contributed to the festschrift in 1974 for Yves Congar's sixtieth birthday (reprinted in *Theological Investigations* XVI (London: Darton, Longman and Todd 1979)), listing the standard pre-Vatican II textbooks, gesturing towards Protestant treatments, recommending above all Karl Barth *Church Dogmatics* II/1: 179–203; Balthasar's favourite volume.
[33] *Theological Investigations* XIII (London: Darton, Longman and Todd 1975): 229. Subsequent page references for quotations are given in the text.

knowledge and the modern understanding of knowing as a process of mastering the object combine to make it impossible to know God at all – which either leads to resignation, to our being imprisoned in our finitude, or else generates practical atheism. Worse, the incomprehensibility might be the other side of fear that God could behave quite differently from the way he actually does – the God who is merciful with sinners could also be a god of sheer wrath or, in neoscholastic terms, a god denying a supernatural destiny.

However, knowledge need not be regarded primarily as mastery. Rather, 'the essence of knowledge lies in the mystery which is the object of primary experience' (236). This does not make the human being 'the event of absolute Spirit' (Hegel); on the contrary, it directs us to 'the incomprehensible mystery, in relation to which the openness of transcendence is experienced'. Nor does the human being become 'the shepherd of Being' (Heidegger) – rather 'the one protected by the mystery', *der von dem Geheimnis Behütete*. 'In the primary realization of his being and in the philosophical reflection derived from it, man comes to be himself and here he does not experience himself as the dominant, absolute subject, but as the one whose being is bestowed upon him by the mystery' – 'the one whose self is granted to him by the Mystery' (236).

'Transcendence' as 'the a priori condition of objective and reflective knowledge and evaluation', 'the a priori condition of all categorial knowledge and of all historical activity', is 'the truth', 'the primary event of the spirit', 'the mystery which endures and unfolds and establishes the essential human capacity for truth' – and here Rahner refers us to his 'studies in the metaphysics of knowledge' – (238), directing us immediately to the essay 'Thomas Aquinas on Truth', a lecture dating from 1938, published only in 1972, noting that it belongs to the period of the 'basic works' but insisting that it is especially valuable for his basic preoccupations *then*.[34]

The first point Rahner makes is that Thomas Aquinas is a theologian, with no philosophy developed on its own (14). In any case there is always the question of interpretation; as with Plato, Aristotle, Kant and so on, we have to reconstruct creatively, since Aquinas's 'justly acclaimed clarity also entails a constant temptation to assume that his philosophy is easier than it in fact is' (15). In a lengthy footnote Rahner refers us to Rousselot, Maréchal, the so-called Transcendental Thomists, but also to Söhngen, Siewerth, Lotz, Pieper and others.

Rahner concludes by citing the prayer traditionally attributed to Aquinas:

---

[34] In *Theological Investigations*, XIII: 13–31. Subsequent page references for quotations are given in the text. Rahner's suggestion is that he himself was always a theologian of the divine mystery, not merely of human self-transcendence.

'Adoro te devote latens deitas, quae sub his figuris vere latitas', insisting that 'Everything is a parable – figura – of God, who is constantly being unveiled yet at the same time constantly concealed in the parable'. (31) From the outset, Rahner regarded Christian life as a kind of mystagogy: a being led by the Holy Spirit into the mystery. Indeed, he sometimes suggested that all Christians in future would be mystics, since none will be born into 'cradle' Catholicism or the kind of Catholic environment to which his family belonged.

Origen Again

Karl Rahner's first major theological work, it is often forgotten, was a documented study of the doctrine of the five spiritual senses in Origen.[35] As his 10 years of neoscholastic formation were ending (he was ordained in 1932), Rahner was devoting himself to patristic and medieval studies, specifically to tracing the history of this doctrine through to the Middle Ages, particularly in Bonaventure.[36] These studies antedate his going to Freiburg to study philosophy. Moreover, in republishing these essays in 1975, Rahner makes two points. The charismatic movements in North America and Europe had brought a long-forgotten Christian theme back onto the theological agenda: non-theologians, the ordinary faithful, were reminding theologians, through this living experience of the Spirit, of what was neglected in the standard theological enterprise. That is to say, Rahner was pointing to the empirically verifiable existence of experientially felt faith in the lives of perfectly ordinary believers.

Second, referring particularly to his study of Bonaventure, Rahner tells us that he includes it because of its fundamental importance in understanding his work in the philosophy of religion – in other words, his first two books, *Geist in Welt* and *Hörer des Wortes*. The doctrine is no mere period piece, Rahner contends, 'a speculative a priori game which has no contact with the real world'.[37] While not uncritical of certain aspects of Bonaventure's thesis, Rahner is persuaded that, by integrating the traditional doctrine of the spiritual senses, Bonaventure greatly clarified the nature of mystical experience. In concluding, Rahner insists on how mystical experience is always described in images derived from the world of sense experience. The

---

[35] 'Le début d'une doctrine des cinq sens spirituels chez Origène', *RAM* 13 (1932): 113–45; much curtailed in *Theological Investigations*, XVI: 81–103.
[36] *Theological Investigations*, XVI: 104–34.
[37] Ibid.: 127.

history of the doctrine of the five spiritual senses belongs to the history of metaphors that are drawn from the sense-perceptible realm and are used to represent mystical realities.[38]

As far as nuptial mysticism goes, however, Rahner does not seem to want to exploit Origen. Whether the modest five-page essay in 1975 in *Stimmen der Zeit* is consciously or otherwise something of a challenge to those, including Henri de Lubac and (as we shall find) Hans Urs von Balthasar, building a whole ecclesiology, a Catholic sensibility and spirituality, on an image of Mary as the archetypal woman, is a moot point. In connection with the 'so called feminine attributes' Rahner sees plenty of room for further thought about the distinction of the sexes, about the nature of woman, determining her existence and thus also her grace-given relationship to God. 'But if we begin to describe concretely the religious character of woman. . . . we are at once involved . . . in great embarrassment'. We are likely to see Mary in historically, culturally and sociologically conditioned ways. Many of the statements made about Mary – rightly enough – in her relationship to God are, Rahner contends, by no means specifically and exclusively feminine, anyway. On the contrary: it is 'human, masculine as well as feminine, to be able to be silent, wholly receptive, self committing, listening in humility and faith, serving and not dominating, in our approach to God'.[39]

Rahner did not find the central thesis in 'Women and the Priesthood' 1976, the statement by the Congregation for the Doctrine of the Faith, approved by Pope Paul VI, beyond discussion.[40] He says, indeed, that the statement cannot be regarded as definitive, thus it is in principle revisable, perhaps erroneous. As regards the significance of the fact that women were not chosen for ordination in New Testament times, he finds the Congregation's statement unconvincing – but he sets aside questions of gender, sexual difference, difference in gender roles, that emerge from a certain philosophical and theological anthropology.

---

[38] For a recent attempt to make use of the doctrine see Sarah Coakley, 'The Resurrection and the "Spiritual Senses": on Wittgenstein, Epistemology and the Risen Christ', in her *Powers and Submissions: Spirituality, Philosophy and Gender* (Oxford: Blackwell 2002): 130–52 footnoting Rahner, arguing (however) much more positively for the possibility of a transformation of normal sense perception through disciplined penance and prayer.

[39] 'Mary and the Christian Image of Woman', in *Theological Investigations*, XIX (London: Darton, Longman and Todd 1984): 211–17. For 'divine maturity', however, read 'divine maternity' (213).

[40] 'Women and the Priesthood', in *Theological Investigations*, XX (London: Darton, Longman and Todd 1981): 35–47.

Self-criticism

Whether Rahner's *Foundations of Christian Faith* should ever have been treated as his attempt at a systematic theology is a moot point.[41] When he reviewed the reviews he began by quoting the commendatory review by Joseph Ratzinger, not yet Cardinal Archbishop of Munich: even if one is not disposed to accept Rahner's 'idea of Christianity' completely, 'this impressive synthesis' will outlast much modern Catholic theology.[42] Actually, Rahner tells us, he wanted the book entitled 'An introduction to the concept of Christianity', not 'The basic course of faith', *Das Grundkurs des Glaubens*, which the publishers preferred. He sees it as a scholarly work, demanding hard thinking. It was, however, never intended as any kind of 'synthesis'.

By describing his theology as 'transcendental', so he says, no more is meant than that to explain this or that faith claim, the question must be asked how and why, in virtue of one's always already graced nature, this or that claim matters. This does not mean that, in his theological work, 'man is a subject of faith . . . only in his abstract transcendentality and not in his historical being in his concrete history'. That is what we have to show – that 'history can really be significant for salvation to the intellectual subject, who is always more than space and time'. Our history is '*not* something in which [we are] involved *over and above* [our] transcendentality to God as the absolute being and mystery'. Rather, 'it is only *as* history of this transcendentality in freedom that history is actually history in which salvation can come about' (8).

Rahner allows that, in *Foundations*, the doctrine of the Trinity gets less attention than it should (13). Moreover, he says too little about 'evil' – which does not mean that he counts on universal salvation – though, after all, one who highlights God's holy goodness is surely better off than those who want to explain why evil has a purpose. But there is so much else left out: nothing about angels, nothing about the sinful Church – which last would have helped readers these days to take 'an uninhibited attitude', *unbefangenes Verhältnis*, towards the Church. Indeed, the ecclesiology is 'perhaps too innocuous, *harmlos*, even somewhat triumphalistic' (14). There is a certain individualism, no 'political theology', no 'liberation theology' –

[41] *Foundations of Christian Faith: An Introduction to the Idea of Christianity* (London: Darton, Longman and Todd 1978, published in German 1976).
[42] 'Foundations of Christian Faith', in *Theological Investigations*, XIX (London: Darton, Longman and Todd 1984): 3–15. Subsequent page references for quotations are given in the text.

here, writing in 1979, Rahner seems determined to break the mould, to insist, in this litany of self-criticism, rare in a theologian, that he never was the author of a 'system', with a position about everything, always referring back to the foundations he allegedly laid out in *Spirit in the World*. He leaves us instead with the self-portrait of a theologian who worked in an *ad hoc*, piecemeal fashion, with many gaps and untreated problems, essentially a pastor, responding to the questions and anxieties of the people of his time and place.[43]

Conclusion

Currently, Karl Rahner is played off against his old colleague Hans Urs von Balthasar, with Rahner regarded as the 'progressive' theologian of the Council and Balthasar the 'conservative' theologian of the post-conciliar reaction. Allegedly, Rahner was shaped by German idealist philosophy, Balthasar more grounded in biblical and patristic theology. Their projects were very different, as we shall see (chapter eight). Yet, since both were rooted in the school of Jesuit spirituality, they were never as far apart as they may seem. Moreover, each was far more complicated than the standard story allows. As time goes by, in the perspective of history, their projects may well come to seem more complementary than conflicting, overlapping much more than their admirers and adversaries think at present.

---

[43] Karen Kilby, *Karl Rahner: Theology and Philosophy* (London and New York: Routledge 2004); *The Cambridge Companion to Karl Rahner*, edited by Declan Marmion and Mary E. Hines (Cambridge: Cambridge University Press 2005).

Chapter Seven

BERNARD LONERGAN

John Henry Newman, who died in 1890, is the only eminent English Roman Catholic theologian.[1] Although unsuccessful in most of his undertakings, his significance for theology was discovered, first by French, then by German and finally by English scholars.[2] Never accepted as much of a theologian by neoscholastics, Newman was, by mid-century at least, recognized as in the first rank of Christian thinkers. So many of the Council's decrees seem to resonate with his ideas (development of doctrine, 'On Consulting the Faithful', liberty of conscience, and so on) that Newman is often hailed as the 'Father of Vatican II'.[3] As far as Vatican II goes, the most effective English-speaking contributor was Basil Christopher Butler (1902–86), one of the few non-episcopal members of the Council, as the elected Abbot-General of the English Benedictine Congregation.[4] Brought up in an Anglo-Catholic family, Butler became a Catholic soon after graduating at Oxford, largely through reading Baron Friedrich von Hügel. A competent New Testament scholar, interested especially in the Synoptic Problem, he

---

[1]   John Henry Newman (1801–90) was invited in 1868 to be an official papal theologian (probably at Cardinal Paul Cullen's suggestion). He refused, saying he was too old (67) and not a theologian anyway. He also refused repeated requests by Bishop Brown of Newport to accompany him.

[2]   Jean Guitton (1933), M. Nédoncelle (1946), Louis Bouyer (1952); Gottlieb Söhngen (1946), H. Fries (1948); Hilda Graef (1967), John Coulson (1970), Nicholas Lash (1975), to name the most significant.

[3]   Not by everyone, however: see P.J. FitzPatrick ('G. Egner'), *Apologia pro Charles Kingsley* (London: Sheed and Ward 1969) and 'Newman's *Grammar* and the Church today', in D. Nicholls and F. Kerr (eds.) *John Henry Newman: Reason, Rhetoric and Romanticism* (Bristol: Bristol Press 1991): 109–34. For the best set of essays see Ian Ker and Alan G. Hill (eds.) *Newman after a Hundred Years* (Oxford: Clarendon Press 1990).

[4]   Appointed in 1966 Auxiliary Bishop of Westminster.

regarded himself as 'estranged from the main current of Catholic opinion', for one reason because of what he saw as 'Roman authoritarianism': 'The trouble, as I saw it, was that centralization was typical of an age of mass-production, and also that Rome had by now obtained such a commanding position that it would take something not far short of a miracle to reverse the centralizing trend in the Church'.[5] As far as Rome was concerned he agreed with Ronald Knox: that a bad sailor keeps clear of the engine room. He approached the Council with 'more foreboding than hope', fearing 'another dose of authoritarian obscurantism'.[6] In the event, however, Butler played quite a distinguished part in the endless drafting and redrafting of the texts. Though he himself says nothing about it, he drafted a text on the role of the Blessed Virgin Mary in the course of the second session (1963) which helped to secure a majority for including the document on Mary in the document on the Church. His account of the theology of the Council is the best in English by a participant.[7]

Like many others, Butler owed a great deal to his study of Bernard Lonergan. In 1958 he discovered *Insight*. Considering himself not much of a philosopher or even of a theologian, he found that this cured him of the 'not quite articulate discomfort' that he felt about the neothomism he had been taught as a young monk.[8] Though by far the most eminent and influential Catholic theologian in the English-speaking world at the time, Lonergan himself played little part in the doings of Vatican II.

Born on 17 December 1904 in Buckingham, an English-speaking enclave in Quebec, he died on 26 November 1984 in Pickering, Ontario.[9] His father, a McGill University graduate in engineering, was third-generation Irish-Canadian. His mother, a Dominican tertiary, was a descendant of one of the British families who moved north when the American colonies rebelled in 1776. He attended a Jesuit boarding school in Montreal, where he received (so he believed) much the same education as the Society had provided since the Renaissance.

---

[5] *A Time to Speak* (Southend-on-Sea: Mayhew-McCrimmon 1972): 139.

[6] Ibid.: 141.

[7] *The Theology of Vatican II*, Sarum Lectures at Oxford 1966, published 1967, revised and enlarged edition 1981 (London: Darton, Longman and Todd): he concludes with the three elements of religion, as in Newman's 1877 Preface to *Via Media*.

[8] *A Time to Speak*: 134.

[9] This chapter depends heavily on information provided on the Lonergan web site www.lonergan.on.ca and particularly on the excellent book by Richard M. Liddy, *Transforming Light: Intellectual Conversion in the Early Lonergan* (Collegeville, MN: Liturgical Press 1993).

In 1922 he entered the Canadian province of the Society of Jesus. In 1926 he studied philosophy at Heythrop College, then near Oxford. The Latin textbooks he came to see as 'Suárezian' in orientation.[10] The professor of natural theology, a convinced Suárezian, celebrated the ferial Mass on the feast of St Thomas Aquinas, somewhat perversely. The professor of metaphysics, who had other duties, gave only three lectures during the whole year – which meant less to unlearn. On his own, Lonergan read Newman, especially *An Essay in Aid of a Grammar of Assent*. During a year at London University he discovered H.W.B. Joseph's *Introduction to Logic*.[11] Such was Lonergan's formation in what was supposed to be neoscholastic philosophy. He was not introduced to the work of Aquinas itself. He was grateful for discussions about mathematics with Charles O'Hara.[12] In effect, he was self-taught in philosophy.

In 1933 Lonergan went to study theology at the Gregorian University in Rome. There were several distinguished scholars on the faculty at the time. Lonergan seems, however, to have continued to make his own way. He was indebted to work by Peter Hoenen.[13] During the course on the Incarnation he discovered that Thomas Aquinas might have something interesting to say.

Lonergan taught young Jesuits in Canada from 1940 until 1953. Called back to Rome, he lectured at the Gregorian, until he resigned for health reasons in 1965. Though an 'expert' at Vatican II, he played little part. He spent the last years of his working life at Boston College, engaged in macroeconomic analysis of modern production processes and monetary circulations, a return to an early interest.

---

[10] According to Liddy, typical reading matter included textbooks by Juan José Urráburu (1844–1904), a Spanish Jesuit, prominent in the neoscholastic revival promoted by Leo XIII: *Institutiones philosophiæ* (Valladolid: I: *Logica*, 1890; II: *Ontologia*, 1891; III: *Cosmologia*, 1892; IV: *Psychologiæ* part 1, op. 1894; V: *Psychologiæ* part 2, 1896; VI: *Psychologiæ* part 2 (continuation), 1898; VII: *Theodiceæ*, vol. I, 1899; VIII: *Theodiceæ*, vol. II, 1900); and *Compendium philosophiæ scholasticæ* 5 vols. (Madrid 1902–4).

[11] Horace William Brindley Joseph (1867–1943) taught at Oxford 1891–1932. He is better remembered for his contribution to moral theory, *Some Problems in Ethics* (1930) and for the book on Leibniz, edited by J.L. Austin (1949).

[12] The same Father O'Hara is mocked by Wittgenstein for treating religious statements like scientific hypotheses, *Lectures and Conversations*, edited by Cyril Barrett SJ (Oxford: Oxford University Press 1966): 57–9.

[13] Anthony Kenny, who attended his lectures 20 years later, regards Hoenen's *La Théorie de jugement selon S. Thomas d'Aquin* 'to this day' as one of the two most illuminating books about Aquinas's philosophy of mind, the other being Lonergan's *Verbum*; see *Aquinas on Mind* (London and New York: Routledge 1993): Preface.

Lonergan and British Empiricism

Lonergan was more truly a philosopher than anyone else in this book apart from Karol Wojtyla. Indeed, Hugo Meynell, in one of the best studies, places Lonergan among 'contemporary philosophers of the first rank', albeit admitted to be 'up to now the most neglected'.[14] *Insight* is 'at a conservative estimate one of the half-dozen or so most important philosophical books to have appeared in the course of the present century'. Study of human understanding is the way to determine the fundamental nature of the world revealed to that understanding.

This is of course the starting point of the classical British empiricists Locke, Berkeley and Hume; but the metaphysical consequences that Lonergan lays out are, needless to say, quite different from theirs. Since Hume and Kant, Meynell reminds us, the intelligible order which we seem to find in the world has been attributed to the activity of the human mind; indeed it can be rightly inferred to be there at all only as a result of the imposition of a conceptual framework in the process of understanding it. According to Lonergan, on the other hand, 'both the phenomena which we experience and the intelligible pattern within which they are found to cohere are aspects of the real objective world which confronts the human inquirer' – the world which would exist, Meynell goes on, 'even if there were no intelligent beings to inquire into it'. Thus, investigating *how* it is and *what* it is that the mind comes to know has implications not only about the nature of the knower but also about everything that there is for us to know.

While Meynell mentions neither Newman nor H.W.B. Joseph, it was in his close study of the *Grammar* and Joseph's *Logic* that Lonergan came to grips with British empiricism and its problematics. Prior to 1914 the philosophical scene at Oxford was dominated by F.H. Bradley, either as a model to follow or a target to attack. Resistance to neo-Hegelian idealism was led by J. Cook Wilson, who held the chair of logic from 1899 until his death in 1915. Joseph should be seen as a major figure in the realist revolt, in the generation of Oxford realists or 'Cook-Wilsonians'. Cook Wilson's legacy at Oxford was no doubt his influence on a certain ethical intuitionism. Through Joseph's *Logic*, we may perhaps say, the Cook-Wilsonian legacy in epistemology was inherited by young Lonergan. This attack on metaphysical idealism was rooted in respect for ordinary language. Distinctions current in everyday language, Cook Wilson insisted, should not be

---

[14] Hugo A. Meynell, *An Introduction to the Philosophy of Bernard Lonergan* (London: Macmillan 1976): 1.

ignored. Rather, the task of the philosopher is to determine the normal use of an expression, a task for which countless examples need to be adduced. Moreover, against idealism, Cook-Wilsonians argued for the distinctness of knowledge from its objects, for the reality of relations, and for the claim that in logic we are not concerned with judgements conceived as the expression of mental acts of judging, but with statements, which may be the expression of diverse 'acts of mind' (knowing, believing, supposing, inferring).

Self-taught Thomism

The impetus for Lonergan to study Thomas Aquinas at first hand, bizarre as this may seem, came from an article (in Latin) on the nature of geometry:

> In 1933 I had been much struck by an article of Peter Hoenen's in *Gregorianum* arguing that intellect abstracted from phantasm not only terms but also the nexus between them. He held that that certainly was the view of Cajetan and probably of Aquinas. Later he returned to the topic, arguing first that Scholastic philosophy was in need of a theory of geometrical knowledge, and secondly producing various geometrical illustrations such as the Moebius strip that fitted in very well with his view that not only the terms but also nexus were abstracted from phantasm.[15]

This is barely intelligible to those never exposed to neoscholastic philosophy. Hoenen's point, briefly, is that the principles of mathematics could not be derived, as neoscholastics generally held, from mere analysis of the terms of those principles. How do we know, say, that the whole is greater than the part? The neoscholastics interpreted such knowledge as a comparison of concepts, such as 'whole', 'part', 'greater than'. On the contrary, Hoenen contended, such principles of the understanding derive from insight into the image, the 'phantasm', in the jargon, together with a grasp of the 'nexus', or relationship, between the terms. *Experience*, then, indeed *imaginative* experience, is necessary for the abstraction of universal principles.

---

[15] *A Second Collection: Papers by Bernard J.F. Lonergan SJ*, edited by William F.J. Ryan SJ and Bernard Tyrell SJ (London: Darton, Longman and Todd 1975): 266–7; see 'A Note on Geometrical Possibility', in *The Modern Schoolman* 27 (1949–50): 124–38, reprinted in *Collection: Papers by Bernard J.F. Lonergan SJ*, edited by F.E. Crowe SJ (London: Darton, Longman and Todd 1967): 96–113.

Hoenen's article directed Lonergan to Thomas Aquinas, for example in the *Summa Theologiæ*, a remark that he often cites:

> Anyone can verify this in his own experience, that when he is trying to understand something, he forms some phantasms for himself by way of examples, and in these he as it were looks at what he wants to understand. It is for the same reason that when we want to have someone understand something, we offer him examples by means of which he may be able to form images for himself to aid his understanding.[16]

Years later, in *Insight*, Lonergan developed this. For Thomas Aquinas, the mind apprehends the intelligible in the sense-perceptible and grasps the universal in the particular.[17] John Duns Scotus, on the other hand, by rejecting this notion of insight into the sense-perceptible, reduced the act of understanding to seeing a nexus between concepts. Contrary to this, the process of coming to know is not a kind of 'metaphysical sausage machine, at one end slicing species off phantasm, and at the other popping out concepts'. The mind is not a 'black box', in which there is sensory input at one end and words as 'output' at the other. On the contrary, our understanding is a conscious process of 'grasping the intelligible in the sensible'. To see this we have only to attend to how we actually understand; as Aquinas said, 'anyone can verify this in his own experience'. Scotus, however, Lonergan contends, thought of knowledge, not as a process that culminates in judgement, but as 'taking a look'.[18]

How well all this would stand up to examination by a medievalist we must leave aside. For Lonergan, never a scholar of medieval thought, always a speculative thinker, there are three key points: knowing occurs in interaction with our physical environment; we can see this by reflecting on our own experience; and knowing is not merely 'taking a look'.

The next piece that helped Lonergan towards his reconstruction of Thomistic philosophy was the doctoral dissertation of his colleague Leo W. Keeler, *The Problem of Error from Kant to Plato* (1934), which he reviewed in *Gregorianum* (1934). Keeler's work is chiefly historical. In discussing Plato's *Theatetus*, he notes Plato's emphasis on the discursive activity of the mind. This was to be Lonergan's key insight. Delightedly he picks up the need for a serious critique of the Suárezian school: this 'intuitionism', as he will call it later, needs to be deconstructed completely.

---

[16] *Summa Theologiae*, 1.75.
[17] *Insight: A Study of Human Understanding* (London: Longmans, Green and Co. 1957): 406.
[18] Ibid.: 372.

Transcendental Thomism?

Lonergan is usually classified as an exponent of Transcendental Thomism.[19] Once again, however, while this was certainly an element in the *bricolage*, Lonergan writes:

> My philosophical development was from Newman to Augustine, from Augustine to Plato, and then I was introduced to Thomism through a Greek, Stephanos Stephanou, who had his philosophic formation under Maréchal. It was in talking with him that I came first to understand St. Thomas, and see that there was something there.[20]

In other words, his young Greek Jesuit friend, who had studied at Louvain, told Lonergan about the thought of Joseph Maréchal, and his five-volume work, *Le Point de départ de la métaphysique*, aimed at bridging the gap that separated the thought of Thomas Aquinas from the Kantian idealism that dominated Continental philosophy.

For Maréchal, Aquinas's thought could complete the 'transcendental turn to the subject' initiated by Kant. A 'critique of knowledge', undertaken as laying bare 'the conditions of the possibility of knowledge', reveals the forms and categories of human knowing, but not the possibilities of objective knowledge. Such objective knowledge would be possible only on the basis of an intellectual intuition, and since he discerned no such intuition, Kant discounted the objectivity of human knowledge. In the famous fifth *Cahier*, mounting a confrontation between Aquinas and Kant, Maréchal maintained that Kant became an idealist because he was not consistent in his own transcendental reflection on the *a priori* conditions of human knowledge. Knowing is an operation, a movement, a tendency towards an end.

Maréchal insisted that a critique of knowledge revealed the objective dynamism of human knowledge, culminating in objective judgements of existence. In other words, as Lonergan would later put it, 'authentic subjectivity leads to objectivity'.

The student of Aquinas, reading him properly, need not fear the Kantian critique of knowledge: on the contrary, appropriately radicalized, it brought us back to Aristotelico-Thomistic metaphysical positions, properly understood.

---

[19] Though David Tracy, in a good study (early but not outdated), *The Achievement of Bernard Lonergan* (New York: Herder and Herder 1970), notes that Lonergan is not 'strictly speaking' a Maréchallian: 28–9.

[20] *A Second Collection*: 264–5.

In the 1920s, this 'turn to the subject' was a risky step in the paranoically anti-modernist climate of Catholic thought. Those who attempted it were often accused of sacrificing the objectivity of human knowledge. Obviously, there was the danger of arriving at the same position as Kant and much of European thought after him, that is, a transcendental idealism. The fear was that by 'turning within' one could never again emerge 'outside'. There would be no possibility of escaping from the clutches of a subjectivism. The first question in neoscholastic theory of knowledge was how to get from 'consciousness' to the 'external world'. To start from analysis of our cognitional activities seemed to risk leaving us trapped inside our own heads. The solution was simply to insist that 'being is what the mind knows', *ens est primum cognitum*. The philosophy of consciousness associated with Descartes, Kant and their successors, should simply be set aside.

Lonergan was inoculated against this by his early acceptance of Cook-Wilsonian realism. On the other hand, there was something more to be learnt from Aristotle and from Aquinas. Largely independent of Maréchal, he began to see that the supposed problem of bridging the gap between consciousness and reality presupposes a highly contestable understanding of human knowledge as *confrontation*. As Lonergan would note in *Insight*: 'Five hundred years separate Hegel from Scotus. As will appear from our discussion of the method of metaphysics, that notable interval of time was largely devoted to working out in a variety of manners the possibilities of the assumption that knowing consists in taking a look'.[21] In other words, picking up Maréchal's key idea, mediated through Stephanou, Lonergan saw the obvious – human knowledge is *discursive*: 'It was through Stefanu [sic] by some process of osmosis, rather than through struggling with the five great Cahiers, that I learnt to speak of human knowledge as not intuitive but discursive with the decisive component in judgment'.[22]

Lonergan's critique of Gilson's position[23] focuses on Gilson's 'perceptionism': his assumption that cognitional activity is confined to phenomena: perception is the one manner in which 'cognitional activity attains objectivity'.[24] Lonergan cites passages where Gilson writes as follows: 'the apprehension of being by intellect consists in directly *seeing* [Gilson's emphasis] in any sensible datum whatever the concept of being'.

---

[21]   *Insight*: 372.
[22]   *A Second Collection*: 265.
[23]   In *Gregorianum* 1963, reprinted as 'Metaphysics as Horizon', *Collection*: 202–20.
[24]   *Collection*: 208. Previously, he had reviewed Gilson's *Being and Some Philosophers* in *Theological Studies* 11 (1950), 122–5.

The World as Language

In his explanation of how human beings gain understanding, in *Insight*, Lonergan analysed not only historical and contemporary philosophical ideas but also recent developments in mathematics, both the natural and social sciences, as well as theology; he also made a thorough study of common sense.

One obstacle for most theologian readers is that the first five chapters broach the question of the nature of knowledge, or of intelligent inquiry, in examples entirely taken from the fields of mathematics and physics. Skipping to chapter six we meet countless examples of intelligence in every walk of life – 'readiness in catching on, in getting the point, in seeing the issue, in grasping implications, in acquiring know-how'[25] – no learning without teaching – 'the communication of insight' – 'It throws out the clues, the pointed hints, that lead to insight. It cajoles attention to drive away the distracting images that stand in insight's way' – 'Talking is a basic human art' – 'We watch to see how things are done' – 'Not only are men born with a native drive to inquire and understand; they are born into a community that possesses a common fund of tested answers' and so on – 'common sense'.

By 1972, Lonergan was insisting that we exist, not just in the infant's world of immediacy, but in the far vaster world mediated by meaning.[26]

Lonergan starts from the simple and evident fact that infants do not speak whereas adults mostly do. In other words: so long as they do not speak, infants do not live in a world mediated by language. 'Their world is a world of immediacy, of sights and sounds, of tastes and smells, of touching and feeling, of joys and sorrows.' As they learn to speak, they are gradually drawn into a world which 'includes the past and the future as well as the present, the possible and the probable as well as the actual, rights and duties as well as facts'. 'It is a world enriched by travellers' tales, by stories and legends, by literature, philosophy, science, by religion, theology, history'.[27] It is, however, also a world in which 'besides fact there is fiction, besides truth there is error, besides science there is myth, besides honesty there is deceit'.

Mostly, we get along without raising philosophical questions as to how this all works. Philosophers, however, raise the questions but, far too often, Lonergan suggests,

---

[25] *Insight*: 173.
[26] *A Second Collection*: 239–61.
[27] Ibid.: 240

they are apt to go into a deep huddle with themselves, to overlook the number of years they spent learning to speak, to disregard the differences between the infant's world of immediacy and the adult's world mediated by meaning, to reach back to their infancy, and to come up with the infantile solution that the real is what is given in immediate experience.[28]

The result follows: 'Knowing, they will claim, is a matter of taking a good look; objectivity is a matter of seeing what is there to be seen; reality is whatever is given in immediate experience'.[29]

This is 'naïve realism', or 'empiricism'. The empiricist confuses the criteria for knowing the world mediated by meaning with the criteria for the world of immediacy – what can be known by merely feeling and touching and seeing. The idealist knows there is more to human knowing than this, but he conceives this 'more' in the same or analogous sensitive terms and so concludes that our knowing cannot be objective.

The critical realist asserts that objective human knowing takes place, not just by experience, but by experience completed by human understanding and correct judgement. 'In the infant's world of immediacy the only objects to which we are related immediately are the objects of sensible intuition'. 'But in the adult's world mediated by meaning the objects to which we are related immediately are the objects intended by our questioning and known by correct answering'.[30]

The objects intended are beings, *entia*, as the neoscholastic jargon says; we need to be clear, however, that these beings are what is to be known by asking questions such as *Quid sit* and *An sit* – what are they and whether they exist – and by coming up with correct answers.

The break from both empiricism and idealism, Lonergan argues, involves the elimination of the cognitional myth: that knowing is like looking, that objectivity is seeing what is there to be seen and not seeing what is not there, and that the real is what is out there now to be looked at.[31]

But knowing is not just seeing. It is experiencing, understanding, judging, and believing.

[28] Ibid.
[29] Ibid.: 241.
[30] Ibid.: 243.
[31] *Method and Theology* (London: Darton, Longman and Todd 1972): 238.

Thomas Aquinas on Grace

Lonergan was not, however, just a philosopher. In *Grace and Freedom*[32] he retrieves the developments of speculative theology on grace from Augustine to Thomas Aquinas, sets out the terms and relations in the latter's notion of operative and co-operative grace, and presents an as yet unsurpassed analysis of Aquinas's theory of divine transcendence and human liberty. He disengages Aquinas's notion of divine causality from the hierarchical cosmology in which it was expressed. He cuts through the difficulties surrounding subsequent theological controversies on grace and freedom, from the voluntarism of Scotus, through nominalism and the disputes on God's grace and human freedom (the *De Auxiliis* controversy between Dominicans and Jesuits),[33] to the Enlightenment and modern variations on determinism and decisionism, indicating how crucial achievements of Aquinas were ignored. The intellectual breakthroughs, which Aquinas effected, were neither understood adequately by his contemporaries nor communicated through subsequent commentators. The 'theorem of the supernatural' in Aquinas expresses the mystery of redemption as gifting humankind with theological virtues and graces natural to God alone, and so absolutely gratuitous and supernatural relative to human nature. Subsequent commentators missed imagined separate realms or planes, one natural and another supernatural. This led to a host of difficulties characterized by supposed contradictions between the supernatural and the natural, grace and freedom, faith and reason.

This work convinced Lonergan that the task of retrieving Aquinas was far more difficult than most theologians had envisaged. For what was needed was not simply historical reconstruction of Aquinas's work but profound changes within the student.

Obviously, in the circumstances of the time, four articles in an American theological periodical in 1941–2 did not make much impact. In 1946, however, reviewing a Latin study on the controversy between Jesuits and Dominicans, Lonergan, tacitly referring to his own work, remarks that the new approach to reading Thomas Aquinas involves 'not only the discredit of baroque procedures but also an unexpectedly quiet funeral for a once celebrated and very passionate debate'.[34] For himself, trained to be Molinist at

---

[32] *Grace and Freedom: Operative Grace in the Thought of St Thomas Aquinas*, edited by J.P. Burns with an introduction by F.E. Crowe (London: Darton, Longman and Todd and New York: Herder and Herder, 1971).

[33] See page 124, note 16.

[34] *Collection*: 67.

the Gregorian, a month on Aquinas's texts freed him.[35] His reading of Thomas put an end to centuries of bitter dispute, or would have done if it had been much studied. Ironically, when the articles were reprinted, in 1972, his reconstruction of Aquinas's theology of grace dropped into a post-Vatican II environment in which younger Catholic theologians barely understood what the debate was ever about.[36]

No Philosophy of Religion

Lonergan distinguishes 'philosophy of God' and 'systematics' as, respectively, thought about God not logically derived from revealed religion and thought about God dependent on revealed truths.[37] The former aims at proving the existence of God and the divine attributes. The latter takes over truths established elsewhere as true and tries to understand them.

In an age dominated by classicism and conceptualism the two have been separated. By classicists Lonergan means people for whom 'the rhetorician or orator of Isocrates or Cicero [sic] represents the fine flower of human culture' (ix). No doubt he has in mind the Renaissance humanism he knew as a schoolboy. Conceptualists, as we have seen, are all those in the long tradition of Western philosophy who picture knowing as taking a look: empiricists and idealists and certainly neoscholastics.

Now, however, so Lonergan thinks, there is no reason to have philosophy of God taught by philosophers in departments of philosophy, and systematics taught by theologians in departments of theology or religious studies. He rejects Pascal's distinction between the god of the philosophers and the God of Abraham, Isaac and Jacob. More specifically, he rejects the conception of philosophy of God, in the recent Catholic past, treating God's existence and attributes in a purely objective way – considering philosophy, and so philosophy of religion, as 'so objective that it is independent of the mind that thinks it' (13). Now, on the contrary, we find we cannot do philosophy of God prescinding from ourselves – 'intellectual, moral, and religious conversion have to be taken into account'.

Now, in 1972, Lonergan declares that he 'taught theology for twenty-five years under impossible conditions' (15). 'The whole set-up', of Scholasti-

---

[35] *Method*: 163.

[36] *Grace and Freedom*.

[37] *Philosophy of God, and Theology: The Relationship between Philosophy of God and the Functional Specialty, Systematics* (London: Darton, Longman and Todd 1973). Subsequent page references for quotations are given in the text.

cism, 'was predicated upon things that were fine in the sixteenth century'; but now we see that divisions introduced by Christian Wolff are 'not sacrosanct'. Lonergan rejects the old distinctions between natural ethics and Christian ethics, between philosophical and Christian anthropology – distinctions operative from an Aristotelian viewpoint but no longer – and the integration has to be done in theology.

We have to move natural theology over into systematic theology: from his experience students are simply bored by a natural theology which isn't 'religious', which leaves aside the involvement of the person (19–20).

For Aristotle philosophy was metaphysics from which all other disciplines derive their basic terms and relations. Now philosophy is basically cognitional theory, and this cannot be conducted independently of hermeneutics and history. This is what forces Catholic theology out of the neoscholasticism (32). Formerly, the dogmatic theologian was expected to establish a system of propositions, from Scripture, patristic writings, the consensus of theologians (he should have added: papal encyclicals), applying *ratio theologica*. Now, however, historical scholarship intervenes between the dogmatician and these sources. There can be no systematic theology now which does not include biblical criticism, history of doctrines, and so on. Above all, however, natural theology and systematics have a common origin in religious *experience*.

This experience varies from culture to culture, class to class, person to person; but, rooted in God's gift of his love, it is antecedent to any knowledge of God: 'Religious experience at its root is experience of an unconditioned and unrestricted being in love' (51). That is, however, only the beginning of the story – 'what we are in love with, remains something that we have to find out'.

This is not incompatible with the decree of Vatican I, to the effect that from the existence of creatures by the natural light of reason we can know with certainty the existence of God – this does not mean that fallen human beings without grace can know with certainty the existence of God – so Lonergan contends. The question of God may begin as a purely metaphysical question but it unavoidably becomes moral and religious, so that there can be no philosophy of God isolated from the cultural and personal background and expectations of the questioner. Indeed: 'It is only in the climate of religious experience that philosophy of God flourishes'.

It is not difficult, Lonergan thinks, to establish God's existence – the hard work lies in refuting all the objections. Not every student of religion needs to be concerned with these arguments. Rather, what matters, Lonergan says, is what he calls 'self-appropriation'. 'The concern of the theologian is not just a set of propositions but a concrete religion as it has been lived, as it is being lived, and as it is to be lived' (56).

Experiential Expressivism?

Lonergan often remarked that theologians previously placed so much emphasis on the objectivity of truth that the subject was overlooked – his point being that there is no truth except in judgements and judgements exist only in *minds*.

Perhaps not surprisingly, given the remarks cited about 'experience', George Lindbeck takes Lonergan's *Method* as an example of the 'experiential-expressivism' that he finds so pervasive in Christian theology and religious studies.[38]

For a start, Lonergan envisages different religions as different expressions or objectifications of a common core experience, which is the experience that identifies them as religions. The experience, while conscious, may be unrecognized for what it is, at the level of self-conscious reflection. It is an experience that all human beings have, potentially. In most religions, the experience is the source and norm of objectifications: it is by reference to the experience that the adequacy or otherwise of these expressions is to be judged.[39]

On the other hand, granted that the universe is intelligible, the question arises whether it could be so without having an intelligent ground (101). For Lonergan, this is what the question of God comes to. He particularizes the question – are cosmogenesis, biological evolution, historical process, and so on, in some way related, favourable or anyway cognate to us as moral beings or indifferent and alien to us? Such questions we human beings cannot avoid asking – we are the creature 'that questions without restriction, that questions the significance of its own questioning' – and so the question of God comes up again. In fact, the human spirit, call it our transcendental subjectivity, 'is mutilated or abolished, unless [we are] stretching forth towards the intelligible, the unconditioned, the good of value'. The reach of our stretching is unrestricted: 'There lies within [our] horizon a region for the divine, a shrine for ultimate holiness'. Atheists may say that this space is empty; agnostics may be unsure; humanists disallow the question to arise. 'But their negations presuppose the spark in our clod, our native orientation to the divine' (103).

Our capacity for self-transcendence, enacted in these questions, 'becomes an actuality when one falls in love'. Admittedly, Lonergan concedes, there

---

[38] George A. Lindbeck, *The Nature of Doctrine: Religion and Theology in a Postliberal Age* (London: SPCK 1984).
[39] *Method*: 101–24. Subsequent page references for quotations are given in the text.

are many ways of 'being-in-love'. However, just as the question of God is implicit in all our questioning, so being in love with God is the basic fulfilment of our intentionality. The absence of this fulfilment 'opens the way to the trivialization of human life in the pursuit of fun, to the harshness of human life arising from the ruthless exercise of power, to despair about human welfare springing from the conviction that the universe is absurd' – but 'being in love with God, as experienced, is being in love in an unrestricted fashion' – 'Though not the product of our knowing and choosing, it is a conscious dynamic state of love, joy, peace, that manifests itself in acts of kindness, goodness, fidelity, gentleness, and self-control' (Gal. 5:22).

Lonergan appeals to an 'experience of mystery' – Rudolf Otto's experience of the holy as *mysterium fascinans et tremendum*; Paul Tillich's experience of being grasped by ultimate concern; and indeed St Ignatius Loyola's consolation that has no cause, as expounded by Karl Rahner. This, no doubt, is the generous acceptance of a fairly heterogeneous array of experiences, which makes Lindbeck nervous. This is sanctifying grace, Lonergan affirms– 'the gift of God's love' – 'an experience' – which is 'only consequently . . . objectified in theoretical categories' (107). More worryingly still, from Lindbeck's viewpoint, Lonergan claims that, before it enters the world mediated by meaning, language, and so on, religion is the prior word God speaks to us by flooding our hearts with divine love. 'This always prior word pertains to the unmediated experience of the mystery of love and awe – this always antecedent gift, in its immediacy, withdraws one from the diversity of history, cultures, out of the world mediated by meaning and into a world of immediacy in which image and symbol, thought and word, lose their relevance and even disappear' (112). On the other hand, this does not mean that the historically conditioned, contextually varying outward word is incidental; it has a constitutive role; a man and a woman are not in love if they have not avowed this to each other; yet, the experience of the mystery 'remains within subjectivity as a vector, an undertow, a fateful call to dread holiness'.

Conclusion

In years of sustained study, Lonergan worked out, on his own, a revolutionary reading of Thomas Aquinas, first in reconstructing the history of Aquinas's doctrine of grace, then his theory of knowledge. With *Insight*, he produced a major work of philosophical thinking, comparable with Rahner's *Spirit in the World*, Balthasar's *Truth of the World*, and Wojtyla's *Acting Person*, much more accessible than any of these, at least to philosophers. In the foreword to Tracy's book Lonergan allowed that he played a modest part, in the wider process of renewal in Catholic thought: 'It crystallized, burst into the open, and startled the world at Vatican II' – a process going on for over a century, in which theologians 'have gradually been adapting their thought to the shift from the classicist culture, dominant up to the French revolution, to the empirical and historical mindedness that constitutes its modern successor'.[40] In his reflections on the mystery of subjectivity, however, on 'the fateful call to dread holiness', Bernard Lonergan (like Chenu, de Lubac and Karl Rahner) calls the reader into a form of theological work which is simultaneously an ascetic discipline – a spirituality, so to speak.

[40] Tracy, *Achievement of Bernard Lonergan*: xi.

Chapter Eight

HANS URS VON BALTHASAR

Greatly influenced by Henri de Lubac and frequently played off nowadays against his one-time colleague Karl Rahner, Hans Urs von Balthasar is widely regarded as the greatest Catholic theologian of the century.

Born on 12 August 1905 at Lucerne, Switzerland, Hans Urs von[1] Balthasar comes of an old patrician family. His younger brother was to serve in the Swiss Guard. His sister became superior general of a congregation of Franciscan nuns.[2] He could have been a professional pianist. He studied German literature and philosophy at Zurich, Vienna and Berlin. His doctorate, on 'the history of the eschatological problem in modern German literature', appeared, considerably rewritten, as *Apokalypse der deutschen Seele* (1938). In 1929, at an age when most seminarians were being ordained, he entered the Society of Jesus, in Germany, since it was still banned in Switzerland.[3] Bitterly hating neoscholasticism, he discovered, from the maverick Jesuit Erich Przywara,[4] a way of reading Thomas Aquinas, against that

---

[1]   The nobiliary particle, correctly employed only with full name or initials; inconsistently, however, we don't say 'von Harnack', yet the Baron is always 'von Hügel'.

[2]   See David L. Schindler (ed.) *Hans Urs von Balthasar: His Life and Work* (San Francisco: Ignatius Press 1991); Edward T. Oakes SJ and David Moss (eds.) The *Cambridge Companion to Hans Urs von Balthasar* (Cambridge: Cambridge University Press 2004), and Ben Quash, in *The Modern Theologians: An Introduction to Christian Theology since 1918*, third edition edited by David F. Ford with Rachel Muers (Oxford: Blackwell 2005): 106–23.

[3]   The ban was lifted in 1973; even then only 55 per cent of the electors voted in favour of doing so.

[4]   Erich Przywara (1889–1972), born in Upper Silesia, entered the Society of Jesus in 1908. He never held an academic post and few of his writings are available in English but see Thomas F. O'Meara OP, *Erich Przywara SJ: His Theology and His World* (Notre Dame, IN: University of Notre Dame Press 2002).

propounded in the lectures he had to attend, and was introduced to the work of the Heideggerian Thomist Gustav Siewerth.[5]

Balthasar was not a happy student: 'My entire period of study in the Society of Jesus was a grim struggle with the dreariness of theology, with what men had made out of the glory of revelation . . . I could have lashed out with the fury of a Samson. I felt like tearing down, with Samson's own strength, the whole temple and burying myself beneath the rubble. But it was like this because, despite my sense of vocation, I wanted to carry out my own plans, and was living in a state of unbounded indignation'.[6] Four years of theology with the Jesuits in France were relieved by meeting Henri de Lubac, who never formally taught him (or any other young Jesuits), but, living in the same house, was able to encourage them – 'he showed us the way beyond the scholastic stuff to the Fathers of the Church. . . . And so when all the others went off to play football', Balthasar and a handful of others 'got down to Origen, Gregory of Nyssa, and Maximus'. By 1942 he had published a book about each of them. Origen, in particular, he discovered, recognizing 'in astonishment that he was the most sovereign spirit of the first centuries, who has set his mark for good or ill on the totality of Christian theology'.[7]

Balthasar worked briefly in Munich, on the Jesuit journal *Stimmen der Zeit*. With Karl Rahner, he composed a plan for the reform of Catholic theology.[8] When the Nazi regime encroached on the freedom of Catholic journalists, he returned to Switzerland, in 1940, to become student chaplain at the University of Basle (a ministry not foreseen when Swiss law banned the Jesuits). In 1940 Balthasar received Adrienne Kaegi-von Speyr into the Church.[9] In 1945, they founded a religious society, the Community of Saint

---

[5]   Gustav Siewerth (1903–63), lay man, and philosopher, studied 1926–31 at Freiburg im Briesgau with Heidegger. As an anti-Nazi, his academic career was blocked, see Peter Reifenberg and Anton van Hooff (eds.) *Gott für die Welt: Henri de Lubac, Gustav Siewerth, Hans Urs von Balthasar* (Mainz: Matthias-Grünewald-Verlag 2001), for his influence.

[6]   Recalling in 1946 the wasted years, cf. Schindler, *Balthasar*: 13; in 1985 he was still attacking 'the rationalism of the neoscholastics', see *Theo-Logic: Theological Logical Theory*, vol. I (San Francisco: Ignatius Press 2000): 20.

[7]   *My Work: In Retrospect* (San Francisco: Ignatius Press 1993): 11 is much the best guide.

[8]   See 'A Scheme for a Treatise of Dogmatic Theology', in Karl Rahner, *Theological Investigations*, vol. I (London: Darton, Longman and Todd 1961): 19–35; for which Rahner takes responsibility though noting it is no longer possible to distinguish his part from Balthasar's.

[9]   Adrienne von Speyr (1902–67) came from a French-speaking Swiss, comfortably-off Protestant family. She went to secondary school, against her mother's wishes, and was the only girl in the class, where her best friend was Heinrich Barth (Karl's brother). She was among the first women physicians in Switzerland, financing her medical training by tutoring fellow students. In 1927 she married Emil Dürr, a professor of history and a widower with

John, for men and women. In 1950, after painful negotiations, he chose to follow this new call and left the Society of Jesus.[10] Dogged by gossip, he remained in the wilderness, ecclesiastically, until he was incardinated in the diocese of Chur in 1956.

Balthasar attended Karl Barth's lectures. His book on Barth appeared in 1951, the product of lectures Barth attended when he could. This book brought Balthasar to the attention of Protestant theologians though it attracted little interest among Catholics.[11] He founded a publishing house, primarily to publish the dictations he was by now taking down from Speyr during her mystical trances. The first round of publications, however, included his own *Schleifung der Bastionen* (1952), a forthright denunciation of the Roman Catholic Church's 'fortress mentality';[12] two comparatively good-tempered calls by Karl Rahner for freedom of speech in the Church; and the 29-year-old Hans Küng's doctoral thesis on Barth (see chapter 9).

Balthasar was not invited to take part in any capacity in the Vatican Council. In 1961 the first volume of *Herrlichkeit* (translated into English as *The Glory of the Lord*) appeared: the first of 15, as it turned out, successfully concluded in 1985, and constituting by far the most impressive work by any twentieth-century Catholic theologian, comparable with Barth's (unfinished) *Church Dogmatics*, in scope and ambition, as well as in bulk.

Honoured in 1965 by the University of Edinburgh (for his book on Barth) and by the Ecumenical Patriarch (for his studies of Greek patristic writers), Balthasar was at last recognized by his co-religionists in 1969, when Pope Paul VI appointed him to the International Theological Commission.[13] While Vatican II brought about most of what Balthasar wanted,

---

two young sons. Dürr died as the result of an accident in 1934 and in 1936 Adrienne married Werner Kaegi, expert on the Renaissance historian Jacob Burkhardt. From 1940 until 1944, she had a series of visions, ecstasies, mystical experiences, including bilocation and stigmatization. From 1944 until 1948 she dictated to Balthasar some 60 volumes. In the early 1950s she fell seriously ill with diabetes, severe arthritis and bowel cancer, and became increasingly blind. Her husband died in 1979. As yet there is little secondary literature on her.

[10] Text of his resignation letter in H. de Lubac, *At the Service of the Church* (San Francisco: Ignatius Press 1993): 370–5.

[11] Listening to Mozart records for nearly 24 hours with Balthasar and Kaegi-von Speyr in winter 1948–9, at Einsiedeln, Barth was so delighted that he bought himself a gramophone and began regular listening, see Eberhard Busch, *Karl Barth: His Life from Letters and Autobiographical Texts* (London: SCM Press 1976): 362.

[12] Hans Urs von Balthasar, *Razing the Bastions: On the Church in This Age* (San Francisco: Ignatius Press 1993).

[13] In 1973 he was elected a Corresponding Fellow of the British Academy.

in terms of a new openness of the Church to the world, a reaffirmation of the place of the laity, and so on, it was not the retrieval of a fuller experience of Catholic tradition, as he had hoped. From *Cordula* (1966, translated into English as *The Moment of Christian Truth*) onwards, polemics poured forth, against Karl Rahner and 'anonymous Christianity', Eastern meditation, Hans Küng, women as priests, modern biblical exegesis, seminary education, and much else.[14] Balthasar was instrumental in founding *Communio*, the 'conservative' counterblast to *Concilium*, the periodical associated with Edward Schillebeeckx, Hans Küng and other 'progressive' and 'liberal' Catholics: countervailing journals which, to this day, exemplify the incommensurable perspectives within which Catholic theology is conducted.

In 1985 Adrienne von Speyr's 'mission' was recognized at an international colloquium in Rome, much to Balthasar's delight. He sought to return to the Jesuits but negotiations failed: they were not willing to undertake responsibility for the *Johannesgemeinschaft*. He died at Basle on 26 June 1988, three days before investiture as a cardinal, having accepted the honour reluctantly, but as recognition of her work.

Suárezianism

According to de Lubac, Rahner, Lonergan and Balthasar, the mandatory Thomism, which they were taught as young Jesuits, was actually 'Suárezianism'. The only extended account by one of them, which would surely have been accepted by the others, is Balthasar's, in his reflections on metaphysics in the modern age.[15]

In the wider world, the Spanish Jesuit Francisco Suárez (1548–1617) is best known for his *De Legibus* (1616), on the principles of natural and international law, which influenced jurists and legislators in Continental Europe and America. He tangled with King James I of England: a copy of his *Defensio fidei* (1613), directed against the Church of England, was solemnly burned in London for doctrines prejudicial to the power of the state.

---

[14] E.g. 'The shorter the skirts, the less exciting the legs. Fashion designers will have to bring out something new if they are to turn up the thermostat on our eroticism', *Elucidations* (San Francisco: Ignatius Press 1998; original German 1971): 227; and much similar needlessly reprinted journalism.

[15] *The Glory of the Lord: A Theological Aesthetics* V: *The Realm of Metaphysics in the Modern Age* (Edinburgh: T&T Clark 1991): 21–9; subsequent page references for quotations are given in the text. The German edition appeared in 1965; cf. Robert C. Miner, 'Suárez as Founder of Modernity? Reflections on a Topos in Recent Historiography', *History of Philosophy Quarterly* 18 (2001): 17–36.

Suárez was, so Balthasar says, 'the father of Baroque- and Neo-Scholasticism' (21). Most significantly, he taught 'the univocity of Being' – the idea of Being as 'the univocal and neutral principle which is beyond both God and world' (560).

One consequence was that his theological system failed to match his Jesuit spirituality. Balthasar takes the view held by Chenu and mocked by Garrigou-Lagrange that the spirituality of a great charismatic figure, such as St Ignatius Loyola, or religious tradition, such as the Jesuits, should be articulable in a correspondingly distinctive theological vision, and indeed that the latter should be inspired by the former. Without explaining this, he holds that Suárezian theology was never an adequate rendering of the Ignatian vision.

Another consequence is that Suárez – not Descartes – laid the foundations for the metaphysics of modernity (25).

More to the point here, however, Suárez's 'naïve point of departure' controls 'the clerical activity of philosophical and theological Neoscholasticism' – whether or not the doctrine of univocity is formally taught (25). Following Scotus, so Balthasar says, Suárez reduces being, reality, to one level plane, fearing that if we allow the concept of being to function analogically then we open the way to uncertainty, since we have no guarantee that the concept of God has any content at all. Without a plainly univocal concept of being that embraces God as well as the angels and all material things, God would slip out of the range of our knowledge altogether, however negative, apophatic and so forth we may claim it to be.

The rot spreads into how the relationship is conceived between divine and human freedom. God and creatures have the same kind of being – that we are on all fours, ontologically speaking – then one seems to be in a position to compare God and creatures. The 'pitiful controversy' which the 'young Society of Jesus' allowed itself to get involved in – the controversy *De Auxiliis*[16] – rests on the presupposition that the theological metaphysician 'can peer from above into the interaction of the *Causa Prima* with the *causa secunda*' (26). The existence supposedly of a concept of being that univocally embraces Creator and creatures is the precondition for the doctrine of Molinism, which leads to the creature's attaining 'an ultimate particularity and freedom which is independent of God's will' (28).

---

[16] In 1597 Pope Clement VIII set up the 'congregatio de Auxiliis' to deal with the bitter dispute between Jesuits and Dominicans over what 'aids', *auxilia*, the operation of divine grace in the soul presupposed or required: for Luis de Molina SJ (1535–1600) the efficacy of divine grace rests ultimately not in the gift itself but in God's foreknowledge of how the soul will co-operate; this *scientia media* or *conditionata* was regarded as a violation of divine sovereignty by Dominicans; never settled, the dispute was suspended in 1609 when Pope Paul V forbade Dominicans to call Jesuits Pelagian and Jesuits to call Dominicans Calvinists.

The 'sense of philosophical mystery' disappears, and with it the 'sense of theological mystery' – which, according to the axiom 'grace perfects nature', should have generated 'an intensified and deepened feeling for the mystery of glory'. Instead, neoscholastic pedagogy, with its 'apologetic all-knowingness' fails to communicate this 'feeling'; indeed it has deleterious effects in preaching and catechesis, affecting the prayer life and contemplative practice of Catholics who have no sympathy with such apologetics. 'What is characteristic here is that in Neoscholasticism, when the feeling for the glory of God was lost – that glory which pervades the Revelation as a whole but which is not perceived by conceptual rationalism, or concerning which it remains silent, or which it wholly removes by means of method – there perished also the sensorium for the glory of Creation (as "aesthetics") which shone through the whole theology of the Fathers and of the Early and High Middle Ages' (26–7). The conceptualization of Being in Suárez's metaphysics 'annuls the experience of reality and encloses thought in a sphere which is characterized by bare, essential predications, by the play of the analysis and synthesis of concepts, and accordingly by the inner-subjective opposition of the act of thought (*noesis*) and the content of thought (*noema*)' (27).

It is no surprise, Balthasar concludes, that 'the sensorium for the glory of Creation' passed to the poets and artists (Dante, Petrarch, Milton, Herder, Hölderlin, Keats) and to the great natural scientists (Kepler, Newton, early Kant, Goethe, Carus, Fechner, Teilhard) – leaving neoscholasticism isolated from imaginative literature as well as from the natural sciences.

Whether Balthasar's assertions are altogether intelligible, we must let pass – together with the genealogy he offers for the rationalism, which, in his experience, had infiltrated the mandatory philosophy, including metaphysics and apologetics, taught in the Jesuit colleges of his day. The 'Suárezianism' which Balthasar denounces seems remarkably like the 'Wolffianism' which we found Chenu detecting in Garrigou-Lagrange's Thomism.[17]

Subjectivity, Language and Truth

For theologians with an interest in philosophy, Balthasar's most interesting and accessible book is *Wahrheit der Welt*, first published in 1947.[18]

---

[17] How much Balthasar's Suárez has to do with the philosopher studied by John P. Doyle, Alfred J. Freddoso, Jorge J.E. Gracia, Bernard Cantens and others, is another matter.

[18] *Wahrheit der Welt* (translated into French in 1952, Spanish in 1953), reprinted in 1985 as the first volume of *Theologik*. English translation published as as *Theo-Logic: Theological Logical Theory*, vol. 1: *Truth of the World* (San Francisco: Ignatius Press 2000). Subsequent page references for quotations are given in the text.

This 'phenomenology of truth as we familiarly encounter it' – 'natural truth' (31) – might profitably be compared with Karl Rahner's *Geist in Welt* (1939 version). While not going in for detailed exegesis of an Aquinas text, Balthasar nevertheless works out what is very much an interpretation of Aquinas's epistemology, with many more echoes of Heidegger's work than one finds in Rahner.

Over against the standard 'Cartesian' problem, Balthasar insists that 'self-knowledge and the disclosure of the world are not just simultaneous but intrinsically inseparable': 'There is no moment when subjectivity monadically and self-sufficiently rests in itself. Rather, subjectivity is a matter of finding oneself always already engaged with the world' (47). Furthermore, 'the revelation of the subject can occur only in an encounter with the object' (62). What this means, however, in the 'event' and 'adventure' of intellectual knowledge, is that 'both subject and object will be fulfilled by coming together, but the fulfilment will be a wonder and a gift for both'. 'The subject's self-knowledge can reach its actuality only by taking a detour by way of the knowledge of another; only in going out of itself, in creatively serving the world, does the subject become aware of its purpose and, therefore, of its essence'.

But it is not only the subject who is 'in the world', dependent on the world for his or her own development, self-discovery, and so on. According to Balthasar, we should not 'suppose that objects form a self-contained world that has no essential, and at best only an accidental, need of the world of subjects'. While the object of knowledge is commonly pictured as 'an already finished, separately established, and stably self-contained thing that remains unaffected by being known', it is better to see that 'the objects of this world need the subject's space in order to be themselves' (63). The subject is like a 'hospitable dwelling wherein things can unfold their potentialities' (108). A tree needs to be seen and heard and smelled: 'Without the subject's sensory space, it would not be what it is . . .. The space of being that is opened and illuminated in the subject makes available to the object an opportunity to be itself in a way that the inferior space of inanimate elements does not'.

Subject and object 'expand within each other'. It is not just that the subject is enriched by the object, a perfectly acceptable thesis in modern philosophy, at any rate when the subject is thought to receive from the world and not to impose all the meaning there is – for Balthasar, the object is enriched by being taken into the subject's space.

Remarkably, for 1947, Balthasar moves from this to consider the animal world. We shall never know what an animal sees, hears and feels. For a start, even when we have senses in common, we do not see in the multifaceted way of some insects, we cannot imagine how the world looks to a bird or a fish: 'Most of all, we cannot imagine what a sensorium without mind would be' (91). 'Alien worlds that we will never know pass right through ours' – we know a dog is angry by its bark, in pain by its whine. Yet, so Balthasar contends, animals are actually further from us than plants – nearer us to the extent that they can express their fears and desires in utterance that bears generic likeness to our language; further, however, because the impossibility of interpreting the animal's 'language' drives home the mysteriousness of life, indeed of existence as such (cf. 93).

What happens with the human animal, in Balthasar's jargon, is that 'being's revelation to itself also immediately enables and thus requires its revelation to others' (94). Being able to know the truth and being able to say it go together; there could be no knowledge of the truth, which is not communicable.

On the other hand, one does not *have to say* what one knows. Predisposed as we are to communication, we are not compelled to communicate on every occasion. In our case, communication begins with a free decision to share with another what belongs to us – 'it is not as if man had to avail himself of deficient, arbitrary signs in order to communicate with others, in order to get "behind the mystery" of another mind, whereas entities having perfect knowledge could somehow dispense with this roundabout means because they could look into one another's minds by an immediate, non-discursive intuition' (95). 'Self utterance is bound to the natural symbolic language of the senses', which is a limit in one way, since we can never overcome the solitude of the sensory sphere; yet mastery of this symbolic expressive language is also a help and an enrichment. Language is not an invention that floats free in a realm of abstraction. Rather, language is grounded in the language of nature and the laws of natural expression – one's countenance, indeed one's whole figure, inseparably expresses one's rootedness in nature as soul and one's freedom as spirit. The boundary between sensible and intelligible expression cannot be strictly defined.

There is much else in this book, which is of great philosophical interest.[19] Balthasar, for example, attacks the dominance in Western culture of the fact/value split, the disjoining of being and value (103). He writes well on time and historicity (195); on shame (213); and on knowledge as primitively receptive, mocking the picture of 'the knowledge-hungry subject that first prowls about in search of prey' (258). Rather, 'a knowing that grasps is

---

[19]   Much that Balthasar says parallels what Ludwig Wittgenstein was writing about the same time: see e.g. posthumously published *Remarks on the Philosophy of Psychology* I (Oxford: Basil Blackwell 1980), dated to 1946–9.

always embedded in a knowing that can let go because it is itself grasped' (259). Above all, however, he writes excellently on language, a lacuna in neoscholastic philosophy – 'The child who wakens to consciousness does not enter into the world as a pure spirit in order to tackle the problem of expression from scratch. Rather, the child awakens from subspiritual life, where there was already a natural relation of expression between inside and outside and where the natural correspondences between signification and signified were always already saturated with human and spiritual expressive relations' (162).

This phenomenology of truth, language and meaning is, in effect, an ontology of the human person, including always already a theology (260). This is not a second-order supplemental discovery. For Balthasar, in any knowing we always already know our creatureliness, which we can then explicate and so conclude to God's existence: 'insofar as all grasping is itself comprehended by God's grasp, the form of faith is traced out already within natural reason. When one freely submits in faith to the knowledge of God as Lord and Creator one is at the same time obeying one's nature, or the command of God engraved in one's nature' (260).[20]

Barth, Beauty and Divine Glory

Throughout the 1950s, Balthasar was a lonely figure, theologically, supported by his friendship with Henri de Lubac (himself marginalized) and especially by Adrienne von Speyr, to whom he said later that he owed his most distinctive theological insights; without her, he claimed, though she had no part in the writing, 'the basic perspective of *Herrlichkeit* would never have existed'.[21]

Perhaps so – yet he also noted, elsewhere, that 'it is almost unnecessary to set out how much I owe to Karl Barth: the vision of a comprehensive biblical theology, combined with the urgent invitation to engage in a dogmatically serious ecumenical dialogue'.[22] Barth 'joyfully greeted and endorsed

---

[20]   See Christophe Potworowski, 'Christian Experience in Hans Urs von Balthasar', *Communio* 20 (1993): 107–17.

[21]   *First Glance at Adrienne von Speyr* (San Francisco: Ignatius Press 1981): 13. 'Adrienne is a world. I believe that the Church will gradually have to adopt substantial parts of her doctrine and, perhaps, wonder why these beautiful and enriching things have not been recognized earlier.' Angela Scola, *Test Everything; Hold Fast to What Is Good: An Interview with Hans Urs von Balthasar* (San Francisco: Ignatius Press 1989): 88–9.

[22]   *Rechenschaft 1965* translated by Kenneth Batinovich, in *The Analogy of Beauty: The Theology of Hans Urs von Balthasar*, edited by John Riches (Edinburgh: T&T Clark 1986): 220.

my book about him, followed my subsequent works with some suspicion, but perhaps never noticed how much a little book like *Love Alone* sought to be fair to him and represents perhaps the closest approach to his position from the Catholic side'.[23]

The book on Barth is a classic, contributing as much to the renewal of Catholic theology as to the reception of Barth, though of course dated, in both respects. Donald MacKinnon remembered a conversation in the autumn of 1952 when Barth praised the book for 'its complete understanding of his most fundamental theological purposes'.[24]

In the introduction to the first volume of *Herrlichkeit*,[25] Balthasar implies that the very idea of contemplating the divine glory, and thus of reconceiving Christian theology in the light of the transcendental of beauty, comes from *Church Dogmatics* II/I. In that volume, published in 1940, Barth deals with the perfections of the divine freedom – God as 'One, constant and eternal, and therewith also omnipresent, omnipotent and glorious'. This culminates in the claim that the biblical concept of God's glory, if it is to mean 'something other and more than the assertion of a brute fact', requires the complement of the concept of *beauty*: to say that God is beautiful is to say 'how He enlightens and convinces and persuades us'.[26]

Barth cautions us against bringing contemplation of God 'into suspicious proximity to that contemplation of the world which in the last resort is the self-contemplation of an urge for life which does not recognize its own limits'.[27] Nevertheless, we have to say that God is beautiful, and in saying this, Barth allows, 'we reach back to the pre-Reformation tradition of the Church', referring to Augustine and Pseudo-Dionysius.[28] Here, Balthasar thinks, Barth achieves a 'decisive breakthrough'.[29] His appeal to 'an authentic theological aesthetics' had 'no roots within the realm of Protestant theology' but required him to retrieve 'those elements of Patristic and Scholastic thought which can be justified from revelation itself and which, accordingly, are not suspect of any undue Platonizing'. In Barth's theology

---

[23] Ibid.; *Love Alone: the Way of Revelation* (London and Dublin: Sheed and Ward and Veritas Publications, 1968) translated anonymously with a few minor additions to the original *Glaubhaft ist nur Liebe* (Einsiedeln: Johannes Verlag, 1963).

[24] *Engagement with God* (London: SPCK 1975): 2. Barth was wrong, according to Bruce L. McCormack, for whom Balthasar's book is 'the massive shadow' occluding correct interpretation for over 40 years, cf. *Karl Barth's Critically Realistic Dialectical Theology: Its Genesis and Development 1909–1936* (Oxford: Clarendon Press 1995): 1.

[25] *The Glory of the Lord: A Theological Aesthetics* I (Edinburgh: T&T Clark 1982): 52–6.

[26] *Church Dogmatics* II/1 (Edinburgh: T&T Clark 1957): 650.

[27] Ibid.: 651.

[28] Ibid.

[29] *The Glory of the Lord* I: 56.

of the glory and beauty of God Balthasar found the strategy to dethrone the neoscholasticism – 'sawdust Thomism' – which he hated so deeply.

In the introduction to the final volume of *Herrlichkeit*, Balthasar reverts to *Church Dogmatics* II/I, at some length, saying that Barth's theology of glory 'agrees with our own overall plan' and that outlining it, as Barth does, offers 'an overview that we ourselves can approach only slowly'.[30] Thus, in effect, *Herrlichkeit* is a rich, slow, patient, and much more elaborate working out of Barth's theology of the divine beauty.

Divine Glory Anticipated in Metaphysical Beauty

In Balthasar's *magnum opus* the three volumes on truth are preceded by five on the 'drama' of God's dealing with the world in the history of the Christian dispensation, and these are in turn preceded by seven on the glory of God, as anticipated in pre-Christian philosophies and revealed in Scripture.

On the basis of the axiom that grace builds on nature, and faith and reason are finally always in consonance, Balthasar explores the history of how the self-revelation of the divine glory in the biblical dispensation was prefigured, as we see in hindsight, in the great works in the Western metaphysical tradition. The history of Western philosophy may be read, with Christian hindsight, as a preparation for, and counterpart to, the history of salvation recorded in the Bible.

Neglect of the 'aesthetic' has had deleterious effects on Christian theology, Protestant and Catholic. The absence of the aesthetic perspective begins with the Reformation itself: 'It appeared to Luther that the Death-and-Resurrection dialectic of the Christ-event had been replaced by the non-dialectical schemata of neo-Platonic aesthetic metaphysics'.[31] The Gospel had been betrayed (Luther thought) by Hellenization. On the contrary, Balthasar contends, the elimination of the aesthetic deprived Protestants of the contemplative dimension of the act of faith (70). On the Catholic side, as late as Nicholas of Cusa (1401–64), 'the normative tradition of thought remains the integrated philosophical and theological method common to both the Platonic-Aristotelian and the Augustinian-Dionysian streams' (72).

After Descartes, however, philosophy yields to the natural-scientific ideal of knowledge; and philosophers, including Catholic apologists, 'become eager to experiment with the question of what reason can accomplish

---

[30] *The Glory of the Lord: A Theological Aesthetics* VII (San Francisco: Ignatius Press 1989): 23.
[31] *The Glory of the Lord* I: 45. Subsequent page references for quotations are given in the text.

without the aid of revelation and what the possibilities are for a pure nature without grace' (72).

The proper sense of theological activity is lost. 'True theology begins only at the point where "exact historical science" passes over into the science of faith proper – a "science" which presupposes the act of faith as its locus of understanding' (75).

Balthasar directs us to Chenu's work on Thomas Aquinas: theology is a 'science', *scientia*, only in virtue of a concept of 'science' which is only analogously like any other science, including philosophy. For Aquinas, theological work is grounded on participation through grace in the intuitive saving knowledge of God himself and of the Church triumphant. In brief, there is no true theology except in virtue of the theologian's personal act of faith, directly, mediated in virtue of the pattern of faith presented by the Church. Few theologians these days, Balthasar hazards, believe this: on the contrary, they split theology from 'spirituality'.

Balthasar's Alternative Canon

The alternative reading list for Catholic theologians is no doubt deliberately provocative. Balthasar offers a series of monographs on figures who have shaped (Western) theology: Irenaeus, Augustine, Denys, Anselm, Bonaventure, Dante, John of the Cross, Pascal, Hamann, Soloviev, Hopkins and Péguy – Denys, whose radically aesthetic world-view 'becomes after that of Augustine, the second pillar of Western theology',[32] an affront to exponents of Aristotelico-Thomistic theology;[33] Bonaventure's 'cathedral-like theology';[34] J.G. Hamann (1730–88) 'the Magus of the North', a Lutheran; Soloviev (1853–1900), whom few neoscholastic theologians would have regarded as 'a thinker of universal genius', and they would not have been delighted at the news that he 'anticipates the vision of Teilhard de Chardin'.[35]

Whether Gerard Manley Hopkins, a poet 'of the highest calibre', may intelligibly be said to represent 'the English theological tradition' is another matter: its difference from Continental thought being that 'there has never

---

[32]   *The Glory of the Lord: A Theological Aesthetics* II (Edinburgh: T&T Clark 1984): 17–18.
[33]   See Wayne Hankey, 'Denys and Aquinas: Antimodern Cold and Postmodern Hot', in *Christian Origins: Theology, Rhetoric and Community*, edited by Lewis Ayres and Gareth Jones (London and New York: Routledge 1998).
[34]   *The Glory of the Lord* II: 18.
[35]   Ibid.: 19.

been any opposition between image and concept, myth and revelation, the apprehension of God in nature and in the history of salvation', so that he is able to 'build a bridge between poetic aesthetics and the Ignatian exercises'.[36] English theology, 'reared in an hereditary empiricism', alive in such works as Austin Farrer's *The Glass of Vision* and Eric Mascall's *Words and Images*, involves mistrust of the value of universal concepts, sensitivity to the uniqueness of the individual, and is traceable back to Milton, Purcell, Shakespeare, and behind them to Duns Scotus.[37]

Charles Péguy, an ardent socialist and Dreyfusard, much influenced by the philosophy of Bergson, and an anti-clerical who remained unreconciled to the Church for domestic reasons (he was killed on the Marne in 1914), had been far too controversial a figure for decades in French Catholic circles for his inclusion in Balthasar's list to be anything but intentionally provocative.

No Philosophy without Christianity

Balthasar's history of philosophy comes to a head in his claim that it is now the Christian who 'remains the guardian of that metaphysical wonderment which is the point of origin for philosophy and the continuation of which is the basis for its further existence'.[38] In other words, philosophy can be practised these days only within the context of faith. It takes a Christian to ask 'the authentic metaphysical question': 'Why is there anything at all and not simply nothing?'.[39]

Thus Balthasar rejects Heidegger's thesis that Christians cannot take seriously the question why there is anything rather than nothing since they already have the answer. On the contrary, Balthasar contends, Christians are the only ones who are capable of the 'wonder at Being', the experience which is fundamental to philosophy.

In short, philosophy has a theological background. The religious *a priori* in Plato, Aristotle and other pagan thinkers, may seldom if ever be uncovered; but it is always operative. It is not just that philosophy grew out of mythology and religion historically; for Balthasar, we need to acknowledge the 'indelible presence' of theological themes and presuppositions in actual

---

[36] Ibid.
[37] *The Glory of the Lord* III: 355. Interesting as Balthasar's reading of Hopkins of course is, the assumptions about Englishness would need attention.
[38] *The Glory of the Lord* V: 646.
[39] Ibid.: 613. Heidegger's thesis is to be found in his *Introduction to Metaphysics*.

philosophical thinking. In modern philosophy (idealism, existentialism, personalism, and so on), it is true, the underlying theological motifs are overlooked or denied. Philosophical work is theologically neutral, most philosophers would suppose. That is not how Balthasar sees it. 'Greek metaphysics was orientated towards the theion and the Christian view of reality took possession of this "natural" aesthetics in order to complete and transcend it on the basis of revelation'.[40]

Holy Saturday

Balthasar is, however, very adventurous in his theological speculations. Few, if any, theologians or philosophers have ever owed anything, intellectually, to any woman.[41] Balthasar, however, insisted that he owed his most distinctive theological insights to Adrienne von Speyr: 'On the whole I received far more from her, theologically, than she from me'; 'her work and mine cannot be separated from one another either psychologically or theologically. They are two halves of one whole, with a single foundation at the centre'.[42]

The most famous of her contributions relates to the doctrine of Christ's descent into hell: an article of the Apostles' Creed. The New Testament evidence is such passages as Matthew 27:52f., Luke 23:43 and especially 1 Peter 3:18–20. According to the received view, Christ visited the 'place', after his death, neither heaven nor hell, where the souls of pre-Christian people awaited the Gospel.

From 1941 until 1965, Speyr relived the Passion during Holy Week. On the afternoon of Good Friday she would fall into a trance until early Easter morning. In this state she would undergo the descent into hell with Jesus. Hell was the place where God was absent, where there is neither faith nor hope nor love. It was the experience of sin in its essence, of the radically

---

[40] *The Glory of the Lord* X: 393.

[41] Karl Barth is the exception: 30 years of companionship ended in the early 1960s when Charlotte von Kirschbaum (1899–1975) fell ill and was then 'put out of action as far as the *Church Dogmatics* was concerned, having taken an immeasurable part in its origin and progress' (Eberhard Busch, *Karl Barth: His Life from Letters and Autobiographical Texts* (London: SCM Press 1976): 473, citing a letter from 1966); see also the handsome tribute dated 1950 in the preface to *Church Dogmatics* III/3.

[42] See Johann Roten SM, 'The Two Halves of the Moon: Marian Anthropological Dimensions in the Common Mission of Adrienne von Speyr and Hans Urs von Balthasar', in *Hans Urs von Balthasar: His Life and Work*, edited by David L. Schindler (San Francisco: Ignatius Press 1991): 65-86, an important discussion for understanding Balthasar's work; Balthasar cited 74-5.

absurd. And because he is without sin he experiences the absurd in all its horror. This is what it means to assume the sin of the world. The disembodied soul of Jesus undergoes the horror of death. Far from being the triumphant liberation of the souls from the power of the devil – the harrowing of hell, in the medieval English phrase – Christ's descent is a total identification with the dead, souls psychologically cut off from others and from God.

Nuptiality

Contemplation of being, practising metaphysics properly, that is to say, is 'a being dedicated and taken up in the mystery of the nuptiality between God and the world, which has its glowing heart in the marital mutuality of Christ and the Church'. Admittedly, 'philosophy', here, is in the ancient patristic sense: 'a Christian life lived in consistent praxis in the world'.[43] Balthasar goes on to quote Philo, Justin, Clement of Alexandria and (of course) Origen, for whom philosophy is 'just as much practical as theoretical, demanding the imitation of the Logos, poverty, celibacy, domination of the passions, strict asceticism' (335). This asceticism, which is the kenosis of God's *agapè*, 'its emptying out into human form, into obedience and Cross', becomes 'the communication of this cruciform pattern of all love to the bride-Church'. Thus 'this sacrifice of the bride to the Bridegroom and together with the Bridegroom [which is the eucharist] is the Christian surmounting and perfecting of the philosophical act' (368). Liturgy is the consummation of philosophy, to coin a phrase.

Indeed, it turns out that Barth saw in the Song of Songs the unfolding of the second creation narrative: 'here we witness the thrill of the man before the woman that has been brought to him, and this thrill is reciprocated by the woman without any reference to family or children' (135). Barth sees only one explanation: the author of the Creation saga and the Song both anticipate the New Covenant of Jesus Christ with redeemed humanity.[44] In the end, whatever the breaches of fidelity – even the most terrible – by the Church on earth, rejection is no longer a possibility, since these breaches are 'undergirded by an indefectible nuptial fidelity' – 'in the resurrection of the bridegroom and, as its necessary consequence, the bodily assumption into heaven of the first fruits, of the bride' (413–14).

---

[43] *Explorations in Theology* II: *Spouse of the Word* (San Francisco: Ignatius Press 1991): 368. Subsequent page references for quotations are in the text.
[44] *Church Dogmatics* III/1 313ff.

The allegorical application of the Song Balthasar traces to Origen's vision of the relation between Christ as bridegroom and the Church as bride. Though the text existed in Greek in the Septuagint (250–150 BC), the allegorical interpretation is not attested until Rabbi Aqiba (d. AD 135); it gets going with Origen (c. 185-c. 254), then begins its 'triumphal march', as Balthasar calls it, through the patristic and medieval-scholastic periods into the period 'even of the Reformation and the Baroque Age'.

This is normative not just for marriage (and virginity) but for all the forms of nuptial intimacy and relationship that he sees at every level in the cosmos.

The doctrines of creation and redemption are radically Christological, Balthasar says – a very Barthian thought, which old-fashioned Thomists would no doubt accept also, though after saying a great deal else first. More controversially, these doctrines are properly expounded only in the light of the analogy of marriage: 'The Fathers . . . saw the formation of the hypostatic union as the real and primordial marriage union, that of God with the whole of mankind . . .. The marriage of Christ and the Church is to be interpreted against the background of an, as it were, fundamental marriage with mankind as a whole'.[45] In other words, what happened in the Incarnation is a wedding of the divine and the human natures of the Son of God. Thus, 'when the Fathers see the actual *connubium* between God and man realized in Christ himself, in the indissoluble union of the two natures, this is also no purely physical occurrence, with its matrimonial character exclusively derived from the side of God and his intention. It is a real two-sided mystery of love through the bridal consent of Mary acting for all the rest of created flesh, to which God wills to espouse himself' – 'the hypostatic union is the carrying out and thus the final indissoluble sealing of the covenant of fidelity'. (163).

Balthasar takes this 'law of theology' from Scheeben for whom everything is related, one way or another, to the structure of this *connubium*, this epithalamic relationship: 'At the centre of his theology is the God-man with the two natures, whose union he interprets, with the Greek Fathers, as the marriage of God with mankind in Mary's bridal chamber'.[46]

---

[45] 'Who is the Church?', in *Spouse of the Word*: 181; an essay, Balthasar tells us, which Yves Congar said he did not understand, cf. Scola, *Test Everything*: 82.
[46] *Explorations in Theology* I: *The Word Made Flesh* (San Francisco: Ignatius Press 1989): 202; originally published in German in 1960. Matthias Joseph Scheeben (1835–88), a seminary professor was an enthusiastic supporter of the definition of papal supremacy in 1870, but his passionate opposition to Enlightenment rationalism issued, not in neoscholasticism, but in his own Catholic version of German Romanticism.

It is not only the relationships between God and creation, Christ and the Church, Christ and the soul, and so on, as well as the union of the two natures in Christ, which reflect the nuptiality. The practice of theology itself 'participates in a special manner in the bridal holiness of the Church'. Indeed, 'theology as dialogue between bride and Bridegroom in the unity and communication of the Spirit', so Balthasar says, expounding Scheeben, is 'contemplation of the bridegroom by the bride, and this becomes more objective, profound and comprehensive, the more light and grace are imparted by the Bridegroom to the bride' (203). This is not the language in which many theologians, Catholic or otherwise, would think of their work. Quite what it would amount to, in practice, is, however, perhaps not all that obscure. The example of Garrigou-Lagrange might well be followed, Balthasar advises us, in the sense that he confronted the theology of Thomas Aquinas with the mystical experience of John of the Cross: 'making them elucidate and complete each other' (204). One may not accept all his conclusions, yet his initiative and method are to be commended. More basically still: 'Theology is essentially an act of adoration and prayer. This is the tacit presupposition of any systematic theology, the air that courses through the systems' (206). What has happened, as 'theology at prayer was superseded by theology at the desk', is that 'scientific' theology 'lost the accent and tone with which one should speak of what is holy', while 'affective' theology 'degenerated into unctuous, platitudinous piety' (208). Many theologians would no doubt endorse this view that Christian theology, however rigorously academic and professional, needs to be practised in the context of Christian life and worship.

There is no call for a revival of patristic theology at the expense of medieval scholasticism, Balthasar adds. In any case, 'it is of the very essence of tradition, and so of theology, that its progress depends on a deeper, bolder exploration of the sources'. In this ongoing return to the tradition, no one has more to offer than Thomas Aquinas – 'what a variety of approaches and aspects he suggests, how numerous the hints and promptings scattered at random through his works, compared with the dry bones of a modern textbook' (208). In other words, Aquinas's own work is incomparably more open-ended and patient of innovatory interpretations and developments than the closed systems of theology *ad mentem sancti Thomæ* suggest.

The Marian Principle

The world's response to God in Jesus Christ takes the feminine form of Mary-Church; a culture, which would be Christian and fully human, would be 'Marian', primarily 'feminine'. According to the medieval theme of the soul as *sponsa Christi*, Christ's spouse, we are all feminine-receptive-virginal.

The Marian principle is decisive in the celebration of the eucharist. The philosophical practice of contemplation comes to a climax in the Holy Mass: 'the bride is sacrificed together with the Bridegroom; she is placed together with him under the one knife of the Father on Moriah; the Mother of the Lord shares in the state of being abandoned . . . with the Son who is abandoned by God on the Cross.'[47]

Among the many patristic and medieval texts Balthasar quotes he likes this from Mechthild von Hackeborn (1241–99): as the time of Holy Communion approaches, in her vision, Mechthild sees

> a table was set down and the Lord sat at it and his Mother sat down beside him. The whole community approached the table, and every one knelt down and, from under the arm of the Blessed Virgin, received the Body of the Lord from the Lord's hand. The Blessed Virgin held out a golden chalice containing the stream of blood that came from the Lord's side, and all drank from it that wondrous drink which flowed from the Lord's side.[48]

From the creation of the 'human' as male and female and thus as God's image and likeness (Gen. 1: 27) to the 'great mystery' of Christ and Church imaged in marriage (Eph. 5: 22–33), the form of the Christian doctrine of creation and of the history of salvation is radically 'nuptial'. The Song of Songs turns out to be the key text, as it were the lens for reading Scripture as a whole.

Against Feminism

According to Balthasar, women who want to play the male role in the Church want something less than they already are.[49] The worldwide offensive of feminism – 'world wide'? – battles for the equality of women with men but does so in a predominantly male-oriented technological civilization. It aspires to an unnatural masculinization of woman. This is a great tragedy: rationalism has taken over, natural things and conditions are seen as raw material for manufacturables (this is pure Heidegger). We have lost the

[47] *Spouse of the Word*: 369.
[48] *Theo-Drama: Theological Dramatic Theory* V: *The Last Act* (San Francisco: Ignatius Press): 468.
[49] 'Women Priests?' in *New Elucidations* (San Francisco: Ignatius Press 1986): 187–98. Subsequent page references for quotations are given in the text.

attitude in which we contemplated nature while being receptive to its essence – the contemplative-receptive gaze has turned into a merely calculating stare. The feminine element that makes a person secure in nature and in being (sic!) is abandoned in favour of a preponderance of the masculine element, which 'pushes forward into things in order to change them by implanting and imposing something of its own' (189). We should not press the analogy of sexual intercourse, of male penetration, too far, Balthasar advises. Moreover, the contemplative attitude of 'letting oneself be gifted and fructified by nature and being' is not, whatever one might be tempted to think, 'feminine in the sense of mere receptivity'. (189). Rather, there is a way of thinking 'which, like the fructified womb, is able to bear patiently the seeds conceived and give birth to them in images, myths and concepts'. In a contemplative person, the active element of the feminine principle is wedded to the passive element of the masculine – passive, since it needs the self-bestowing womb in order to be able to give itself freely and fully.

Where positivistic technocratic thinking dominates, the female element vanishes from the attitude of the man, leaving him with no other hope than to appeal to the woman, 'who perceives and understands her role as counterpoise to and spearhead against man's increasingly history-less world' (191).

In fact, the Catholic Church is perhaps the world's last stand in valuing the difference between women and men. In the eucharist above all, the extreme oppositeness and complementarity of their functions guarantees the fruitfulness of human nature. It is to men that the masculine tasks of initiation and leadership are given – always within the all-embracing Marian Church. These men – bishops and priests – represent Christ: in the surrender of his entire substance on the Cross he gathers the people of God to himself eucharistically, while the men who represent him have a specifically masculine function, which is 'the transmission of a vital force that originates outside itself and leads beyond itself'. The fruitfulness of the woman always depends on a prior fructification by the man. Christ as man brings about the fruitfulness of his bride the Church, above all in the celebration of the eucharist, the marriage feast; thus it takes men to represent him, in an analogous and of course much diminished manner.

Ultimately, fundamentally, Balthasar insists, the Church is feminine: receptive, nurturing; giving birth to what she receives from Christ. The Church continues, more intensely, the relationship of the people of ancient Israel with the Lord God. From the early Fathers of the Church into the Middle Ages the Church is imaged as a woman: 'mother Church', 'the bride of Christ'. This image prevailed despite the fact that the hierarchy was composed solely of men. 'These men are the agents of Christ the Bridegroom within the Church's all-embracing femininity' (211).

Balthasar sweeps aside the erroneous idea of woman as a *mas occasionatum*, a defective man; as well as the related biology according to which, in pro-creation, the man alone plays an active role while the woman remains passive and receptive. Considering the months of pregnancy, birth, nurturing, and so on, it would be better to say that the woman's role is significantly more active than that of the man. Citing recent biologists, Balthasar observes that we might better say that the embryonic structure of all living creatures, including humans, is basically feminine. This resonates with the ancient view that nature is feminine. We might reverse the patristic and medieval view and say that men are defective women. All created being, we might say, is feminine in relation to the creator God. The ultimate relationship of creature to Creator is embodied in the relationship of the Church to her Lord.

Paul VI's Encyclical

Balthasar defends Pope Paul VI's condemnation of artificial contraception but contends that only Catholic Christians can understand the challenge thrown out by the encyclical, and among them perhaps only a tiny minority of married couples who practise a certain asceticism.[50]

At one stage, however, Balthasar, while recognizing that with the encyclical Paul VI had opted for 'the ideal of the small, loving devoted community', against the majority of his advisors, stated that he 'was burdening and biding the consciences of married Catholics in an issue that had serious consequences' – here Balthasar aligns himself explicitly with Hans Küng. He grants that we can all see 'the devastation created in the sexual area by the separation of pleasure from the risk of self-giving' (pregnancy, that is to say). Yet, he suggests, the form of the encyclical 'needs to be criticized' – it would have been better, he clearly thinks, 'to point to the ideal as a "normative goal" to satisfy the objective, eschatological emphasis of the Christian concept of selfless and self-renouncing love, the personal ideal of the committed, while at the same time both stimulating and reassuring those who were either unable or too perplexed to follow this course'.[51]

The relationship between Christ and the Church is repeated, analogously, and thus with all due qualifications, in the relationship between husband

---

[50] 'A Word on *Humanæ Vitæ*', originally a lecture at a symposium in San Francisco, 1978; in *New Elucidations*: 204–28.
[51] *The Office of Peter and the Structure of the Church* (San Francisco: Ignatius Press 1986; German original 1974): 330.

and wife in marriage (Eph. 5:25). There are, of course, immense differences. 'Christ does something that a husband can in no way do: Christ brings forth the Church from himself as his own fullness, as his body, and, finally, as his Bride'.[52] Husbands do not bring forth their wives; they encounter them as separate persons, with their own freedom and their own act of surrender.

Nevertheless, in sexual intercourse, it is the man who initiates, while the woman, active in her own way, is essentially passive. 'We could almost say (very nicely) that, through the man, the woman is somehow awakened to herself, to the fullness of her feminine self-awareness' (216).

'Such an order of things holds true even if we may smile at the incidental, marginal and transitory character of the male's function in procreation, a function that certainly cannot be compared with Christ's extraordinary act of self-surrender' (216). 'The begetting power of Jesus Christ, which is what creates the Church, is his eucharist'. . . . Christ neither 'holds [anything] back for himself', nor 'places any reservations on his own self-surrender' – he has 'no fear of losing' himself 'through the perfect outpouring and lavishing of himself' – 'Unlike the man in the act of intercourse, Christ does not give away just a little of his substance' (217).

Sexual orgasm, a climax in the coming together of man and woman, ecstatically for a moment, seems to be the analogy here. No doubt the analogy of sexual intercourse should not be pressed too far, as Balthasar says. One might think, however, that denying any comparison between Christ's act of self-surrender in the eucharistic sacrifice and a husband's self surrender in the act of sexual intercourse, 'incidental, marginal and transitory' as it is, is already going quite far.

Supersexuality in the Trinity

The last volume of *Theodramatik*, entitled 'The Last Act', *Das Endspiel*, which appeared in 1983, draws heavily on Scripture, interweaving hundreds of quotations from Adrienne von Speyr, such that, when the prefatory note refers to 'our theology', Balthasar means exactly that: 'I quote her to show the fundamental consonance between her views and mine on many of the eschatological topics discussed here'.[53]

The purpose of the prefatory note is to twit Karl Rahner for dubbing Balthasar's theology 'gnostic' and 'neo-Chalcedonian'. These insults mean

---

[52] 'A Word on *Humanæ Vitæ*': 215; subsequent page references for quotations are given in the text.
[53] *Theo-Drama* V: 13. Subsequent page references for quotations are given in the text.

that, for Rahner, Balthasar's speculations about the interior life of the triune God verge on denying the traditional doctrine of God's immutability; and, second, his endorsement of the thesis 'One of the Trinity has suffered in the flesh', defended in the early sixth century by monks in Constantinople, borders on the heresy of 'theopaschism' (holding that 'God suffered'). Balthasar allows that he and Adrienne go as far as revelation permits – 'some may feel we have gone one step too far'; but they are only following Thomas Aquinas: 'we have tried to erect theology on the articles of faith (and not vice versa): on the Trinity, the Incarnation of the Son, his Cross and Resurrection on our behalf, and his sending of the Spirit to us in the apostolic church and in the *communio sanctorum*' (14).[54]

The first step is to insist that the God revealed in Jesus Christ 'exists in himself as an eternal essence (or Being), which is equally eternal (that is, not temporal) "happening"' (67). While the distinction in seminary courses *de Deo uno* and *de Deo trino* is of some use in apologetics, Balthasar notes, to the extent that one may have to address people who believe in God and need to be confirmed in this faith before they are introduced to the doctrine of the Trinity, this division has no New Testament basis. For Balthasar, it is no way to conduct the theology of God among Christians: 'Jesus does not speak about God in general but shows us the Father and gives us the Holy Spirit' (67). The only picture of the divine 'essence' for us who are Christians is always already of 'the triune process'. The two apparently contradictory concepts – 'absolute being' and 'happening' – we have to see as a unity.

Here, Balthasar recalls patristic texts. Gregory of Nyssa, for example, writes of God, paradoxically, as 'rest that is eternally in motion and constant motion that is at rest'. He interweaves such texts with formulations by recent theologians. Klaus Hemmerle, for example, thinks of God as 'happening, action, consummation'. Balthasar includes paradoxes by Adrienne von Speyr: since love as we know it is always enlivened by an element of surprise, something analogous must be predicated of God. God as Trinity is 'a communion of surprise': 'from the outset [the Son] surpasses the Father's wildest expectations'; 'God himself wishes to be surprised by God, by a fulfilment that overflows expectation'; and so on.[55]

This insistence on the 'sublime transactions' (80) within the triune Godhead certainly dislodges the 'static' God of so-called 'classical theism'.

---

[54] The implication is, of course, that Rahner, with his interest in creating 'short formulas of faith', in effect rewrites the Creed on the basis of his theology; Balthasar is also claiming Thomas Aquinas as precursor and patron, albeit an evidently much richer Thomism than the seminary textbooks or the emphasis on Aquinas as philosopher provided.

[55] *Credo: Meditations on the Apostles' Creed* (Edinburgh: T&T Clark 1990): 78.

For Balthasar, there is no giving which is not also receiving and vice versa, as also there is no initiative which is not also consent. He directs us to the analogy of the duality of the sexes:

> In trinitarian terms, of course, the Father who begets him who is without origin, appears primarily as (super-) masculine; the Son, in consenting, appears initially as (super-) feminine, but in the act (together with the Father) of breathing forth the Spirit, he is (super-) masculine. As for the Spirit, he is (super-) feminine. There is even something (super-) feminine about the Father too, since, as we have shown, in the action of begetting and breathing forth he allows himself to be determined by the Persons who thus proceed from him; however, this does not affect his primacy in the order of the Trinity. (91)

'The very fact of the Trinity', Balthasar hastens to say, 'forbids us to project any secular sexuality into the Godhead (as happens in many religions and in the gnostic *syzygia*)' – which no doubt is meant to head off Rahner's kind of worries.[56] On the face of it, however, the attribution, however analogically, of super-masculine and super-feminine postures to the intra-Trinitarian Persons seems more confusing than enlightening. It even seems a little forced. It does not help that the feminine is construed as essentially passive, being-done-to rather than doing, receiving rather than giving, being determined by another; while the masculine is essentially active, initiating, doing and donating – all very much on analogy with male/female sexual coupling, as traditionally conceived.

Balthasar warns us against the error of projecting sexual difference on God and especially against seeing in the Holy Spirit the feminine, indeed the 'womb' in which generation occurs. 'If one wishes to go further', however,

> then the feminine would best be sought in the Son, who, in dying, allows the Church to emerge from himself, and who, in the whole of his earthly existence, allowed himself to be led and 'fertilised' by the Father; but in such a way that, at the same time, as a man, he represents the originally generative force of God in the world. And since the Son proceeds from the Father, the different sexes are, in the end, present in the latter [the Father] in a 'preternatural' way; it was for this reason that, in the Old Covenant, his love could also be described in terms of feminine qualities.

---

[56] Syzygy: 'pair' – in ancient Gnostic parlance the cosmos was brought about through the interaction of such opposites as male and female.

Balthasar then cites Lateran IV – even in this respect God is 'more dissimilar than similar' – yes indeed![57]

The Father, Balthasar has said earlier, 'is no statically self-contained and comprehensible reality, but one that exists solely in dispensing itself' 'a flowing wellspring with no holding-trough beneath it, an act of procreation with no seminal vesicle, with no organism at all to perform the act'.[58]

Conclusion

From the *Phenomenology of Truth* in 1947 to the 15 volumes of the trilogy *Herrlichkeit, Theodramatik,* and *Theologik,* and the scores of ancillary writings, Hans Urs von Balthasar created an entirely different version of Catholic theology from anything ever imagined by regular disciples of Thomas Aquinas. With sources as diverse as Karl Barth, Adrienne Kaegi-von Speyr, Greek fathers such as Origen and Maximus the Confessor, and Gustav Siewerth's Heideggerianized Aquinas, Balthasar's work is clearly unique, idiosyncratic and inimitable. He is by far the most discussed Catholic theologian at present, as the ever-expanding secondary literature shows, overwhelmingly positive in tenor, which is perhaps surprising – unless critics do not know where to start.

[57] *Credo*: 78–9.
[58] Ibid: 30.

Chapter Nine

HANS KÜNG

Books by popes are best sellers. Otherwise, by far the most widely read twentieth-century Catholic theologian is Hans Küng. His attacks on the doctrine of papal supremacy, and eventually on the authoritarian style of Pope John Paul II, led to the withdrawal of his right to teach as a Catholic theologian by the local bishop in 1979, which did not hurt sales. Ironically, with the exception of Chenu (one of his heroes), Küng is the only one of the theologians we are considering in this book who completed the seven-year-long course in neoscholastic philosophy and theology at a Roman university.

Küng revels in Swiss intransigence. Born on 19 March 1928 in Switzerland, by the Sempacher See, where the Habsburgs were defeated in 1386, he had a traditional Catholic upbringing, in a happy family.[1] He felt called to the diocesan priesthood while still at school. He studied in Rome at the Jesuit-staffed Gregorian University from 1948 to 1955, dashingly dressed in the red soutane favoured at the German College. Far from feeling oppressed in the intellectual climate of the last decade of Pius XII's pontificate, he seems to have enjoyed himself. In 1950 Küng was 'enthusiastically present' at the solemn proclamation of the dogma of the Assumption of the Virgin Mary. The encyclical *Humani Generis*, issued in 1950, reaffirming Scholastic philosophy against modern trends, did not intimidate him, as it did so many others. Küng celebrated Mass for the first time in the crypt of St Peter's, the day the inoperable brain tumour, which was to kill his only brother, made its presence felt.

---

[1] See the first volume of autobiography: Hans Küng, *My Struggle for Freedom: Memoirs* (London: Continuum 2003); Hermann Häring, *Hans Küng: Breaking Through* (London: SCM Press 1998), and Werner G. Jeanrond, in *The Modern Theologians: An Introduction to Christian Theology in the Twentieth Century*, edited by David F. Ford, second edition (Oxford: Blackwell 1997): 162–78.

Morning lectures, of course in Latin, were followed in the afternoons, back at the Germanicum, by going over the material with a young Jesuit ('no sense of humour'), whose neoscholastic Thomism Küng brushed off easily.[2] He writes appreciatively of some of his teachers, Paolo Dezza among others. He found Bernard Lonergan's lectures on Christology tedious. He took a course on Hegel. He wrote his licentiate dissertation on Sartre (there were always Jesuit professors who secured students permission to study 'prohibited books'). In sum, Küng had the full neoscholastic course in its heyday, in Rome, during the apotheosis of Pius XII and under the shadow of the encyclical *Humani Generis*.

He remained unscathed. Choosing to work for his doctorate on the theology of Karl Barth, his eminent compatriot, Küng moved to Paris, to the Institut Catholique, where Louis Bouyer supervised his thesis. The resulting book came out in 1957, endorsed by Barth himself and published by Hans Urs von Balthasar. As transpired later, the Vatican opened a file on the young theologian, not surprisingly, since nothing enraged the ecclesiastical watchdogs in the 1950s more than the idea that Catholics might learn from Protestants.

In 1960, aged 31, Küng was offered the chair in fundamental theology in the Catholic faculty at Tübingen.[3] He never taught anywhere else. Küng took an active part as an officially appointed *peritus* in the work of the Vatican Council (1962–5). The book that he wrote as soon as he knew of the forthcoming Council inspired many of those who hoped that reform would facilitate reunion.[4]

Two major works of ecclesiology appeared, in 1962 and 1967, but also, in 1970, a study of Hegel's Christology. However, Küng's career as an academic heavyweight was diverted, after Vatican II, into ecclesiastical politics. He protested against Pope Paul VI's encyclicals on celibacy of the clergy (1967) and contraception (*Humanæ Vitæ*, 1968). Then, in 1970, with *Unfehlbar?*, a radical critique of papal claims, he set off a furious controversy, which led in 1979, after Karol Wojtyla became pope, to Küng's 'mandate' – *missio canonica* – to teach as a Catholic theologian being withdrawn.[5] His status as a priest

---

[2]   Peter Gumpel SJ, currently judge in the cause of the canonization of Pope Pius XII, see Peter Gumpel, 'Pius XII as He Really Was', *The Tablet*, Saturday, 13 February 1999.

[3]   This chair had been turned down by Bernhard Welte (the philosopher/priest who was to give the address at Heidegger's funeral in 1976), but was also refused by Hans Urs von Balthasar, knowing that his appointment would be blocked.

[4]   *Konzil und Wiedervereinigung* (1960) translated as *The Council and Reunion* (London and New York: Sheed and Ward 1961).

[5]   On his first anniversary as pope, Karol Wojtyla was offered some fraternal criticism by Hans Küng, in *The New York Times*, 19 October 1979, questioning whether 'the darling of the masses

was never in question. The practical effect was that he could no longer examine seminarians: attendance at his lectures increased. From then until he retired in 1996 he held a chair for ecumenical theology, independent of the Catholic faculty.

Hans Küng has published three substantial, widely read works of Christian apologetics: *On Being a Christian, Does God Exist?*, and *Eternal Life?* He has made equally substantial contributions to interfaith studies: *Christianity and the World Religions: Paths of Dialogue with Islam, Hinduism and Buddhism* (1984), *Theology for the Third Millennium: An Ecumenical View* (1987) and *Christianity and Chinese Religions* (1988). More recently, he has tackled moral questions raised by globalization: *Global Responsibility: In Search of a New World Ethic* (1990).

The Barth Book

In the 1950s the justification of the unrighteous by faith alone was the doctrine assumed to lie at the heart of the split between the churches of the Reformation and the Roman Catholic Church: the doctrine over which no agreement would ever be possible.[6] Sinners do not find their way into God's grace and favour on the basis of their own efforts, we do not earn salvation by our works – as Catholics were assumed by Protestants to believe (not entirely without reason). It looked to Catholics, on the other hand, that the emphasis that Reformed Christians placed on the divine act of justifying the sinner, as it were *ex nihilo*, ignored the process of the individual's sanctification. For Catholics, justification could not be other than a transformation, involving responsive co-operation on the sinner's part. The righteousness of Christ, to quote the jargon, is not only imputed to the sinner, as Protestants were held to believe; it is imparted, in a process of divinization.

While acknowledging Hans Urs von Balthasar's 'masterful book' on Barth, Küng confronts the Swiss Calvinist's doctrine head on, in *Justification*,[7] rather

---

and the superstar of the media' was 'truly free from the personality cult of former Popes, for example Pius XII', questioning whether he was 'sufficiently familiar with recent developments in theology', rebuking him for approving of 'the inquisitorial proceedings against other streams in contemporary Catholic theology, and this in spite of his call for human rights outside the church': 'Many Catholics and non-Catholics seriously doubt whether this Pope from a country with a totalitarian regime, with a closed, authoritarian church (understandable for domestic reasons), will in all instances be a guarantor of freedom and openness in our church'.

[6]   See A.E. McGrath, *Iustitia Dei: A History of the Christian Doctrine of Justification* (Cambridge: Cambridge University Press 1986).

[7]   *Rechtfertigung: Die Lehre Karl Barths und eine katholische Besinnung* (1957) translated as *Justification: The Doctrine of Karl Barth and a Catholic Reflection* (London: Burns and Oates 1964).

than reading Barth in the light of current debate in Catholic theology, as Balthasar does. He quotes Barth's damning characterization of Catholicism as 'a system embracing God and the creature', 'the attempt to see and correlate them on the same level', which is nothing but

> the kind of act in which the creature arrogates to itself the ability to control itself and therefore God . . . But this act precisely is the ground, the basic outlook of the entire Roman Catholic system down to its every detail. This act is the basic act of its doctrine of grace, of the Sacraments, of the Church, of Scripture and tradition, of the Roman primacy and the infallibility of the Pope, and above all of its Marian doctrine.[8]

According to Küng, this harsh attack (in 1940) gave way to a more sympathetic account, after Balthasar's book. In the same chapter of *Church Dogmatics*, in fact, Barth acknowledges an interpretation of the *analogia entis* he could accept, by Gottlieb Söhngen, whom (however) he discounts as unrepresentative of Catholic teaching. After Balthasar's book, which amply confirmed Söhngen's approach, we have no more polemic about the Catholic *analogia entis*.

In the wake of Balthasar, Küng explores how far Barth's doctrine of justification may be compatible with 'a' Catholic doctrine – explicitly not offering 'the' Catholic interpretation.[9] The book was well received. Karl Rahner, reviewing it, concludes that on all essential points Küng expounds a theology of justification, which is in accordance with Catholic doctrine. Thus, if Barth was happy with Küng's exposition of his doctrine, as he declared in his prefatory letter ('your readers may rest assured – until such time as they themselves might get to my books – that you have me say what I actually do say and that I mean it in the way you have me say it'), then, on this issue at least, a breakthrough in reconciling Catholic and Protestant doctrine had been achieved. Barth was, of course, only one theologian (and anyway not a Lutheran); Küng's was only one Catholic interpretation of the doctrine – yet, considering how divisive the doctrine of justification was since the Reformation, one could be cautiously optimistic about eventual reconciliation.

Küng's account of the Catholic doctrine of justification was found satisfactory – 'orthodox' – by an array of Catholic theologians, listed by Rahner.

---

[8]   *Church Dogmatics* (Edinburgh: T&T Clark) II/1, 582–3.
[9]   Of course Barth is not the only or the most characteristic Protestant theologian: for the probably far more influential Dutch-American Presbyterian Cornelius Van Til (1895–1957), 'Barthianism' is 'the higher humanism', barely Christian, precisely because of its affinities with Balthasar and Küng, see *Christianity and Barthianism* (Phillipsburg, NJ: Presbyterian and Reformed Publishing Co. 1962).

His exposition, as Rahner notes, was guided by two principles: to show that the truths that Barth finds absent in Catholicism are actually there; and to make truths that are unpleasant to Protestants as intelligible as he can, without diluting or avoiding them. There is no 'false eirenicism' here.[10] 'One can be a Catholic and hold this doctrine of justification, which Barth has declared to be the same as his own' (198).

Rahner's discussion is the best starting point to assess Küng's book. His criticisms, as he insists, do not in any way amount to a withdrawal of his acceptance of the main argument. Indeed, his discussion culminates in a defence of Küng against Heinrich Stirnimann, a Swiss Dominican, who, while insisting that his criticisms were *intra muros*, nevertheless, as a good Thomist, attacks one of Küng's key moves as little better than 'Gnosticism' (211). What this means, according to Stirnimann, is that, for Küng, the order of creation, of the world and of mankind, as actually existing, is founded, even as a natural order, on the Word yet to become incarnate and now incarnate – thus the world, even in its natural state, is in fact and everywhere and always a 'Christian thing' (210). It is possible to prescind from this, to entertain the thought experiment of a world without Christ. Yet, since in fact all sin, for example, is sin against Christ, what remains of the natural good of the fallen creature is always already a grace of Christ. This goes a long way, Rahner observes, towards Barth's doctrine of the priority of the covenant to creation, and of Christology to anthropology. The creation of 'nature' takes place in the grace of the Incarnation, so to speak.

Rahner finds this thesis very congenial. Nevertheless he worries at some length that it fails to do justice to the Catholic distinction between nature and grace. He allows that Küng wants to show that the Catholic doctrine of the persistence of the human creature's nature (including power of choice) after the Fall does not trade on quasi-Pelagian assumptions about the crea-ture's autonomy, as Barth kept lamenting. Against this charge, Rahner thinks, there may be some other way of securing the Catholic position. The outcome, anyway, of Küng's book, so Rahner concludes, is that, even when one sticks to the neoscholastic distinction between nature and strictly super-natural grace in humankind as we actually are, as Stirnimann does, it remains possible to regard the existence and activity of this fallen, though of course redeemable, nature as already graced, in the actual historical order of things. It was always God's absolute and irrevocable will that the Word should become flesh as a member of the one, though fallen, humanity. 'This

[10] 'Questions of Controversial Theology on Justification', in *Theological Investigations*, vol. IV (London: Darton, Longman and Todd 1966): 189–218 at page 191. Subsequent page refer-ences for quotations are given in the text.

"grace" is conceivable', so Rahner concludes (218), 'as the deficient mode of the grace which must presuppose this "grace" as the condition of having anybody at all who can be endowed with grace'. While the discussion needs much more unpacking; the upshot, anyway, so Rahner maintains, is that Küng's Catholic doctrine of justification returns us to *la nouvelle théologie*: an unsurprising conclusion.

Leaving this rather technical discussion hanging, we may note that, according to Barth, much else remains to be done, 'to make somewhat plausible to us matters like transubstantiation, the sacrifice of the Mass, Mary, and the infallible papacy, and the other things with which we are confronted – pardon me, I could not resist picking up Denzinger again – in the Tridentine profession of faith'.

Correspondingly, Küng remains critical of Barth's 'dangerous inclinations',[11] apart from his lamentable anti-Catholic polemics, such as pushing the theology of election towards *apokatastasis*, that is, towards the salvation of all; but, above all, devaluing creaturely independence in the theology of creation; neglecting creaturely co-operation in the event of redemption – all put down to 'his idealistic faith and . . . his anti-humanistic, dialectical existentialism' (266). Here Küng goes in for typical Catholic polemic against Barth in those days.

Much of this need not be more significant than differences of opinion within Catholicism, Küng allows, as for example between the Greek patristic and medieval Scholastic theologies of the Trinity and of grace. Yet Barth's emphasis on the gracious sovereignty of God, which of course Catholics endorse, does not seem to them, as it obviously does to him, to entail 'a negative and subversive calling into question of the primacy of Peter and his successors, of the soteriological status of Mary, of the normative character of tradition, of the effective character of the sacraments and the "natural" knowledge of God' (266).

However, in 1957, Catholics had much to learn from the first two volumes of Barth's *Church Dogmatics* (1932 and 1939), which he devotes to the theology of the Word of God. Catholic textbooks offered no serious doctrine of the Word of God, saying little about what the Bible says about the subject, let alone what is to be found in patristic and Scholastic theologies. Moreover, neoscholastic treatises *de revelatione* were tame and quite uninspiring compared with Barth's exposition of the concept of divine revelation. Finally, Barth's insistence everywhere on the primacy of Scripture should challenge Catholics to reconsider the relationship of Bible to Church.

---

[11] Küng, *Justification*: 265. Subsequent page references for quotations are given in the text.

Reform for Reunion

In the 1950s, few remembered that the First Vatican Council was only suspended, and that the bishops who had voted in favour of the decree on the
primacy of the pope expected to return to Rome in September 1870
to consider the draft texts on the role of the episcopacy, among other things.
In any case, the doctrine of papal jurisdiction, many believed, in the ultramontanist climate of the 1950s, rendered further councils of the Church
unnecessary. Very few knew that Pius XII, who seemed happy to regard
himself as the sole exponent of Catholic theology, considered reconvening
the Council but never felt the moment opportune.[12] Everyone was amazed,
and many were dismayed, when the elderly, 'transitional' Pope John XXIII
announced his decision, on 25 January 1959, to hold a Council, foreseeing
an agenda which would renew the life of the Church, bringing its teaching,
discipline and organization up to date (*aggiornamento*) in order explicitly to
facilitate the reunion of all Christians.

Early in 1960, Küng brought out *Konzil und Wiedervereinigung*, the third
edition of which was translated as *The Council and Reunion* (1961). The
preface by Franz König, then cardinal archbishop of Vienna reads as follows:

> It is a happy omen to find a theologian responding to the stimulus provided
> by the Holy Father when he announced the holding of an Ecumenical
> Council; to see, with his help, in all loyalty to the Church, the perspectives
> that are opening before us concerning the divisions in Christendom and the
> hopes offered by the coming Council. I hope that this book, and the chal-
> lenge which it presents, will be received with understanding, and spread far
> and wide.[13]

Like it or not, *The Council and Reunion* is the key for beginning to understand what happened at Vatican II. As Küng notes, the book largely
recapitulates Yves Congar's *Vraie et fausse réforme* (1950) – popularizing it,
we may say.[14] Following Congar, Küng retrieves the word 'reform' from the
Reformation. In the liturgy and in patristic and Scholastic theology, as he

---

[12] Just as well: imagine what the result would have been in the 1950s!
[13] Hans Küng, *The Council and Reunion* (London: Sheed and Ward 1961).
[14] For what Congar thought about Küng see *Mon Journal du Concile* I (Paris: Cerf 2002): 101:
the draft texts, representing the Roman professors' theology, needed to be rejected but he
warns Küng against the 'danger' of what might look like 'a para-council of theologians', September 1962; I, 465–7: Küng is 'revolutionary', 'impatient', Congar wonders if he himself has
been 'too timid', but 'suspected, pursued, sanctioned, limited, crushed' since 1938, he is now
aware of 'unavoidable delays and the power of active patience'.

shows, it has always been taken for granted that the Church is called to permanent 'reformation'. The Fourth Council of the Lateran, in 1215, for example, was summoned, 'for the reformation of the universal Church, *propter reformationem universalis ecclesiæ*'.

Renewal in the Church will always be a tricky course, steering between accommodationist worldliness and introverted unworldliness – 'really serious dangers'. The basic requirements for the right kind of reform, so Küng says, are first *suffering* – out of love of the Church; second, *prayer*; third, *criticism*, as practised by Bernard of Clairvaux – criticism based on *love*, though, he concludes, since 'there is always more occasion for thankfulness in the Catholic Church than for blame'.

Surveying episodes in the history of reform, Küng asks why the sixteenth-century 'reform' – the Reformation – was rejected by the greater part of the Catholic Church. While there were misunderstandings of both sides, the pope had no alternative to rejecting Luther, so Küng argues. Moreover, in the climate of the time, the strengthening of papal authority in the Counter-Reformation was inevitable.

The interruption of the Vatican Council in 1870 was disastrous, Küng says. Nevertheless, a process of renewal was initiated by Pope Leo XIII (something of a hero in Küng's book), which means that, in 1960, so Küng thinks, surveying the scene, there evidently was a reformed and renewed Catholic Church. He details some of the achievements. Catholic historians had at last stopped denigrating Luther. Catholics had returned to reading Scripture. Liturgical renewal dated as far back as Pope Pius X. The recovery of the Catholic doctrine of universal priesthood allowed many new lay ministries and activities to flourish. With inculturation of Catholicism in non-European societies, the disengagement of the papacy from politics, reform of the Curia and of canon law, a new tolerance, respect for conscience, the ordination of married men, and the interiorization of popular devotion – all in all, the pre-Vatican II Church, according to Küng, was in a good state.

In the English-speaking world, where the book was widely read, this upbeat account seemed more visionary than descriptive. Yet, even there, the state of things was not as dismal as some now suppose – though never as wonderful as others like to think. On the other hand, it seems disingenuous to speak of the papacy as disengaged from politics (Pius XII, lately deceased, and the Cold War!), or of the incipient internationalization of the Curia as 'reform'. The married priests, all former Protestant pastors, could have been counted on the fingers of Pius XII's hands.

Anyway, according to Küng, the Catholic Church was in good enough shape to engage in reconciliation with the churches of Eastern Orthodoxy

and the churches of the Reformation. In ecumenical discussions, conver-
gence – not complete identity – in matters of doctrine, was enough to aspire
to. Assuming fundamental unity as regards the doctrine of the Trinity,
Christology and creation, Küng points to ongoing ecumenical discussion of
the doctrine of sin and grace, the relation of Scripture and Tradition, and
the sacraments. Much remained to be discussed, on these and other contentious topics. While he insists that there must be no compromising of the
truth, he is very optimistic when he considers the prospect of Christian
reunion.

Nevertheless, there are two major stumbling blocks. As regards Catholic
doctrine about the Mother of God, so Küng says, there are deplorable
excesses: a certain 'Marian maximalism'. Yet, among Protestants, he sees a
'sin of omission'. Is the lack of Marian piety in Protestantism, he asks, merely
anti-Catholicism?

Second, there is the question of papal authority. Luther's existential opposition to the papacy made it impossible for him and his followers to see the
nature of the Petrine ministry. Today, even friendly Protestants fear papal
authority as they see it exercised. For that matter, many Catholics fear, if
they criticize anything, having their loyalty impugned and their orthodoxy
suspected. To see the true nature of the Petrine ministry is a matter of faith –
but do the successors of Peter always behave in ways that would make their
claim to be 'vicars of Christ' easily believable?

The book concludes with the Declaration issued by the German bishops
in 1875, contradicting Prince Otto von Bismarck's claim, on behalf of the
newly founded German Empire, that the doctrine of papal jurisdiction rendered bishops mere vicars of the pope. This text was largely unknown to
most Catholics in 1960. As Küng was implying by reprinting it, the ultramontanist conception of papal autocracy so widely taken for granted by
Catholics and others was not what was defined in 1870. Finally, even more
suggestively, Küng lists the 20 General or Oecumenical Councils recognized
by the Church, including the Council of Constance (1414–18).

In retrospect, Küng was far too optimistic about the state of the Catholic
Church on the eve of the Council. As regards the two stumbling blocks, the
partisans of the two radically opposed Mariologies compromised, in the
end. The minority – a very large minority – accepted the incorporation of
the chapter on the Blessed Virgin with which the dogmatic constitution on
the Church, *Lumen Gentium*, concludes, rather than hold out for a separate
text devoted to Mary. At the final ballot on 18 November 1964, a ceremonial event, there were only 23 negative votes, yet at the last ballot which
might have affected the outcome, on 29 October 1964, a quarter of the
voters had reservations. Throughout Vatican II the presiding officers sought

to avoid or gloss over disedifying conflict among the bishops about the place of the Mother of God in Catholic doctrine and devotion. It took great skill to achieve the final result.

As regards the role of the papacy, there was never an atmosphere during the Council to allow anything like the radical reconsideration Küng envisaged. To recall the moderate interpretation of papal authority by the German bishops in 1875 was one thing. Retrieving the Council of Constance from oblivion was altogether more audacious. This was tantamount to raising the spectre of 'conciliarism'.

Conciliarism

The authoritative *Dictionnaire de Théologie Catholique* (1938) omits the Council of Constance altogether from the list of Oecumenical Councils, passing straight from the Council of Vienne (1311–12) to the Council of Florence (1439–45), skipping the years the latter sat at Basle (1431–9). Nowadays, however, standard Catholic lists count Constance (1414–18) as the sixteenth Oecumenical Council – though disputing its 'oecumenicity' before the election of Oddo Colonna as Pope Martin V in 1417.

This is not as arcane as it may seem. In its fifth session, on 6 April 1415, the Council of Constance passed a decree, declaring that 'this Council holds its power direct from Christ; everyone, no matter his rank or office, even if it be Papal, is bound to obey it in whatever pertains to faith, to the extirpation of the above-mentioned schism, as well as to the reform of the Church in its head and in its members'. In short, the decree 'Haec sancta' located supreme authority in the Catholic Church in the bishops-in-council – supreme over the successor of Peter as well. Yet, as the text shows, the question remained whether the supreme authority was recognized as residing in the bishops-in-council henceforth and for ever, or only during the crisis at the time.

The Western Church had been split since 1378. The Cardinals met at Pisa in 1409. They deposed the two rival Popes and elected a third, who died within a year. They met again and elected another, Baldassare Cossa, who took the name John XXIII.[15] Under pressure from King Sigismund,[16]

---

[15]   Cardinal Baldassare Cossa, a Neapolitan, once a pirate and a highly successful Curial official, was long listed as an antipope and definitively brushed out when Cardinal Angelo Roncalli took the name and style of John XXIII in 1958.
[16]   Sigismund (1368–1437) King of Hungary and eventually of Bohemia, and Holy Roman Emperor, sought to unite Christendom against the Turks.

he convoked the Council of Constance, presiding at the opening on 5 November 1414. By February 1415 he was ready to resign, if the other two claimants, deposed at Pisa but still reigning in their constituencies, would do so also. He bargained for a week but then fled, seemingly to disrupt the Council. Sigismund kept the bishops together, determined to bring about an end to the Schism. During the absence of John XXIII, whom everybody present regarded as the legitimate pope, the Council promulgated the decree 'Haec Sancta'. Brought back at the behest of the Council, John XXIII accepted the decision, before the Council deposed him on 29 May 1415.[17]

Gregory XII, formerly Cardinal Angelo Correro, elected by the Roman cardinals in 1406, deposed by them at the Council of Pisa in 1409, when they appealed over his head to Christ and a general council to bring about reunion in the Church, was still on the scene, now aged 90 and regarding himself as the legitimate successor of Peter. At Sigismund's instigation, the Council entered into negotiations with Gregory XII. He agreed to abdicate, to clear the way for the election of a pope acceptable all round, provided he was allowed to convoke the assembled prelates and dignitaries afresh as a general council. Regarding himself as pope since 1406, he could not recognize a council called by Cossa, whatever the Roman Cardinals believed. On 4 July 1415, therefore, he convoked the Council at Constance, abdicated, and was declared ineligible for election as pope. Finally, on 11 November 1417, more than two years later, and three months after Gregory XII's death, Oddo Colonna was elected, as Martin V, by a unique conclave of 22 cardinals and 30 delegates appointed by the Council. The Great Schism was over.

The tricky question that Küng sought to raise remains. While now including Constance on the list of Oecumenical Councils, which may pass decrees binding on the Church and irreformable, theologians differ as to whether its oecumenicity dates from its convocation by John XXIII (9 December 1413), from its (re)convocation by Gregory XII (4 July 1415), or only from the election of Martin V (11 November 1417). The nub of the matter is, obviously, that, if the assembly convoked by John XXIII was a truly Oecumenical Council, then the decree of 6 April 1415, placing the pope, like everyone else, under the authority of a general council, would

---

[17] When the deposed John XXIII paid homage to Martin V he was appointed Cardinal Bishop of Tusculum (Frascati); his magnificent tomb, in the baptistery at Florence, bears the papal insignia, describing him as 'formerly pope'; now usually listed among the antipopes, as by J.N.D. Kelly (1986), Cossa is sometimes described as a 'council pope', *Konzilspapst*, for example by Georg Schwaiger (*Lexikon für Katholische Theologie* 1960).

have the same weight as any other decision by an Oecumenical Council. In that case, however, the question would remain whether this was a decision of permanent validity for the internal structure of authority in the Church (as Küng was suggesting), or only a temporary expedient to deal with the unique situation of there being three rival popes and none universally recognized.

There is much more to 'conciliarism' than this; but an essential part of the case is that this decree, if passed by a truly Oecumenical Council, defined, as a truth of the Catholic faith, that a general council of all Christians has authority over even a legitimately elected and universally recognized pope.

Martin V seems to have taken the decree 'Haec Sancta' seriously: he closed the Council of Constance on 22 April 1418 but in a constitution of 22 May 1418, which was not published, he forbade any appeal from the pope to a future council.

In *The Council and Reunion* Küng refers in passing to the struggle of the papacy against 'the strong Conciliarist movement, which placed the Council above the Pope' (100); but does no more with the decree 'Haec Sancta' than note its existence. The theory that supreme authority in the Church lies, not with the papacy but with a general council, was generally regarded as obsolete and was refuted finally in 1870. One could not revive a theory that advocated the authority of the bishops gathered in general council over that of the Bishop of Rome. Nevertheless, by 1962, something needed to be worked out about the authority of the bishops as a whole, gathered in general council or in lesser assemblies, never of course acting independently of the successor of Peter, the Bishop of Rome, or exercising authority over him.[18] The question about the authority of the bishops, left undiscussed in 1870, was back on the agenda. As we saw (in chapter 3), the language of college and collegial action was introduced into the debate, in the revision of the draft *de ecclesia* undertaken at the behest of Cardinal Suenens, in October 1962, by Gérard Philips, priest of the Liège diocese and professor of dogmatic theology at the University of Louvain.[19] The word 'collegiality' itself does not appear in any Vatican II texts. In the constitution *Lumen Gentium*, however, on the internal structure of the Church, Christ is said to have established the Apostles as a 'college or permanent assembly', with

---

[18] The literature is immense; for a start see Francis Oakley, *The Conciliarist Tradition: Constitutionalism in the Catholic Church 1300–1870* (Oxford: Oxford University Press 2003).
[19] One of the most influential theologians at the Council, Gérard Philips (1899–1972) priest of the diocese of Liège, a co-opted Senator for the Flemish Christian Democratic Party), educated at the Gregoriana in Rome, professor of dogmatic theology at the Catholic University of Louvain.

Peter as head (§19). The bishops take the place of the Apostles (§20). The order into which bishops are ordained has a 'collegiate character and structure', which is said to be shown in many ways, including holding councils to make decisions on questions of major importance – though, in any 'collegiate action', the college or body of bishops 'has no authority other than the authority which it is acknowledged to have in union with the Roman pontiff' (§22). Nonetheless, bishops are 'vicars and legates of Christ'; they are not to be regarded as 'vicars of the Roman Pontiff' (§27), as they were quite commonly perceived to be.

Most of the bishops who voted in favour of this concept no doubt envisaged the development, in the not too distant future, of practices and even institutions to counterbalance the centralization of authority and power in the Vatican. Only 10 voted against the constitution as a whole, on 19 November 1963, the final ballot. On the other hand, in the last week of September, there were still 841 objections and proposals for amendment to be dealt with. Some doubted, on biblical grounds, if the Twelve formed a 'college'. Many questioned whether the bishops formed a 'college', if that meant they were equal, juridically. The same number queried whether bishops received their authority from the sacrament of their ordination or by delegation from the pope.

No special role in this debate can be ascribed to Küng. In his book *Structures of the Church*, published in 1962 (in English in 1964), however, he made a major contribution to the discussion, in the flood of scholarly books, on the interconnection of the concepts of papacy, episcopacy, conciliarity and collegiality. He spells out the significance of the relationship between pope and council if we agreed that the Council of Constance was truly oecumenical when it passed the decree asserting the superiority of council over pope.[20] It is not the case, Küng insists, in his later book, *The Church*, that the Catholic Church is 'saddled for better or worse with a pope, even if he acts in a way contrary to the Gospel'. Clearly, whatever Catholics sometimes assume, the Church is not 'relieved from the responsibility of acting itself'. Nevertheless, 'despite all the justified criticisms that are made of the present "system", one thing can be said: if the Catholic Church today, after all its difficulties and defeats, still exists as it does, relatively well thought-of, unified and strengthened in faith and order, then it has to thank not least the Petrine ministry'.[21] Nevertheless, the way in which this ministry is exercised needs reform. Küng

[20] *Structures of the Church* (London: Burns and Oates 1964).
[21] *The Church* (London: Burns and Oates 1967, original 1967), with imprimatur, dedicated to Archbishop Michael Ramsey, and with gratitude among others to his then colleague Professor Joseph Ratzinger: 454, 455.

concludes The *Church* with a page about Pope John XXIII (Angelo Roncalli), plainly his ideal of how the Petrine ministry should be exercised.

From Infallibility to Indefectibility?

For Küng, Pope Paul VI's 1968 encyclical *Humanæ Vitæ* on birth control is the 'Achilles' heel' of the doctrine of papal infallibility. The Church should leave infallibility 'to the one to whom it was originally reserved: to God'; and be content with a more modest 'indefectibility', a state of being generally held in the truth of the Gospel with no guarantee that any conciliar or papal statement, even if solemnly declared binding in faith, is necessarily free of error.[22]

In 1979 Hans Küng introduced a book by the Swiss Church historian August Bernhard Hasler, contending that the Council fathers in 1869/70 were so intimidated by Pope Pius IX that they were not free to take any decisions and that, consequently, the definition of papal infallibility was of questionable validity.[23] A doctrine with no basis in Scripture or Church tradition, so Hasler contends, was forced on the Catholic Church by an insane pope.

Many scholars would accept that Vatican I was manipulated by a highly autocratic pope, as indeed Newman among others noted at the time. However, that the decisions taken by the bishops were any more invalidated by the intimidatory behaviour of the pope than the decisions of the First Council of Nicaea (held in 325) were undermined by the determination of the Emperor Constantine to force a result, is hard to see. For that matter, without pressure from Sigismund, the Council of Constance would not have been held or kept going at all, nor would the Great Schism have ended when it did.

The decision, Küng contends, is not only invalid; the doctrine is simply erroneous. The susceptibility of the term 'infallibility' to misconstruction,

---

[22] *Infallible? An Enquiry* (London: Collins 1970; expanded edition London: SCM Press 1994, with a valuable summary of the debate as at 1979).

[23] Translated as *How the Pope Became Infallible: Pius IX and the Politics of Persuasion* (New York: Doubleday 1981). The scholarly work behind this book is Hasler's Munich doctorate thesis: *Pius IX (1846–1878), Päpstliche Unfehlbarkeit und I. Vatikanisches Konzil: Dogmatisierung und Durchsetzung einer Ideologie*, 2 vols, no. 12 in the series Päpste und Papstum (Stuttgart: Verlag Anton Hiersemann 1977). Hasler served for five years in the Secretariat for Christian Unity, concentrating on work with Lutheran, Reformed and Old Catholic churches, with access to the Vatican Archives, including diaries, letters and official documents relating to Vatican I which few others had studied; he died prematurely in 1980, deflecting attention from his work.

he notes, is widely acknowledged. Indeed, as was pointed out at Vatican I, the term German term *Unfehlbarkeit* could easily be confused with 'faultlessness' and thus with 'sinlessness'. Much effort at the Council went into distinguishing 'infallibility' from 'impeccability'.

The root of the problem, however, in Küng's view, lies in the philosophical assumptions made by neoscholastic theology about what propositions actually do. He does not mean that propositions are incapable of stating the truth, or that propositions are both true and false, or that they cannot be measured against the reality to which they claim to refer, or any other such wild idea.[24] Nevertheless, a certain degree of ambiguity is inherent in all propositions, so he claims, in the sense that they can always be understood differently by different people. With the best will in the world, all misunderstanding and misuse of a true proposition cannot be ruled out. To claim, then, that the Church or the pope can, even in special circumstances, deliver a proposition which would be 'infallible', 'irreformable', is a piece of nonsense. *No* proposition is ever free of ambiguity.

As a philosophical argument against the very idea of an infallible proposition, this requires clarification. Obviously, context is important: the same words in a quite different situation may well mean something quite different. Küng, however, makes no distinction between a proposition and a propositional formula, a truth and the sentence in which it is expressed.[25] Thus, quite a routine philosophical point about the nature of propositions seems to rule out Küng's claim that propositions are inherently ambiguous.

As Küng claimed, however, his questioning of the nature of infallible statements was 'not an attempt to bring unrest and uncertainty into the Church, but only to give expression to the unrest and uncertainty already to be found on all sides'.[26] Whether the ordinary Catholic is much bothered may be doubted. In practice, papal infallibility seems as empty to most Catholics as biblical inerrancy does now to most Protestants, rightly or wrongly.[27] Few expect any more *ex cathedra* definitions of truths that Catholics should believe, though anxiety continues in some quarters about the status of the condemnation by a series of popes of artificial contraception.

The ferocity of the debate set off by Küng's book, especially in German theology, was quite remarkable. Without spelling out the issues in detail let

---

[24] *Infallible?*: 132.
[25] See Patrick McGrath, 'The Concept of Infallibility', *Concilium* 83 (1973): 65–76.
[26] *Infallible?*: 11.
[27] The emphasis on biblical inerrancy in the schema *De Revelatione* submitted to Vatican II is absent from the final Constitution *Dei Verbum*. The Lutheran Church (Missouri Synod) was torn apart in the 1970s, with Concordia Seminary in St Louis taking a strong stand on biblical infallibility, and the Southern Baptist Convention similarly in the 1980s.

us simply note the discussion by Karl Rahner.[28] Setting aside the attempt by
Küng to interpret infallibility as the 'indestructibility' of the Church's faith,
grounded on the abiding union of the Church with Christ, taking this as a
single whole, such that, even in 'definitions', errors can occur here and there
and exist for years,[29] Rahner concentrates on the dogma of infallibility in
the traditional sense, that is, as relating to the truth of a proposition. The
dogma makes no sense in isolation. It has nothing to do with arriving at
new knowledge by the intervention of an authority external to the process.
There is historical development. The Church is not a totalitarian system, so
to speak, capable of being fixed and frozen by an element within the system.
The Church is 'a *free* believing community': no one has to believe anything
against his or her will. There can be absolute assent to a proposition, which
does not exclude criticism of it. One does not accept any such proposition
without belief in the assistance of the Holy Spirit at the point of decision.
And so on.

Turning to the dogma of infallibility as relating to the papacy, Rahner
insists that it too has a history, indeed it is a relatively late development.
Here, however, he concentrates on the development since 1870. After the
definition in 1950 of the dogma of the Assumption of the Blessed Virgin
Mary, so Rahner allows, many theologians looked forward with glee to new
statements of Marian doctrine being defined; 'Today no one any longer
thinks of such a thing' (72). One reason for this abandonment of the desire
for more dogma that Rahner gives – 'Nothing was defined at the Second
Vatican Council' – would need more discussion than he grants it. The conflict over episcopal collegiality was understood, by the leaders of the
opposition to it at any rate, as defining a doctrine complementary to (or
undermining of, as they feared) the dogma of papal primacy.

Mainly, however, Rahner sees such pluralism in culture, theology and
philosophy, that no single, common and universally acknowledged theology
exists, which would be the prerequisite for a dogmatic statement (73). If
there were a new definition, it could not be false, since the legitimate range
of interpretation would be so wide that no room for error remains (80). If
any conceivable new dogma entails such a range of possible interpretations
that it cannot be false, this does not make it devoid of content or tauto-

---

[28]   Once the oecumenicity of Vaticans I and II is 'unconditionally affirmed', it may be 'freely discussed' whether the confusing associations of the term 'infallible', 'not unjustly noted' by Hans
Küng, should not lead to its being abandoned in favour of some more easily understood word,
such as *Verbindlichkeit* (obligation, commitment, binding character), see Hans Urs von Balthasar,
The Office of Peter and the Structure of the Church (San Francisco: Ignatius Press 1986): 221–2.
[29]   Rahner, *Theological Investigations*, XIV (London: Darton, Longman and Todd 1976): 66–7.
Subsequent page references for quotation are given in the text.

logical. We are more aware now than our predecessors were that no process of interpretation is ever concluded (82). Any 'new' definition, we should see immediately, would be 'old' from the outset: no 'advance' but rather the introduction of 'a certain perfectly reasonable and respectable authorized parlance and a new reference to the basic historical experiences and basic historical realities of Christianity' (82).

In what Rahner says here, as well as in what Küng seems to say about inherently ambiguous propositions, there is surely room for further philosophical discussion of the concepts of a proposition, truth and interpretation, before debate on papal infallibility is resumed.[30]

Conclusion

Hans Küng's recent books on non-Christian religions and on the ethics of globalization may have more impact in opening Christian sensibility in the West to the widest issues facing the Church in the world today, and thus to extending the intentions of Vatican II. Apart from his being demonized in some quarters, too much controversy will always surround his name, for his books on matters internal to the structure of the Church to be influential. Sooner or later, however, the Catholic Church will have to return to the agenda he did so much to dramatize, to clarify what episcopal collegiality and papal infallibility mean.

When Hans Küng asked for a meeting, the recently elected Pope Benedict XVI, his old friend and sparring partner, immediately invited him to the papal summer residence at Castel Gandolfo, in the hills outside Rome, where, on 24 September 2005, they talked for several hours, had dinner together, and jointly approved a statement, composed by the pope himself, announcing and describing their meeting for the whole world to read. The Vatican Press Office released a statement three days later, describing the meeting as having been held 'in a friendly atmosphere'. The discussion concentrated on two subjects: the question of global ethics and the dialogue between science and faith.

Benedict XVI welcomed Professor Küng's contribution to these, affirming that the commitment to a renewed awareness of the values that sustain

---

[30] It would be difficult to find anything more enlightening on this whole debate than the three articles by Garrett Sweeney, then Master of St Edmund's House, Cambridge, published in *The Clergy Review* between 1971 and 1975 and reprinted in *Bishops and Writers: Aspects of the Evolution of Modern English Catholicism*, edited by Adrian Hastings (Wheathampstead: A. Clarke 1977): 161–234.

human life is also an important objective of his own pontificate, and affirming his agreement with Küng's attempt to revive the dialogue between faith
and the natural sciences. For his part, so the press release concludes, Küng
expressed his praise for the pope's efforts in favour of dialogue between religions and towards meeting the different social groups of the modern world.
Some topics, once — and no doubt still — dear to Hans Küng's heart, were
evidently not on the agenda.

Chapter Ten

KAROL WOJTYLA

When an extraordinarily gifted man is pope for nearly 27 years, with a clear vision of how to lead the Church, his contribution simply as one of the innovative theologians of the twentieth century might easily be overlooked. Elected pope on 16 October 1978, John Paul II died on 2 April 2005.

Karol Wojtyla was born on 18 May 1920 at Wadowice, near Krakow.[1] The Polish Republic had just been created, at the Versailles Peace Conference. Marshal Józef Pilsudski was fighting to secure the eastern frontier against the new Soviet Union.[2] Wojtyla's father, drafted into the Austro-Hungarian army in 1900, and eventually posted to Wadowice, married into a comfortably well-off family. The Austrians were on the losing side; the Habsburg Empire collapsed; and Karol's father, who had a desk job throughout, emerged as an officer in the new Polish army.

Wojtyla did not intend to become a priest. His humanistic studies at the Jagiellonian University in Krakow were soon disrupted by the German invasion. Hundreds of the professors were taken to concentration camps, where more than half died. In the Katyn forest, the Soviet Communists shot 25,700 military officers, landowners, civil servants, factory owners, clergymen and policemen. Between them, Hitler and Stalin sought to exterminate the entire Polish middle class. Wojtyla was lucky to survive.

By 1942 he had decided on the priesthood. Working in a factory, he embarked on the required philosophical course. He found metaphysics hard:

---

[1]   See Jonathan Kwitny, *Man of the Century: The Life and Times of Pope John Paul II* (London: Little, Brown and Company 1997) and George Weigel, *Witness to Hope: The Biography of Pope John Paul II* (New York: HarperCollins 1999).

[2]   There is a good account of 'The Polands of the Pope' in George Hunston Williams, *The Mind of John Paul II: Origins of His Thought and Action* (New York: Seabury 1981), an excellent study by an eminent Protestant scholar with expertise in Polish history.

For a long time I couldn't cope with the book, and I actually wept over it. My literary training centred around the humanities [and] had not prepared me at all for the scholastic theses and formulas. I had to cut a path through a thick undergrowth of concepts, without even being able to identify the ground over which I was moving. . . . After hacking through this vegetation, I came to a clearing, to the discovery of the deep reasons for what until then I had only lived and felt. But in the end it opened a whole new world to me. It showed me a new approach to reality, and made me aware of questions that I had only dimly perceived. This discovery has remained the basis of my intellectual structure. So it all really began with the book of Wais.[3]

Wais deals with being, act and potency, existence and essence, and so on, the standard neoscholastic topics, albeit in a historical context, ancient, medieval and especially nineteenth century, according to G.H. Williams, who also says that the author was fully aware of the rethinking of Thomism in the light of the philosophy of Kant.[4] The book, another commentator says, 'reflects the influence of transcendental Thomism, the school of Louvain, which attempted to reconcile Kant and St Thomas'.[5] Since Wais studied at Innsbrück, Rome, Fribourg and Louvain, where he counted Mercier as his master, he seems to have been acquainted with the entire range of pre-1914 versions of Thomism.

Narrowly escaping arrest by German soldiers, in August 1944, Wojtyla moved into the clandestine seminary in the archbishop's palace in Krakow.[6] In January 1945, the Germans fled and the Russians arrived. Wojtyla was ordained priest on 1 November 1946. His ordination course, including the private study of metaphysics, was not the typical initiation into neoscholasticism.

---

[3]   The book, in Polish and not in Latin, by Kazimierz Wais (1865–1934), was published in 1926; for the quotation see Kwitny, *Man of the Century*: 77.
[4]   Williams, *The Mind of John Paul II*: 87; though even if Wais knew much about 'transcendental Thomism', Williams is mistaken in ascribing that version of Thomism to Mercier.
[5]   So Rocco Buttiglione, *Karol Wojtyla: The Thought of the Man Who Became Pope John Paul II* (Grand Rapids, MI: Eerdmans 1997): 31.
[6]   Archbishop Adam Stefan Sapieha (1867–1951), Polish nationalist, reported to the Vatican in 1940 via Innocenty Bochenski OP the ruthlessness of the German occupation, and again in 1942, about the concentration camps. He allowed Jews in hiding to have baptismal certificates. He was appointed Cardinal only in 1946 by Pope Pius XII (Pius XI thought he had been slighted by Sapieha back in 1921).

Thomism?

Two weeks after ordination Karol Wojtyla enrolled at the Dominican College in Rome. The Dominicans at the Angelicum were famous for their pure version of Thomism, untouched by efforts to relate Aquinas to Kant or (perhaps even worse) to situate him in his historical context. Thirty years had gone by but Réginald Garrigou-Lagrange was still there to supervise Wojtyla's doctorate research as he once had Chenu's.

According to some authorities, Wojtyla received 'rigorous training in the most traditional form of Thomism', from Garrigou-Lagrange.[7] In fact, however, Wojtyla spent from November 1946 until June 1948 at the Angelicum: three semesters. During the first semester he wrote a paper (in Latin, for Mario Luigi Ciappi) on the theology of Aquinas, in order to demonstrate his grasp of the underlying metaphysical principles. The remaining two semesters were devoted to the doctoral dissertation, 'The essence of faith in John of the Cross', supervised, indeed, by Garrigou-Lagrange. Wojtyla never studied Thomistic philosophy and theology under the usual conditions. Composing a long essay in four months was not the 'rigorous training' that resulted from attending lectures on Aquinas for seven years, as Dominican students did then (and into the 1960s). Moreover, one wonders how much any supervisor could have affected his project. Garrigou-Lagrange, it is true, was the obvious person at the Angelicum to direct a thesis on John of the Cross. However, Wojtyla had been studying John of the Cross since 1940, under the guidance of Jan Tyranowski (1900–47), an unmarried tailor in Krakow, widely read and deeply contemplative, a quite extraordinary man. In the dissertation, Wojtyla contends that mystical encounter with God is for everyone; we can know God through mutual self-giving, and the goal of the Christian life is for us to become 'God by participation'. This mysticism, far from being exceptional or peripheral, is central: we cannot know others unless we know them as persons in communion with God; God is part of understanding persons; take God out and we lose what is most truly human in us.[8]

With this thesis Garrigou-Lagrange would not have disagreed: his own great contribution as a writer on spirituality was to insist that contemplative prayer is not for an elite but for everyone. He criticized Wojtyla, however, for several reasons, but particularly for insisting on speaking of God as a

---

[7] Buttiglione, *Karol Wojtyla*: 34.
[8] *Faith according to St John of the Cross*, translated by Jordan Aumann (San Francisco: Ignatius Press 1981); unfortunately without Garrigou-Lagrange's observations, for which see the Italian translation, *La Fede secondo S. Giovanni della Croce* (Rome: Angelicum-Herder 1979).

'subject', and for being unwilling to speak of God as 'object'. This is significant. Here, clearly, Wojtyla was moving well beyond the Thomism reigning
at the Angelicum.[9] Aquinas has no problem about speaking of God or of
one's neighbour as an 'object' – for example, as the 'object of charity', *objectum caritatis* (*Summa Theologiæ* 2–2. 23). In pre-modern philosophy, an
'object' is some reality other than the 'subject': an object evokes, challenges,
or polarizes the activity of a subject, in one way or another. In the case of
charity, then, the 'subject' is a human being engaged, in the actualizing of
his or her capacities and endowments, with the 'object' – who is God or
neighbour. In premodern parlance, that is to say, human beings were not
'subjects', cherishing their subjectivity, over against 'objects', passively facing
them, as we are tempted to believe. Thus, for Thomists, such as Garrigou-
Lagrange, Wojtyla's refusal to speak of God as *objectum* in the context of
expounding Aquinas, could not but seem an unnecessary and even a gravely
mistaken move, all part of the putative post-Cartesian turn to subjectivity.

Phenomenology

In 1951, Wojtyla returned to academic life, unwillingly. The seminary professor, who recommended this career change, selected the topic for his
dissertation: the ethics of Max Scheler.[10] First he had to translate Scheler
from German into Polish, which he found a painful experience. However,
he was soon telling friends that Scheler 'opens up a whole new world, a
world of values and a fresh view of mankind'.[11]

Max Scheler (1874–1928) argued, against Kant, that values are objective,
unchanging, and *a priori*, albeit objects of emotions and feelings rather than
reason. Wojtyla was unhappy with this last claim. On the other hand, there
was much in Scheler's philosophy that he liked. For Scheler, a person is
neither a substance nor an object, but (in the jargon) the concrete unity of
acts. Moreover, persons are essentially both individuals and social beings.
Most people, Scheler thought, lack feeling for higher values; they cannot
participate in communities devoted to such values; yet everyone should have
adequate, perhaps even equal, access to what they do value. Values, Scheler
believed, are better promoted by aristocracy than by liberal democracy.[12]

---

[9]   Weigel, *Witness to Hope*: 85–6; 128.
[10] The dissertation was published in 1959; there is an Italian translation (1980).
[11] Kwitny, *Man of the Century*: 125.
[12] Scheler, a Jewish convert to Catholicism at the age of 14, eventually decided that his anti-
Thomist version of Augustinianism was incompatible with Catholicism.

One of Wojtyla's examiners was Roman Ingarden (1893–1970), the most eminent Polish philosopher of his generation. He had studied with Edmund Husserl at Freiburg. While accepting the phenomenological method of 'eidetic reduction', he rejected the transcendental idealism. That is to say, he accepted that acts of consciousness need to be analysed by being 'reduced' to their essence (or *eidos*): the phenomenologist is concerned, not with particular acts of perception (say), but with the essential features common to some class of such acts. On the other hand, Ingarden, and of course Wojtyla, did not accept Husserl's conclusion, at least at one stage, namely that objects are constituted by consciousness, a thesis which seemed to them (rightly) a form of idealism.

One of the best books about Ingarden is by Anna-Teresa Tymieniecka.[13] Familiar with the phenomenological school, when she hit on Wojtyla's book, *Osoba i czyn* (*Person and Act*), published in 1969, the fruit of a decade's thought, she saw it as a major contribution to the phenomenological tradition. The book had been so badly received in Poland, where philosophy was still dominated by Marxism, that Wojtyla set it aside. With her enthusiasm, they worked together, in Krakow, Rome and at her home in Boston, Massachusetts, on an English version, which appeared as *The Acting Person* in 1979.[14]

How true the translation is to the original is much disputed. The Vatican attempted to stop publication when Wojtyla became pope. Tymieniecka threatened to sue, deposited a cache of letters at Harvard University, showing Wojtyla's support of the enterprise, and went ahead with publication.[15] Advertised as the 'definitive text', 'established in collaboration', the book includes a facsimile of the preface, dated March 1977, in Wojtyla's own hand, explicitly thanking her for giving his text 'its final shape'. The book appeared in Analecta Husserliana, a distinguished series edited by Tymieniecka, which includes four other volumes to which Wojtyla contributed. Wojtyla's participation in conferences, as well as these publications, established him as a considerable figure in the development of philosophical anthropology, according to the phenomenological style that comes from Husserl and Scheler.

Because of the dispute over the faithfulness of the translation, it is also disputed how 'Thomist' Wojtyla's book is. Tymieniecka seems to have smoothed out some of the Thomistic terminology, making the book look less Thomistic than, according to readers of the original, it actually is.

---

[13] Born in 1925, in Poland, she has long been settled in the United States of America.
[14] *The Acting Person* (Dordrecht: D. Reidel 1979).
[15] Her husband Hendryk Houthakker was in the Harvard economics department.

G.H. Williams hesitates between calling Wojtyla a 'phenomenological Thomist' or a 'thomasizing phenomenologist'.[16] In over a dozen articles published between 1982 and 1993, the authors range from ascribing to his philosophy a 'fundamental Thomistic core', albeit his notion of 'experience' is 'not Aristotelian-Thomistic', to hailing it as 'a dynamic Thomism', 'Thomistic personalism', Thomism 'but not in the usual sense', and such-like.[17] For those who read Thomas Aquinas in company with the likes of Garrigou-Lagrange, obviously, the concession that Wojtyla's notion of 'experience' is not 'Aristotelian-Thomistic' means that his philosophy is not Thomist at all.

Doxological Metaphysics

In 1980, on his return to the Angelicum as by then its most eminent alumnus, Pope John Paul II hailed Jacques Maritain as interpreter of Thomas Aquinas, going on to insist that the 'philosophical patrimony which is forever valid' can have *all* modern schools of philosophy as 'natural allies' and 'partners' – provided that they share an interest in the metaphysics of the *actus essendi* or of *esse ut actus*, and understand that 'that which subsists as sheer Existing' – God – calls the world into being and pours love into all created beings as into 'precious jewel-boxes full of treasures', and especially into human beings who are autonomous and have access to truth. Aquinas's philosophy is

> a philosophy of *being*, of the *actus essendi* whose transcendental value paves the most direct way to rise to the knowledge of subsisting Being and pure Act, namely to God. . . . On account of this we can even call this philosophy the philosophy of the proclamation of being, a chant in praise of what exists . . . *filosofia della proclamazione dell'essere, il canto in onore dell'esistent*.[18]

This wonderful phrase probably has no connection with G.K. Chesterton – yet, in his book on St Thomas (1933), the praise of Being is equated with the praise of God as the creator of the world. This doxological consumma-tion of the philosophy of Being, as we may say, no doubt takes us more rapidly into theology than the framework of the Twenty-four Thomistic Theses was intended to allow – metaphysics disappears into liturgy; but, as

---

16 Williams, *The Mind of John Paul II*: 117.
17 Buttiglione, *Karol Wojtyla*: 323–30.
18 'The Perennial Philosophy of St Thomas', *Angelicum* 1980: 121–46.

an alternative perspective in which to recall philosophy to its original destiny as 'love of wisdom', *philo-sophia*, such phrases are surely inspiring.

Persons as Agents

Not that Wojtyla has done much that might count as metaphysics – his main contribution, as a philosopher, has more to do with his discussions of human moral agency, rather than any attempt to spell out a doxological conception of the metaphysics of being. Difficult as it certainly is, however disputable the translation, *The Acting Person* is most accessibly approached as one of the many efforts in the middle of the twentieth century to deal with the legacy of the modern picture of the self as the detached observer of the passing show – such as *The Self as Agent* by John MacMurray, *Thought and Action* by Stuart Hampshire, *The Concept of Mind* by Gilbert Ryle, *Phenomenology of Perception* by Maurice Merleau-Ponty, as well as Heidegger's *Being and Time* and (perhaps) the later Wittgenstein's *Remarks on the Philosophy of Psychology*.

Persons are *agents*, actively engaged in the hurly burly of life, long before ever they disengage in order to observe things with scientific detachment or to stand back in wonder with an artist's eye or in contemplation. Moreover, persons are social beings, never isolated in quasi-solipsistic interiority, a position leaving us vulnerable to scepticism about knowledge of one another's minds. Persons are always already 'in the world', reacting to the environment and interacting with others. On the other hand, unlike Ryle, for example, Wojtyla is not inclined to play down or even eliminate our capacity to withdraw into inwardness – he is not attracted by any form of behaviourism. Plainly, also, for Wojtyla, the human agent develops in interaction and communication with others – which, however, does not lead to his endorsing any conception of totalitarian collectivity.[19]

In the encyclical *Fides et Ratio* (§13), on the crisis in philosophy, John Paul II's focus is on the concept of the human being – for all that he recommends the philosophy of being he seems in practice to be much more at home with the modern concern with subjectivity. Philosophy since Descartes and Kant, as he rightly says, has been more interested in cognition

---

[19] The best introductions to his philosophical work are by Peter Simpson, *On Karol Wojtyla* in the Wadsworth Philosophers Series (Belmont, CA: Wadsworth/Thomson Learning 2001), and, much more advanced, by Kenneth L. Schmitz, *At the Center of the Human Drama: The Philosophical Anthropology of Karol Wojtyla/Pope John Paul II* (Washington, DC: The Catholic University of America Press 1993), with excellent bibliography by John M. Grondelski.

theory than in ontology – yet, with appropriate caveats, he seems happy with the turn to the subject as the starting point in the search for truth (§5).

The traditional Thomist cannot but be somewhat disconcerted by John Paul II's references to Aquinas. According to the encyclical, 'The Church has no philosophy of her own nor does she canonize any one particular philosophy in preference to others . . . [because] even when it engages theology, philosophy must remain faithful to its own principles and methods' (§49). For a hundred years, at least, so it was generally believed, Thomistic philosophy was indeed the official philosophy. It sounds strange to hear that the principles and methods of some other philosophy have to be respected in the exposition of Catholic doctrine – which other philosophy? one hears the Thomist enquire. True, Aquinas 'has always been regarded by the Church as a/the master of teaching and a/the model of how to do theology' (§43: no article in the Latin, obviously) – a model, note, of how to do *theology*, not philosophy. We can understand 'why the Magisterium has praised the merits of St Thomas's philosophy and regarded him as leader and model of the discipline of theology' – yet this has nothing to do with 'embracing certain philosophical positions, nor requiring particular views to be held' (§78). It is simply because in his work he kept the balance between reason and faith, safeguarding the particularity of revelation at the same time as never reducing the proper course of reason.

Reforming the Papacy

Much more could be said about Karol Wojtyla as a philosopher. Since becoming pope in 1978 most of what he published obviously falls into the category of exhorting fellow Catholics to remember the faith that they have received, or admonishing fellow bishops to be faithful to their office. However, he also took two immensely important initiatives, one as regards the future of the papal ministry, when he invited interested parties to help reshape the office, and the other, even more remarkable, in theological anthropology, when he made nuptial mysticism the centre of his teaching.

Many decisions that he took as pope have theological implications that will resonate for decades if not centuries. For example, in 1986 he visited the synagogue in Rome, affirming that Jewish/Christian relations rest on respect for each tradition in its own distinctive identity, thereby declaring an end to the supersessionism which has dominated Christian attitudes to Judaism from New Testament times. In 2000, visiting the state of Israel, John Paul II prayed at the Wall in Jerusalem and left his *qvittel* (written request) for forgiveness for the past. Obviously, these deliberate, highly symbolic gestures do not by themselves put an end to the existence of anti-Semitism, which (alas) remains visible in most supposedly Christian societies in Europe, let alone elsewhere. Nonetheless they confirm the aspirations set out in *Nostra Ætate*, the Declaration on the Church's relation with non-Christian religions passed at Vatican II (1965). Following on from the tentative beginnings of his predecessors, John XXIII and Paul VI, John Paul II made decisive advances towards healing the rift between Jews and Christians, and cauterizing the virulent disease that defaces the Catholic Church.

Given how much a theologian like Yves Congar suffered from the authorities in his own Order and in the Vatican for his vocation to promote Christian reunion, we should note that, in his encyclical *Ut Unum Sint* (1995), John Paul II decisively reaffirmed the Catholic Church's commitment to ecumenism, here again going far beyond what was established at Vatican II in *Unitatis Redintegratio*, the Decree on Ecumenism (1964). For example, he begins by praising 'The courageous witness of so many martyrs of our century, including members of Churches and Ecclesial Communities not in full communion with the Catholic Church'. Good Catholics, even today, have never believed that heretics and schismatics (as they would think) could ever be truly martyrs for the faith. 'Believers in Christ, united in following in the footsteps of the martyrs', however, 'cannot remain divided' (§2, cf. §84). Ecumenism, for John Paul II, is grounded in shared suffering for Christ's sake.

Taking Catholic commitment to the principles of ecumenism for granted, perhaps a little optimistically (most Catholics remain lukewarm, especially those who talk most about their loyalty to the Holy See), John Paul II's main concern in this encyclical is to invite all Christians to share his prayer, as 'Successor of the Apostle Peter', for 'that conversion which is indispensable for "Peter" to be able to serve his brethren' (§4). This is quite unprecedented. He appeals to Christians who are not now, and perhaps are never likely to be, in full communion with Rome, to help in reshaping the papal ministry. Paul VI once lamented that the papacy was the greatest obstacle in the way of Christian reunion. John XXIII showed a side of the papacy which made it believable that it might be a focus of unity for all Christians. For Pius XII, Pius XI, Pius X, or Pius IX, the very idea of consulting non-Catholic Christians about *anything*, let alone about the future of the papacy, would have been unthinkable; they regarded most of them as barely Christians at all.

John Paul II takes a radically different line: 'It is not that beyond the boundaries of the Catholic community there is an ecclesial vacuum. Many elements of great value, which in the Catholic Church are part of the fullness of the means of salvation and of the gifts of grace which make up the Church, are also found in the other Christian Communities' (§13). There are 'true Church' elements in non-Catholic church structures – not just in certain individuals. 'The elements of this already-given Church exist, found in their fullness in the Catholic Church and, without this fullness, in the other Communities, where certain features of the Christian mystery have at times been more effectively emphasized' (§14). Things have sometimes been done better by non-Catholics.

John Paul II takes up an idea expressed by John XXIII: 'Ecumenism is an organic part of [the Church's] life and work, and consequently must pervade all that she is and does' (§20). He recounts his own contribution in his many 'pilgrimages'. He hails the progress of many ecumenical conversations, and so on. 'A century ago who could even have imagined such a thing?' (§45), he rightly asks.

Much more is said about reconciliation with the Churches of the East (§50ff), and with the non-Chalcedonian Churches (§62ff), than with the Churches and Ecclesial Communities of the West (§64ff). 'The ecumenical movement', he nevertheless allows 'really began within the Churches and Ecclesial Communities of the Reform' (§65).

Of course, there are divisive questions in need of further study before a true consensus in faith can be achieved (§79). John Paul II notes the significant contribution which theologians and faculties of theology are called to make by exercising their charism (§81). Discussions and agreements reached by ecumenical commissions are noted as having responsibilities and tasks as regards promoting Christian unity.

The Petrine Ministry

Finally, turning to the contribution of the Roman Catholic Church to the quest for Christian unity, John Paul II says this (§88): 'Among all the Churches and Ecclesial Communities, the Catholic Church is conscious that she has preserved the ministry of the Successor of the Apostle Peter, the Bishop of Rome, whom God established as her "perpetual and visible principle and foundation of unity" [a phrase from Vatican I] and whom the Spirit sustains in order that he may enable all the others to share in this essential good'.

The papacy, that is to say, far from being something which should be changed out of all recognition or simply eliminated, is precisely the unique gift which the Catholic Church has to offer. John Paul II refers to 'the Catholic Church's conviction that in the ministry of the Bishop of Rome she has preserved, in fidelity to the Apostolic Tradition and the faith of the Fathers, the visible sign and guarantor of unity' – going on, however, to confess that it 'constitutes a difficulty for most other Christians, whose memory is marked by certain painful recollections'. There is much in the history of the papacy to deplore, no doubt including corruption and nepotism as well as arrogant triumphalism and refusal to collaborate with other Christians: 'To the extent that we are responsible for these, I join my Predecessor Paul VI in asking forgiveness'.

On the other hand, the question of the primacy of the bishop of Rome is now on the agenda, not only in conversations between Catholic theologians and others, Orthodox and Reformed; but, in the ecumenical movement as a whole, the issue comes up unavoidably in connection with authority, communion and unity (§89).

The ministry of the bishop of Rome is to 'ensure the communion of all the Churches'. The post holder is, indeed, 'the first servant of unity'. What the office involves is explained:

> This primacy is exercised on various levels, including vigilance over the handing down of the Word, the celebration of the Liturgy and the Sacraments, the Church's mission, discipline and the Christian life. It is the responsibility of the Successor of Peter to recall the requirements of the common good of the Church, should anyone be tempted to overlook it in the pursuit of personal interests. He has the duty to admonish, to caution and to declare at times that this or that opinion being circulated is irreconcilable with the unity of faith. When circumstances require it, he speaks in the name of all the Pastors in communion with him. He can also – under very specific conditions clearly laid down by the First Vatican Council – declare *ex cathedra* that a certain doctrine belongs to the deposit of faith. By thus bearing witness to the truth, he serves unity.

In all this, obviously, John Paul II is doing no more than repeat the affirmations of Vatican I. He is, however, careful to reject ultramontanist exaggerations that isolated the papacy from the episcopacy: 'All this however must always be done in communion. When the Catholic Church affirms that the office of the Bishop of Rome corresponds to the will of Christ, she does not separate this office from the mission entrusted to the whole body of Bishops, who are also "vicars and ambassadors of Christ"' (§95). He endorses the doctrine of collegiality as promulgated at Vatican II. Nevertheless, the papacy has a special role: 'I am convinced that I have a particular responsibility' – which turns out, perhaps surprisingly, to reside 'above all in acknowledging the ecumenical aspirations of the majority of the Christian Communities and in heeding the request made of me to find a way of exercising the primacy which, while in no way renouncing what is essential to its mission, is nonetheless open to a new situation'.

For a whole millennium – the first thousand years of church history – Christians were united in 'a brotherly fraternal communion of faith and sacramental life'. 'If disagreements in belief and discipline arose among them, the Roman See acted by common consent as moderator.' Here, John Paul II quotes from an address that he made to the Ecumenical Patriarch Dimitrios I, acknowledging that 'for a great variety of reasons, and against the will of all concerned, what should have been a service sometimes manifested itself in a very different light'. For all the harm that popes have done over the centuries, John Paul II insists that he has a ministry – praying, however, 'the Holy Spirit to shine his light upon us, enlightening all the Pastors and theologians of our Churches, that we may seek – together, of course – the forms in which this ministry may accomplish a service of love recognized by all concerned'.

He has no illusions (§96):

> This is an immense task, which we cannot refuse and which I cannot carry out by myself. Could not the real but imperfect communion existing between us persuade Church leaders and their theologians to engage with me in a patient and fraternal dialogue on this subject, a dialogue in which, leaving useless controversies behind, we could listen to one another, keeping before us only the will of Christ for his Church and allowing ourselves to be deeply moved by his plea 'that they may all be one . . . so that the world may believe that you have sent me' (John 17:21)?

Here, asking the help of 'Church leaders and their theologians' not in communion with Rome, John Paul II obviously has the Orthodox mainly in mind. He invites them to engage, 'in a patient and fraternal dialogue', in the 'immense task' of seeking the forms in which the papal ministry may be practised credibly in this ecumenical age.

Since this appeal, according to good sources, proposals have been sent to the Vatican from many different quarters. Little has been published, though it is not difficult to guess that some books and articles represent some of the submissions.[20]

John Paul II cannot have done much to reshape the Petrine ministry in ways that might meet the concerns of the Orthodox, let alone other Christian leaders and communities. None of his symbolic gestures went significantly further than those by Paul VI, as regards Constantinople and

---

[20]   For the beginning of a response see James F. Puglisi (ed.) *Petrine Ministry and the Unity of the Church* (Collegeville, MN: Liturgical Press 1999); and Olivier Clément, *You Are Peter: An Orthodox Theologian's Reflection on the Exercise of Papal Primacy* (London: New City Press 2003), foreword by Avery Cardinal Dulles SJ.

Canterbury for example. Nevertheless, the encyclical *Ut Unum Sint* goes far beyond anything envisaged by Vatican II or by John XXIII and Paul VI. Yves Congar, and the many other pioneers of Catholic ecumenism, would have been astonished that an incumbent of the Roman see would himself envisage what would have to be quite radical reform of the papacy, however wishful and far in the future it seems.

In 1996, at vespers in St Peter's in Rome celebrating the fourteen-hundredth anniversary of Gregory the Great's sending Augustine and his fellow monks to England, John Paul II invited George Carey, Archbishop of Canterbury, to walk in procession with him, in cope and mitre, and gave him a gold episcopal pectoral cross. In 2000, he invited the Archbishop and a representative of the Orthodox Church to assist him in the opening of the Holy Door of St Paul's Outside the Walls to inaugurate the Jubilee Year 2000. Such actions were certainly not spontaneous, their implications not unconsidered. What John Paul II *did*, on these and many other occasions, exhibited an understanding of the papal office, of the Catholic Church, and of the principles of Catholic ecumenism, with which the theological schools have not yet quite caught up. As the French philosopher Paul Ricoeur used to say, in an almost untranslatable phrase, *le symbole donne à penser:* it may take years but the eloquence of a symbolic act will eventually change ways of thinking.

Theological Anthropology

From September 1979 to November 1984, however, John Paul II gave a series of addresses to large audiences of pilgrims, known as the Wednesday Catecheses, on 'The Theology of the Body'.[21] These addresses fall into six cycles: 'The Beginning', 'The Redemption of the Heart', 'The Resurrection of the Flesh', 'Christian Virginity', 'Christian Marriage' and 'Love and Fecundity'. How far back into earlier years these ideas go is a matter of dispute. Anyhow, he develops a theology of the human body, a Christian anthropology of sexual difference, which breaks new ground in Catholic Christian tradition, going far beyond received doctrine, and signalling the most remarkable theme in turn-of-the-century Catholic theology – *nuptiality*.

The distinction between statements of church doctrine by pastors and the

---

[21] Gathered as *The Theology of the Body: Human Love in the Divine Plan* (Boston, MA: Pauline Books 1997), with an introduction by John Grabowski. Cf. www.theologyofthebody.net for the Internet's best documented resource for Pope John Paul II's theology of the body.

ideas of private theologians is usually easier to draw, in the Roman Catholic Church, than it sometimes seems in other churches. Here, however, John Paul II's ideas are by no means simply repetition of long-established common teaching. On the contrary – according to George Weigel, for example, John Paul II's 'longest-lasting theological contribution to the Church and the world might well be something that very few people have ever encountered: his innovative "theology of the body"' – 'a bit of a theological time bomb, something that [will] explode within the Church at some indeterminate point in the future with tremendous effect, reshaping the way Catholics think about our embodiedness as male and female, our sexuality, our relationship with each other, our relationship with God – even God himself'.[22]

As far as the implications of this innovative theology of the body are concerned, there is no departure from received Catholic teaching. John Paul II, as many of his writings indicate, adheres to the traditional doctrine of the indissolubility of marriage, and thus condemns divorced persons who remarry without an annulment. Couples employing *in vitro* fertilization are guilty of reducing procreation to something that happens in the laboratory, thus separating the life-giving potential of the body from the person. Couples who separate the unitive and procreative aspects of love-making by using drugs or barriers enjoy real bodily union in the conjugal act without personal communion. If the conclusions are no surprise, they are, however, reached by a quite new line of argument.

Nuptiality

Back in 1969, reflecting on the Pope Paul VI's encyclical *Humanae Vitae*, the then Cardinal Wojtyla drew support for the condemnation of artificial contraception from the autobiography of Mahatma Gandhi.[23] By the time that, as pope, he brought out his apostolic exhortation *Familiaris Consortio* (1981) on marriage and the family, he preferred to rely only on the high doctrine of the married state in Scripture (§13):

> The communion between God and His people finds its definitive fulfillment in Jesus Christ, the Bridegroom who loves and gives Himself as the Savior of

---

[22]   See the foreword by George Weigel to Christopher West, *Theology of the Body Explained: A Commentary on John Paul II's Gospel of the Body* (Leominster: Gracewing 2003), an invaluable exposition.
[23]   *L'Osservatore Romano*, weekly edition in English, 16 January 1969: 6.

humanity, uniting it to Himself as His body. He reveals the original truth of marriage, the truth of the 'beginning', and, freeing man from his hardness of heart, He makes man capable of realising this truth in its entirety. This revelation reaches its definitive fullness in the gift of love which the Word of God makes to humanity in assuming a human nature, and in the sacrifice which Jesus Christ makes of Himself on the Cross for His bride, the Church. In this sacrifice there is entirely revealed that plan which God has imprinted on the humanity of man and woman since their creation; the marriage of baptized persons thus becomes a real symbol of that new and eternal covenant sanctioned in the blood of Christ.

John Paul II goes on to cite 'a deservedly famous page' from the African church father Tertullian (c. 160–c. 225) expressing 'the greatness of this conjugal life in Christ and its beauty'.

In the brief addresses between 1979 and 1984 to his weekly general audiences (the Wednesday Catecheses), John Paul II further expounded his 'theology of the body' in the light of this biblical and ancient patristic doctrine of the nuptial relation between Christ and the Church, God and his people.[24]

In the Wednesday Catecheses, the key word is *nuptiality*: we human beings were created 'male and female' (Gen. 1:27), such that, in God's good time, heterosexual marriage would be revealed as a sacramental sign of Christ's union with the Church. The human body, inherently and necessarily either male or female, exhibits its readiness for the nuptial relationship which is fulfilled in the union between Christ the bridegroom and his bride the Church.

This is not just an *idea*, John Paul II insists; rather, it is our *experience* of our bodies as a gift and as a symbol of God's love – and, in turn, it is our actually sharing this love with one another in and through our bodies, our masculinity and femininity.

In the first place, the human *body* is the expression or revelation of the human *person*. Expounding Genesis 2.18, which speaks of 'the man' being 'alone', John Paul II claims that the solitude in question is that of 'man' understood as male and female, as yet undifferentiated sexually – not of man the male, lonely for lack of woman. The solitude deriving from the human's very nature enables us to link the human's original solitude with consciousness of the body – which is how the human is distinguished from the animals. In virtue of this experience of original solitude, the human creature

---

[24] Gathered as *The Theology of the Body: Human Love in the Divine Plan* (Boston, MA: Pauline Books 1997).

has consciousness at one and the same time as awareness of the meaning of the body. Man's awareness of the body as different from the bodies of other animals enables him (including her) to grasp the truth that he (and she), alone among visible creatures, is a person, gifted with self-consciousness and self-determination.[25]

Second, reflecting on Genesis 2:18–24, the man's cry of joy at the sight of the woman, 'This at last is bone of my bones and flesh of my flesh', John Paul II finds the expression of 'the subjectively beatifying beginning of man's existence in the world'. This is the revelation of the meaning of the human body as 'nuptial'. The man's body is a sign of the gift of the man as person to the woman as person, and *vice versa*. The 'nuptial' meaning of the body shows man, male and female, that there can be fulfilment as a person only in the mutual self-giving in the act of love.[26]

Concupiscence, however, 'veils' the nuptial meaning of the human body. In the third chapter of Genesis we learn of the sin of the original human, and its dreadful consequences for human existence. John Paul II highlights the contrast between the lack of shame about their nakedness experienced by Adam and Eve in the state of original innocence and the shame about their nakedness that they experience after their 'fall'. In the state of original innocence nakedness expressed full acceptance of the body in all its human and personal truth. It was 'a faithful witness and a tangible verification of man's original "solitude" in the world, becoming at the same time, by means of his masculinity and femininity, a limpid element of mutual donation in the communion of persons' (27.3). Now, however, as a result of original sin and of the concupiscence that has entered his 'heart', man has lost 'the original certainty of the "image of God", expressed in his body' (27.4). The 'cosmic shame' that man experienced with regard to his Creator makes way for another form of shame, the shame produced in humanity itself: the woman's shame with regard to the man and *vice versa*.[27]

In these extraordinary meditations John Paul II argues that the triune God of love made man, male and female, to image Himself fully in their communion of persons, a communion made possible precisely because of their sexual complementarity as revealed in the nuptial meaning of their bodies, the sign that the male person is intended by God as a 'gift' to the female person and *vice versa*. Male and female are shaped physically so as to give themselves away to each other in love, to become one flesh, and in so

[25]   Ibid.: 37ff.
[26]   Ibid.: 25–7.
[27]   Ibid.: 51–4.

doing, to open themselves to the gift of fertility and thus to image even more fully the God who made them. In the state of original innocence the nuptial meaning of their bodies was transparent to them: the man and the woman had no shame about their nakedness since neither feared that the other would view him or her, not as a person to be loved but as an object to be *used*. As a result of the loss of innocence, however, concupiscence 'veiled' the nuptial meaning of the body. But God so loves man, male and female, that, in the person of Jesus Christ, God enables man, male and female, to become – once again – pure of heart, and thus to own his/her desires, rather than being possessed by them, with the result that man, male and female, can rediscover the nuptial meaning of the body and give himself/herself away, unreservedly and totally, in the mutual self-donation of marital intercourse.

Many are baffled by such reflections. Some are inclined to regard this new theology of the body as a belated argument in support of conclusions they already reject. They think of the teaching of the encyclical *Humanæ Vitæ* (1968), reaffirming the teaching of Pope Pius XI, in the encyclical *Casti Connubii* (1930), and thus condemning, in particular, any act of marital intercourse which, by artifice, is deprived of its natural power of procreating life. This teaching – it is commonly assumed – is grounded in the claim that to separate the unitive and procreative aspects of sexual intercourse is transparently contrary to natural law. After decades during which this argument has evidently failed to convince most people, John Paul II has replaced the appeal to what is supposedly 'against nature', with a radically biblical doctrine of nuptiality. While there has been a remarkable revival of interest in natural law thinking at the cutting edge of anglophone moral, legal and political philosophy, the idea that the rightness or wrongness of this or that activity, especially in sexual ethics, may be measured by conformity or otherwise to 'natural law', in most ordinary people's eyes, seems quite unpersuasive. In any case, it has long been debated whether natural law ethics ever stands independently of theological considerations.[28] John Paul II's faith-based doctrine of nuptiality seems to render non-theological natural law thinking in sexual ethics quite redundant. Putting this another way, we may say that it looks as if Catholic Christian ethics, in regard to marriage, depends entirely on the nuptial meaning of the body as revealed in the opening chapters of the Book of Genesis.

---

[28] See *St Thomas Aquinas and the Natural Law Tradition: Contemporary Perspectives*, edited by John Goyette, Mark S. Latkovic and Richard S. Myers (Washington, DC: Catholic University of America Press 2004).

Thomistic–Wojtylan Anthropology

As we noted, considering his sketchy seminary formation and his penchant for phenomenology, as well as his somewhat tentative recommendations about reading Thomas Aquinas, John Paul II may seem not much of a Thomist. Consider, however, the recent work of Graham McAleer.[29] Writing as a medievalist, he argues that Aquinas offers a distinctive theory of the human body which is of great interest in the context of current politics on sexual issues in the Catholic Church, but also is found in John Paul II's theological anthropology.

The argument may seem somewhat arcane. In the key concept of *concreatum*, Thomas held that matter and form are always already internally related – as body and soul thus are, which means, down the line, that sensuality and rationality are naturally suited to relate harmoniously with each other, 'concreated' so to speak. Historically, so McAleer argues, Aquinas was reacting to the concept of *congregatum*, the key term employed by Ibn Rushd (1126–98), the Spanish Muslim philosopher whose work became known in Aquinas's student days: matter, here, is regarded as existing prior to form, which, unsurprisingly, rules out anything like the Christian doctrine of creation. Matter and form, hence body and soul, as the expression suggests, were brought together, 'con-gregated' as it were – but not created simultaneously.

Thomas may well have been more interested in challenging the positions of neo-Augustinians among his colleagues at Paris, McAleer suggests, rather than in anything that Ibn Rushd taught. Anyway, the theory that counts would be that of Aquinas's own student, Giles of Rome (c. 1250–1306/9), a highly regarded theologian who eventually became General of the Hermits of St Augustine. He opted for the concept of *aggregatum*, which means that he pictured matter and form, world and God, body and soul, as ultimately united – brought together, however, through *violence*. As the etymology suggests, the picture includes a certain 'aggression'.

McAleer works this out in detail, documenting every move. His interest, however, is not simply in these three medieval theories. Down the line, so he contends, self-mastery on the part of the human creature is conceivable on the *aggregatum* theory only in terms of an aggressive overcoming of sensuality by rationality, of the human body by the soul. The healing gift of divine grace, according to this logic, becomes ruthless conquest of fallen human nature, and so on.

---

[29] G.J. McAleer, *Ecstatic Morality and Sexual Politics: A Catholic and Antitotalitarian Theory of the Body* (New York: Fordham University Press 2005).

The historical reconstruction by the professional medievalist of this seemingly obscure late-thirteenth-century debate has, obviously, an ulterior motive. As it turned out, Aquinas's notion of matter and form, sensuality and rationality, as *concreatum*, failed to carry the day, even in the Dominican Order. The 'Aegidian' view triumphed, so McAleer maintains, turning up, anonymously, in such well-known dualist metaphysicians as Descartes, Kant and Karl Rahner. For such thinkers, body and soul, sensuality and reason, are never naturally fitted to each other, as on Aquinas's view, but rather always in conflict.

This thesis may be no surprise to admirers of Aquinas's famously anti-Manichean attitude to the body.[30] McAleer, it is true, has a nasty surprise for one variety of Thomist: Catholic social thought, in papal encyclicals as well, so he claims, is largely inspired by Jacques Maritain's 'equalitarianism', a natural rights theory concocted from what Aquinas says about natural law. Invoking Aurel Kolnai, a profound student of Aquinas, who argued that genuine political pluralism must acknowledge hierarchies of natural and social privilege, McAleer declares Aquinas's position incompatible with as elaborate a theory of equal rights as Maritain's ('Christian-leftist social fantasies').

However all that may be, and without claiming that Wojtyla took it directly from Aquinas, let alone that he ever read Ibn Rushd or Giles of Rome, McAleer contends that John Paul II belongs with the minority in Catholic theology over the centuries who work with Aquinas's theology of the body – however unaware they may be of doing so.

The upshot is as follows. In his justifications of the account of marriage in Paul VI's encyclical *Humanæ Vitæ*, John Paul II could not be more authentically Thomist. This is not because he concentrates on the natural law doctrine that sexual activity is ordered to procreation. Rather, in contradiction to the dualisms in Catholic asceticism and spirituality, as well as in modern philosophies, all of which take violence for granted, as we achieve self-mastery by submitting our sensuality to our reason, he expounds a sexual ethics that, founded on the belief that body and soul are created for each other, entirely repudiates resort to violence in our personal development. According to McAleer, John Paul II says exactly what Thomas meant: 'The person, by the light of reason and the support of virtue, discovers in the body the anticipatory signs, the expression and the promise of a gift of self, in conformity with the wise plan of the Creator'.[31]

---

[30] Aurel Kolnai, 'The Sovereignty of the Object: Notes on Truth and Intellectual Humility', in *Ethics, Value and Reality* (Indianapolis, IN: Hackett 1978): 28–43.
[31] *Veritatis Splendor*, Encyclical Letter regarding Certain Fundamental Questions on the Church's Moral Teaching, 6 August 1993: §48.

Down the line, so McAleer's story goes, the 'violence against the stranger in the womb' is the inevitable result of the 'violence against the flesh' which is the use of contraceptive barriers or drugs.[32] No wonder, then, that, according to John Paul II, a liberal democracy that sanctions abortion and encourages abortifacient contraception is a 'tyranny and totalitarianism', as wicked as Nazi Germany and Soviet Russia – a claim that would seem a little exaggerated both to leftists and to patriotic neo-conservatives, of course for different reasons.

Conclusion

When popes die their teaching is soon forgotten. John Paul II's invitation, in the encyclical *Ut Unum Sint*, if it returns to the agenda, would have immense significance for ecumenism and ecclesiology. Whether his distinctive theology of nuptiality will pass into the common teaching of the Catholic Church, as he obviously hoped, it is surely too early even to guess.

---

[32] McAleer, *Ecstatic Morality*: 187

Chapter Eleven

JOSEPH RATZINGER

Metropolitan Damaskinos of Switzerland, who studied with him in Germany before Vatican II, wrote to the Prefect of the Congregation for the Doctrine of the Faith in October 2000 to seek clarification of the recently issued declaration *Dominus Jesus*.[1] This document appeared to imply, he feared, that the Roman Catholic Church alone must be regarded as the only true Church, meaning that the Orthodox Church must be something less, in Catholic eyes. Cardinal Ratzinger replied that the Roman Catholic Church also is 'wounded' by the lack of full communion between the two. Of interest here, however, is the question put to him by his former student as to whether there was any continuity between Professor Joseph Ratzinger and the Prefect of the Congregation in regard to their teaching – Damaskinos clearly thought there was a certain reversal of view. To this, Ratzinger replied that professor and Prefect were still the same person, yet these are titles that refer to different tasks. What a professor teaches 'springs from his personal journey of faith and understanding and locates him in the shared journey of the Church'. The CDF Prefect, on the other hand, 'is not supposed to expound his personal views'; on the contrary, any text to which he attaches his name 'is purged of everything that is merely personal and truly becomes the common message of the Church'.[2]

Born on 16 April 1927, in picture book Catholic Bavaria, Joseph Ratzinger is the son of a police officer, whose career was curtailed by his quiet

[1] *Dominus Jesus*: Declaration on the Unicity and Salvific Universality of Jesus Christ and the Church, issued by the Congregation for the Doctrine of the Faith, 6 August 2000.

[2] *Pilgrim Fellowship of Faith: The Church as Communion* (San Francisco: Ignatius Press 2002): 217–41; includes complete bibliography of Ratzinger's publications until 2002.

resistance to anti-Catholicism among local National Socialist officials.[3] The Concordat signed between the Vatican and the Nazi State in 1933, supposedly to secure the Church's freedom, soon gave way to severe political and social tensions, so that Ratzinger's boyhood was overshadowed by the regime's increasingly anti-Catholic policies.

Conscripted in 1943 with his classmates, he served in the anti-aircraft corps, defending Munich, then in the infamous Austrian Legion ('fanatical ideologues who tyrannised us without respite'), digging trenches near the Hungarian border. Ratzinger never had to fight. In April 1945, as his country descended into chaos, he deserted, heading home only to find US troops billeted in his house. He was held in a prisoner-of-war camp for about a month.

In November 1945 Ratzinger returned to his ordination studies. The seminary rector had spent five years as a prisoner in Dachau. Alfred Läpple, another of his teachers, just back from prisoner-of-war camp in England, was one of the German scholars who were to bring Newman to the fore in Catholic theology. He got Ratzinger to read de Lubac's *Catholicisme*, 'a key reading event'. He read Heidegger, Jaspers, Nietzsche and Bergson, with a freedom unusual in a seminary at the time. Reading the Jewish thinker Martin Buber was 'a spiritual experience that left an essential mark' which he later compared with reading Augustine's *Confessions*.

Thomas Aquinas, however, was a problem: 'I had difficulties in penetrating the thought of Thomas Aquinas, whose crystal-clear logic seemed to me to be too closed in on itself, too impersonal and ready-made'.[4] He was taught 'a rigid, neoscholastic Thomism', by a professor who had been a worker in the Ruhr, Arnold Wilmsen, an interesting man, who had studied Husserl and phenomenology at Munich, but, dissatisfied, had gone to imbibe the *philosophia thomistica* imparted in the Roman universities. He seems to have been an exponent of the neoscholastic Thomism espoused by the enemies of *la Nouvelle Théologie*. In short, from his first years in seminary, Ratzinger, like so many others, was put off the study of Aquinas by having neoscholasticism imposed on him; but, unlike some we have considered, he was never required to invent his own version of Thomism.

At the University of Munich, in 1947, Ratzinger found a wonderful group of professors already re-established. Richard Egenter was rethinking

[3]   Aidan Nichols OP, *The Theology of Joseph Ratzinger: An Introductory Study* (Edinburgh: T&T Clark 1988); Laurence Paul Hemming, *Benedict XVI: Pope of Faith and Hope* (London: Burns and Oates 2005), and John L. Allen, Jr., *Pope Benedict XVI: A Biography of Joseph Ratzinger* (London: Continuum 2005).
[4]   *Milestones: Memoirs 1927–1977* (San Francisco: Ignatius Press 1998): 44.

Catholic moral theology on the basis, not of natural law, but of following Christ. Michael Schmaus, who had 'parted ways with neoscholastic schemas', was reconstructing systematics in the spirit of the liturgical movement and the return to Scripture and the Fathers. Friedrich Wilhelm Maier the New Testament professor, whom Ratzinger admired, was among the first Catholic scholars to accept the 'Q' hypothesis – that Matthew and Luke composed their gospels out of Mark and a hypothetical lost source – for which the Holy Office required him to leave his post. Reinstated in 1924, he 'never quite got over the trauma', indeed 'he harboured a certain bitterness against Rome',[5] so the Congregation Prefect records, perhaps with a wry smile.

Gottlieb Söhngen was, however, the greatest influence.[6] He chose Ratzinger's doctorate thesis for him ('People and House of God in Augustine's Doctrine of the Church') as well as the topic for his *Habilitationsschrift* – a study of the then fashionable concept of *Heilsgeschichte*, 'salvation history', in the light of Bonaventure's theology of history and revelation.[7] According to most Protestant theologians, at the time, the 'Hellenization' of Christianity replaced the God who acts dynamically in historically dateable events (and so on) with the statically conceived deity of Greek metaphysics, the unmoved Mover (and so on). At Munich, with its strong tradition of historical theology, Ratzinger could deal with this question only by studying a classic text – and Bonaventure was 'naturally a more likely subject for study than Aquinas'. Unlike Aquinas, Bonaventure, as Minister General, had to come to terms with the theology of history represented by Joachim of Fiore, since it was so deeply attractive to many of his Franciscan colleagues; he could not just dismiss it as easily as Aquinas did.[8]

Approved by Söhngen, the thesis was referred back at the behest of Schmaus – who judged it defective from the scholarly point of view but, much worse, considered that it betrayed a 'dangerous modernism', leading to the 'subjectivization of the concept of revelation'.[9]

---

[5] Ibid.: 50–3.
[6] Ibid.: 106–13.
[7] Gottlieb Söhngen (1892–1971) little known outside German theological circles, contended, as Barth says, that 'the *analogia entis* is to be subordinated to the *analogia fidei*' – a conception Barth cannot accept as 'authentically Roman Catholic', indeed expects to be repudiated by the Magisterium, which allows him to go on mocking what he, somewhat unfairly, takes to be typically Roman Catholic theology, attempting 'to unite Yahweh with Baal, the triune God of Holy Scripture with the concept of being of Aristotelian and Stoic philosophy', see Karl Barth, *Church Dogmatics* II/1 (Edinburgh: T&T Clark 1957, original 1939): 81–4.
[8] Unfair to Aquinas, see *Summa Theologiæ* 1–2, 106, but let it pass.
[9] *Milestones*: 106–13.

Ratzinger was at all the sessions of the Council. He found himself
working closely with Karl Rahner – an experience, so he recalled 35 years
later, during which he realized that Rahner and he 'lived on two different
theological planets': 'Despite his early reading of the Fathers, his theology
was totally conditioned by the tradition of Suárezian scholasticism and its
new reception in the light of German idealism and of Heidegger'.[10] This
seems a rash judgement of Rahner. But then, comparing what Ratzinger
says in *Milestones* (1977) with what others remember of his record at
Vatican II, one cannot but be struck by the spin that he puts on things.
Aged only 35 when the Council opened in October 1962, he was personal
theologian to Joseph Frings, Cardinal Archbishop of Cologne, aged 76,
nearly blind, formerly a distinguished Scripture scholar, and one of the
great men of the Church, let alone at Vatican II. Ratzinger had no great
problem with the texts drafted by the neoscholastic theologians for the
bishops to consider (or, preferably, ratify): in April 1961, however, Frings
wrote to Pope John XXIII to suggest delaying the start of the Council,
because the drafts were (he thought) so inadequate. It is hard to believe that
Frings would have gone so far if his advisor had thought very differently. In
1962 Ratzinger spent weeks drafting an alternative to the official document on the Church, then one on revelation, working with Karl Rahner.
Perhaps he sat quietly, allowing Rahner to dictate everything. The book
they wrote together on the relationship between episcopacy and papacy,
obviously the fruit of their work together, shows no signs of their living on
remotely alien theological planets.[11] Moreover, in his commentary on the
second session of the Council (published in 1964) Ratzinger deplores the
obstacles some of the bishops seemed to want to place in the way of ecumenical relations with their exaggerated Marian piety; he comments
ironically that some seem concerned only with Joseph, the rosary, the consecration of the world to Mary, devotion to the sacred heart of Mary, and
so on – which betrays their lack of theological enlightenment.[12] In this and
several other ways the evidence is that at Vatican II Ratzinger was a good
deal more revolutionary than he remembers. Finally, in the context of
gossip about 'dangerous experts', recorded by Yves Congar, in October
1963, Rahner, Ratzinger and Gustave Martelet were fingered as 'dangerous' by Cardinal Ottaviani (then Prefect of the Holy Office, the future

---

[10] Ibid.: 128.
[11] *The Episcopate and the Primacy* (English translation London: Herder 1962; original 1961).
[12] Devotion to Saint Joseph, foster father of Jesus, remains strong, in Canada, Mexico, Poland
and elsewhere, see James J. Davis, *A Thomistic Josephology* (1967), and the vast bibliography at
www.jozefologia.pl.

Congregation for the Doctrine of the Faith), admittedly because in a paper on collegiality, with three lines at the end on the diaconate, they failed to mention *celibacy*![13]

In 1966, through the good offices of Hans Küng, Ratzinger secured a professorship at Tübingen. Shocked by student unrest and Marxist ideas in the faculty he resigned in 1969, going to the much less prestigious university at Regensburg In 1977 Pope Paul VI named him Archbishop of Munich-Freising. In 1981, at the second time of being asked, he accepted Pope John Paul II's call to take over as Prefect of the Congregation for the Doctrine of the Faith.

According to George Weigel, this was the first head of the former Holy Office who did not take Thomas Aquinas as his master: 'The Pope [John Paul II] respected Thomism and Thomists, but he broke precedent by appointing a non-Thomistic Prefect of CDF. It was a clear signal that he believed there was a legitimate pluralism of theological methods, and that this pluralism ought to be taken into account in the formulation of authoritative teaching'.[14]

'Non-Thomistic' is one thing; to regard Ratzinger as 'anti-Thomist' would, of course, be absurd. He bore no resentment against the two years of 'rigid neothomism'; they were soon forgotten in the splendid tradition of historical theology that he inherited at Munich.[15]

[13] *Mon Journal du Concile* I: 490; Gustave Martelet SJ, advisor to francophone African bishops, subsequently credited with drafting the encyclical *Humanæ Vitæ*; Congar worked on *Ad Gentes*, the document on the missionary activity of the Church; in March 1965 in a dismally inadequate group, as he thought, he rejoiced to have Ratzinger present, 'He is reasonable, modest, disinterested, a great help', II: 355–6; on 17 September 1965 Congar notes Ratzinger's criticisms of the draft that would become *Gaudium et Spes* – 'too much on the natural ahistorical plane', 'too optimistic', II: 395.

[14] George Weigel, *Witness to Hope: The Biography of Pope John Paul II* (New York: Harper-Collins 1999): 444; Ratzinger was certainly the first *theologian* in recent times to be Prefect; how Thomist his predecessors were, is disputable: Franjo Seper (1905–81) and Alfredo Ottaviani (1890–1979) trained largely on Billot's books; none of his speeches at Vatican II was noticeably 'Thomist'.

[15] Going back to Johannes Joseph Ignaz von Döllinger (1799–1890): excommunicated rather hastily by his bishop in 1871, continued to regard himself as a Catholic, ceased saying Mass, took part in some Old Catholic events, chairing the Bonn Congress in 1875 but never acted as a priest or took Holy Communion in Old Catholic eucharists. Amazingly, his assistant from 1863 to 1867 was Georg Ratzinger (1844–99), Benedict XVI's great-uncle, hitherto the best-known member of the family, who resigned the priesthood in 1888, to pursue a career in politics in the *Bauernbund*, the 'small farmers' party', in Bavarian and Federal German legislatures.

History and Ontology

In his *Principles of Catholic Theology*, Ratzinger includes an extensively revised paper on the problem of 'salvation history', *Heilsgeschichte*, first published in 1969.[16] While anticipated in late medieval thinkers, this way of regarding the relationship between history and salvation, so Ratzinger says, originated with Martin Luther: 'Whereas the very continuity of history had previously been the constitutive factor for the understanding of Christendom as salvation history, Christendom now appears under the sign of discontinuity' (157). Moreover, he says, Christianity, which previously depicted itself as community, now becomes individualistic, subject-centred, *pro me*: 'the ultimate discontinuity of a personalist orientation'. This transition from continuity to discontinuity comes out in many ways: in place of apostolic succession, the expression and safeguard of continuity, we find the charismatic power of the Spirit supervening unpredictably here and there; in place of typological interpretation of Scripture which relies on the continuity of history in promise and fulfilment, we find the contradiction between law and gospel, Old Testament versus New; and ontology, the fundamental metaphysical expression of continuity, is first opposed as medieval-scholastic (Aristotelian), then as a Hellenistic perversion; and by the 1960s the concept of *Heilsgeschichte* was the slogan, proclaiming the Protestant alternative to the metaphysics in which Catholic theology was immersed.

One way of dealing with this discontinuity, Ratzinger contends, is to regard history as salvation only on the basis of eschatology – in terms of hope, revolution and the future. In the 1982 version of the essay he denounces 'political theology', and in particular the work of Johannes Baptist Metz – 'in which the enthusiastic option for history represents, at the same time, an equally decisive rejection of the past, a suspension of all reference to tradition in favour of a programme of what is to be done' (157).

Political theology, so called, in its most radical forms, Ratzinger claims, ignores ontology: 'To maintain the existence of human nature as such is, for them, the essence of alienation; no human nature exists for which history is the mediator but only the rough-draft *man*, the ultimate form and scope of which is determined by *this* particular individual who, out of the rough draft, creates a man' (160). The option for discontinuity reaches its extreme here – 'man as the measure of all human realities simply does not exist; man is what he makes himself to be; there are ultimately no limits to this manipulation except those set by his own ability' (160).

---

[16] *Principles of Catholic Theology: Building Stones for a Fundamental Theology* (San Francisco: Ignatius Press 1987). Subsequent page references for quotations are given in the text.

This is a familiar discussion. In analytic philosophy, for example, the question is whether human beings constitute a natural kind, or, as many philosophers since Locke have held, whether personal identity and animal identity are quite disconnected – as if the distinctive features of persons – self-consciousness, freedom, and so on – conflict with the form of animal life.

Ratzinger turns to the work of Karl Rahner, in particular his *Hearers of the Word*, revised by Metz (1963); and the concept of 'anonymous Christian' built on it. He is happy with Rahner's description of human beings as 'hearers of the word', that is, as beings who wait for the word that comes from beyond ourselves, a word spoken in history, by revelation. We do not find fulfilment in ourselves, from the resources of our nature; but in virtue of that nature, we remain open to what can come to us only from without and in freedom of grace. The paradox is that what is necessary for our being to become most fully itself comes from without, contingently, as an historical accident (163).

All of this Ratzinger endorses. To this extent it could have come straight out of de Lubac and Balthasar also. Where he departs from Rahner – citing the *Grundkurs* of 1975 – is in the claim, 'which became more and more the principal motif of his later work' – that our being is itself historical in character. In effect, history is always already *Heilsgeschichte*: 'revelation history is coextensive with world history'. Christianity is 'only . . . the most successful instance of the necessary self-explication of transcendental revelation'. For Rahner, then, according to Ratzinger, every human being is a self-transcending being, and the Incarnation of God is merely the supreme instance of the transcending of the self towards the absolute – 'the successful form of human self-transcendence'. The implication is that, whether explicitly aware of this or not, any and every human being is always already within the relationship of this transcendence. Put the other way round, 'the Christian is not so much an exception among men as simply man as he is'.[17]

Metaphysics and salvation history need not be played off against one other. Ratzinger rejects the standard Protestant line, which is – still, to some degree – to regard the ontological as unavoidably a projection upon and subversion of the history of salvation. On the other hand, he does not want to see the ontological and the saving-historical collapsed into one another, as with Metz's political theology and Rahner's transcendental theology, as Ratzinger fears. Once again, that is to say, we meet the problem of how faith and philosophy, divine grace and human nature, are to be related – neither excluding the claims of ontology, as classical Protestantism appears

---

[17]   Ibid.: 166 citing Rahner, *Grundkurs*: 388.

to him to do, nor reducing salvation history to human progress, as Rahner-inspired liberation theology seems to Ratzinger to do.

Catholic Apologetics

While he clearly wants to avoid falling into the trap of identifying nature and grace, Ratzinger's version of Catholic apologetics seems not to do the kind of justice to natural theology and the use of reason which an old-fashioned Thomist would desire, especially one fearful of residual modernist tendencies.

In his *Introduction to Christianity*, for example, the product of lectures to students from all faculties at Tübingen, published in German 1968, explicitly imitating Karl Adam's *Spirit of Catholicism* for a new generation, Ratzinger certainly avoids any sign of neoscholasticism.[18] He begins with the idea of the theologian as clown, a picture taken from the great Danish religious thinker Kierkegaard by way of a quotation from Harvey Cox, an American theologian in vogue in the 1960s: what the theologian has to say is indeed unintelligible – provocatively and disorientingly. Turning to Thérèse of Lisieux (1873–97, 'The Little Flower'), the Carmelite nun, and her famous temptations to atheism, and to the shipwrecked Jesuit in the first act of Paul Claudel's play *Le Soulier de satin* (1929), Ratzinger ratchets up this notion of how bizarre and disturbing theological questions are. Martin Buber, he recalls, the great Jewish thinker, teaches us that faith is always a leap, an adventure, a turnabout that can be achieved only by an effort of will.[19] Yet there is also 'the ineradicable positivity of Christianity', we are always already inserted in an existing and ancient tradition. Vico, not a familiar name in neoscholastic seminary philosophy, has shown us that the old metaphysics is ended; nowadays we think *historically*.[20] Finally, 'Christian belief is not an idea but a life' – Catholic Christian faith, anyway, takes a social-ecclesial form, it is a practice, we might say, not merely a set of propositions – though these are not Ratzinger's terms here.

No doubt this approach is meant to wean or shock his mainly Catholic student audience out of their assumption that the only proper introduction

---

[18]   *Introduction to Christianity* (London: Burns and Oates 1969).
[19]   Ibid.: 25.
[20]   Giovanni Battista Vico (1668–1744), Italian philosopher, responded to Descartes's attack on the value of historical study by the first attempt in modern times to expound a philosophy of history, in his *Scienza nuova* (1725); see John Milbank, *The Religious Dimension in the Thought of Giambattista Vico*, 2 vols (Lewiston, NY: Mellen 1991–2).

to Christianity had to be the sort of neoscholastic apologetics they most likely encountered at school in those days. In the immediate aftermath of Vatican II schools, as well as seminaries and Catholic colleges, reacted strongly against neoscholasticism – these students were no doubt the last generation to be trained on old fashioned apologetics. Believing certainly means belonging: Catholics have inherited a certain historical tradition; it is immersion in a kind of life, not merely an intellectual game. Moreover, the ideas that we may call on as we seek to understand what faith involves come from a variety of sources, far more exotic and 'ecumenical' than anything envisaged in the newly discarded textbooks.

Ratzinger turns to the prolegomena to the question of God. Here, where a traditional Thomist would expect natural theology, metaphysical arguments for the existence of God, and so on, Ratzinger appeals simply and solely to anthropology and the history of religions. To understand what the word 'God' means we need to recall and analyse the sources of religious experience. In a lengthy, careful analysis he shows that the God self-revealed at the burning bush (Exod. 3:14) is indeed to be identified with the Father of the one who says 'I am'. What Ratzinger is doing, however, without saying so, is denying that we have to accept the idea that it takes Greek metaphysics to enable us to speak of God as 'being'. Given the near-obsession with the claim that, when the Lord God tells Moses that His name is 'I am', we have the first word of 'the metaphysics of Exodus' (Gilson's famous phrase), Ratzinger's avoidance of all mention of Thomas Aquinas at this point cannot be an oversight.

Indeed, Aquinas is never mentioned in this book, anywhere. We hear of Johann Adam Möhler as the great Tübingen theologian (184) and, even more, of the great Munich theologian Franz Baader – the one who memorably reversed the Cartesian 'cogito ergo sum' with his 'cogitor ergo sum' (185) – not 'I think, therefore I am' but 'I am thought about [by others], therefore I am'. Demonstrating here that the solitary subject does not exist – always an exercise early in the neoscholastic philosophy course – Ratzinger offers some interesting reflections, insisting that mind depends on language – not so common in neoscholastic philosophy. He is very much in tune, here, with philosophy at the time (1960s), with Heidegger, Merleau-Ponty, Wittgenstein, and so on, though never mentioning them.

Ratzinger neither attempts nor even alludes to any kind of natural theology as envisaged by the Twenty-four Theses. The meaning of the word 'God' is to be explored in the context of religious tradition and experience, not established by logical analysis and demonstrations.

Besides Karl Adam, the other theologians to whom Ratzinger refers with obvious respect, in this book, are Romano Guardini, Gottlieb Söhngen,

Henri de Lubac, Hans Urs von Balthasar and Karl Rahner. Remarkably, he
shows considerable enthusiasm for the work of Pierre Teilhard de Chardin.

Prefect

Obviously, when he became archbishop in 1977, Ratzinger's career as an
academic ended. From then on we should expect him to practise theology
in a significantly different way, as a pastor and not as a professor. Then, after
1981, as we noted in his exchange with Metropolitan Damaskinos, he saw a
further definition of his role, as Prefect of the Congregation for the Doctrine of the Faith. The theological texts which he signed as Prefect should
be regarded as 'purged of everything that is merely personal', and thus as
'the common message of the Church'.

Whether the Prefect merely carried out the pope's wishes, or pushed the
pope to take a hard line, or, as some have suggested, sometimes moderated
the pope's rage against dissent, or even deterred him from condemning contraception 'infallibly', we do not, as yet anyway, have the evidence to say.
The most notable theological acts during these two decades included the
campaign in 1984–6 against liberation theology and the silencing of the
Brazilian Franciscan theologian Leonardo Boff and cowing of many others
(we have just seen why he might have been personally engaged in the
policy); the pressure from the Congregation for the Doctrine of the Faith in
1986 which led to the dismissal of Charles Curran from his chair at the
Catholic University of America in Washington, DC, on account of his views
on a range of issues in sexual ethics, dissenting from papal teaching; the document in 1990 'On the Ecclesial Vocation of the Theologian', which was
perceived by many as an attack on the autonomy of Catholic academic
theology, an attempt to stop 'dissent' by forcing Catholic universities to sack
dissenting theologians; a series of documents between 1986 and 2003 insisting on the intrinsic immorality of homosexual love-making; and in 2000
the document *Dominus Jesus*, insisting on the uniqueness of Christ and the
centrality of the Catholic Church to salvation – the text, as we saw, that distressed Damaskinos.[21]

Assuming that the pastors of the Catholic Church will always want some
authoritative organ to control deviations from orthodox doctrine and
respond to the no doubt unstoppable flow of delations for heresy, something
like the Congregation has to exist; and the documents signed by Ratzinger

---

[21] The best account is by Rupert Shortt, *Benedict XVI: Commander of the Faith* (London:
Hodder and Stoughton 2005).

between 1981 and 2005 do not seem particularly characteristic of his mindset or likely to have differed substantially if someone else had been Prefect.

Image of God and Nuptiality

Consider, however, the *Letter on the Collaboration of Men and Women in the Church and in the World*, issued in 2004, signed by Cardinal Ratzinger and his deputy. Offered as 'a starting point for further examination in the Church, as well as an impetus for dialogue with all men and women of good will', the style is not only utterly different from the coarse, brutal rhetoric that characterizes documents issued by the Holy Office during the modernist crisis, brooking no possibility of debate, it also actually invites 'dialogue'.[22] This turned out to be the last major doctrinal text to appear over Ratzinger's signature. It cannot be described as doing any more than repeat 'the common message of the Church'. Anticipated to some degree in the work of Henri de Lubac and Hans Urs von Balthasar, the doctrine in this document originated in Pope John Paul II's Wednesday Catecheses.

The document was evidently prompted by the challenge of feminism. No doubt the Congregation has been inundated with angry letters, denouncing some rash punter who wants women ordained as priests, or another who cannot stand 'inclusive' language in the liturgy, or whatever. The document aims to get to the roots of the question and to offer a balanced account.

One current approach to 'women's issues', we are told, emphasizes the abuse of women by men, in order to provoke women into becoming totally independent of men. The alternative would elide gender difference altogether, thus inspiring ideologies which 'make homosexuality and heterosexuality virtually equivalent, in a new model of polymorphous sexuality'. Thus, according to the first tendency, women and men are radically alien to one another; according to the second, they are virtually identical. Whether this is a fair account even of extreme positions in feminist thought we need not linger over here. The letter's purpose is to outline the theological framework for a properly Catholic understanding of the relationship between women and men. Obviously, this could only be a balanced view of the difference between men and women and the complementarity for which they are naturally formed.

This essay in the theology of gender difference starts from Pope John

---

[22] *Letter to the Bishops of the Catholic Church on the Collaboration of Men and Women in the Church and in the World*, issued by the CDF, on 31 May 2004.

Paul II's reflections on the first three chapters of the Book of Genesis – the 'immutable basis of all Christian anthropology' (his phrase).

This already challenges those theological studies that began with the questions on the soul in Thomistic philosophy courses. For us, the starting point was the conception of human beings as rational animals, as any of the standard seminary textbooks would show. Thomas Aquinas considers the nature of the human creature theologically with respect to the soul, *ex parte animæ* (*Summa Theologiæ* 1.75 prologue); which is disclosed, at the next stage, as 'intellective', *intellectiva* (q.76). As Aquinas proceeds, the 'image of God', *imago Dei*, is found in the human being 'solely in virtue of mind', *solum secundum mentem* (93.6). In due course, as we enter what is effectively Aquinas's exposition of Christian ethics, we find the whole treatise introduced by an appeal to the teaching of John of Damascus (c. 655–c. 750), always the voice of the Greek patristic tradition for Aquinas: 'human beings are said to be made in the image of God', and by image, here, is meant that the human creature is like God, 'an intelligent being endowed with free will and self movement', *intellectuale et arbitrio liberum et per se potestativum* (1–2 prologue).

According to the Congregation document, however, when it is said in the first creation narrative that God makes man 'in His own image' – '*adam*' grammatically masculine but sexually undifferentiated – He made them '*male and female*' (Gen. 1:26–7). The human creature, as 'image of God', in other words, is 'articulated in the male–female relationship'. It is not in our rationality but in sexual difference that we image God – in our genitalia, not in our heads, so to speak.

According to the second creation story (Gen. 2:4–25) the sexually undifferentiated creature of the first narrative was originally male. Surrounded by plants and animals, which fail to afford him companionship, he is put to sleep and gives birth to the female, so that his life 'does not sink into a sterile and, in the end, baneful encounter with himself'. Again quoting John Paul II: 'Woman is another "I" in a common humanity. From the very beginning they appear as a "unity of the two", and this signifies that the original solitude is overcome'.

Whether the first human being is actually envisaged as a solitary male *historically*, or this is a flight of fancy on the part of the egocentric solipsist of existentialist epistemology, we need not decide. In any case, the whole approach is quite adventurous. If this is 'the common message of the Church', it is not what theologians have classically taught.

Taken on their own, it is true, the two verses (Gen. 1:26–7) certainly say that the male–female difference is what makes humankind 'image and likeness of God'. Yet, from first-century Jewish commentators such as Philo of Alexandria through the Church Fathers, such as Athanasius and Augustine, into the Middle Ages, and right into our own day, in Orthodox and Protestant as well as neoscholastic Catholic theologies, the common teaching has been that what is defining for human beings created in God's image is our exercise of authority over the earth and all living things, in virtue of our being endowed with intellect and will.

For Thomas Aquinas, for example, it is by our powers of knowing and loving that we may be said to reflect the divine nature (*Summa Theologiæ* 1.93; 1–2 prologue). More than this, as he meditated on Augustine's *De Trinitate*, Aquinas moved, in one of the most significant developments in his thought, from a view of the image of the Trinity in the soul as consisting of the three faculties of memory, intellect and will, to a dynamic conception of the image as actually happening, so to speak, in acts of remembering, understanding and willing. For him, the image of God in the human being is a kind of *event*: an 'imitation' of God's eternal acts of knowing and willing according to which there are two processions within the Godhead: the processions of the Son as Word and of the Holy Spirit as Love. In its own 'processions' of word and love, analogically speaking of course, the human soul 'images' the divine Trinity. The capacity to participate in this way in the dynamic life of the Trinity is grounded in human nature, Aquinas thinks, yet it is only when the mind is actively engaged in acts of knowing and willing that the two 'processions' actually occur in the human soul, thus imitating (however remotely) the interior life of God: 'an image of the Trinity is to be looked for in the mind first and foremost in terms of activity, in so far as out of the awareness we have we form an internal word by thinking, and from this burst out into actual love' (93.7).[23]

This dynamically Trinitarian anthropology obviously goes far beyond any neo-Aristotelian philosophy of the rational animal (if that was what was on offer in the seminary textbooks). Given its classical status in Catholic Christian tradition, indebted to Augustine and Aquinas especially but in neoscholastic theology also, it is surprising that it should simply be set aside, silently, in favour of this innovatory doctrine of sexual difference as the human creature's way of imaging God.

Obviously, the 'image of God' doctrine has, for centuries, been understood in one particular hermeneutical tradition – prompted and controlled no doubt by the earlier reference to humankind's being in God's image as

---

[23]   According to Angelo Scola, following Balthasar, the best analogy for the life of the Trinity is the conjugal act of man and woman in begetting a child – thus in the Trinity there is a nuptial relationship, the reciprocal love between Father and Son is the bond that begets the Spirit – such that the authentic *imago Trinitatis* is the family: father, mother and child – and Aquinas at I 93 6 ad 2 'cannot be opposed to this reading' (*The Nuptial Mystery* (Grand Rapids, MI: Eerdmans 2005: 368).

'having dominion' (Gen. 1:26). From the outset the doctrine has been connected with our freedom and intelligence, our authority to rule the rest of the animal kingdom. This tradition has been blamed, in recent times, for providing a justification for the ruthless exploitation of the earth. The Hebrew verb *radah* – to hold sway, to rule – often suggests, in many other contexts in Scripture, an absolute and even fierce mastery. On the other hand, since the Reformation, the notion of 'dominion' has been glossed in terms of stewardship, with thoughts of management, cultivation, and so on, and images of shepherding, tending, caring, etc., which open the way to current ideas about ecology, saving the planet, and so on. Now that Roman Catholic concerns with 'Justice and Peace' have been extended to include 'the Integrity of Creation', this 'image of God' theology seems to provide exactly the appropriate rationale.

This 'image of God' theology is to be found in the Catechism of the Catholic Church (1992), twice (§§355–61; and §§1699ff), where it is developed at length, beautifully and entirely in accordance with the tradition. The Catechism, no doubt, was by far the most important exposition of Catholic doctrine that appeared during the decades when Ratzinger headed the Congregation for the Doctrine of the Faith. These paragraphs are little more than a repetition of what was said at Vatican II, in *Gaudium et Spes*.

Later in the Catechism we hear that it is in virtue of being created in God's image that human beings make works of art (§2501); and in a quite different connection that, though we have lost our resemblance to God through sin, we remain the image of our Creator, we retain our desire for the One who calls us into existence – indeed, that is why we may say that 'All religions bear witness to this essential human quest' (§2566).

Of course Genesis 1:26–7 is quoted in the introduction to the section on the sacrament of matrimony (§1602): from the creation of man and woman to the wedding feast of the Lamb (Apoc. 19) the Bible is centrally concerned with marriage – but the theme is not developed. The text is cited again in the introduction to the section on property – the earth belongs to man (§2402). Nowhere in the Catechism, however, is there anything to suggest that the 'image of God' theology in terms of sexual difference even exists, let alone that it is the common teaching of the Catholic Church.

Something has happened since 1992. The teaching of Pope John Paul II in the Wednesday Catecheses was evidently not ripe for inclusion in the Catechism. In the Congregation document of 2004, however, this entirely new doctrine has become the only one. Amazingly, with that characteristic Roman Catholic talent for creative amnesia, the *imago Dei* theology that has held sway for 2,000 years is never even mentioned!

To be fair, the 'image of God' theme, studied by the International Theological Commission, during 2000–2, was published in 2004 with Cardinal Ratzinger's approval in *Communion and Stewardship: Human Persons Created in the Image of God* – a magnificent text, entirely in line with the traditional doctrine. It reaffirms the truth that 'human persons are created in the image of God in order to enjoy personal communion with the Father, Son and Holy Spirit and with one another in them, and in order to exercise in God's name responsible stewardship of the created world' (§4). While the emphasis throughout is on the traditional doctrine of rule and sovereignty, our enjoying the privilege of sharing in the divine governance of visible creation (cf. §57), a good deal is also said about the dialogical or relational structure of the image of God (cf. §§45, 46). While union between human beings is realized in a variety of ways, 'Catholic theology today affirms that marriage constitutes an elevated form of the communion between human persons and one of the best analogies of the Trinitarian life' (§39). 'The procreative union of man and woman . . . mirrors the creative communion of Trinitarian love' (§56). Only in one paragraph out of over 90 are we reminded of John Paul II's teaching, that 'the nuptial meaning of the body finds its realization in the human intimacy and love that mirror the communion of the Blessed Trinity' (§40).

Barth's Theological Anthropology

The tradition may, of course, be ripe for abandonment. Back in 1948, indeed, Karl Barth, in his theological anthropology, dismissed the rational animal as a 'phantom', a 'ghost', asserting that this concept overlooks the most distinctive thing about human beings, namely that they exist in a definite history grounded in God's attitude to them.[24] In other words, there can be no authentic theological anthropology which is not based on the history of salvation – *Heilsgeschichte*, rather than Aristotelian philosophy (the alternative, as he supposes).

In that case, so Barth thinks, we cannot say 'human' without saying 'male and female'. In his exegesis of the Genesis chapters in the previous volume, he insists that the climax is the creation of human beings as male and female.[25] The Song of Songs, he thinks, is a celebration of the covenant of husband and wife, anticipating fulfilment in the covenant of grace between the Lord God and the people of Israel, and between Christ and the Church.[26]

---

[24] *Church Dogmatics* III/2: §44.
[25] Ibid.: III/1: §41.
[26] Ibid.: 288–324; brief exegesis at 324–9.

Ultimately, for Barth, the image of God in the human's being sexually differentiated is not merely an image of the covenant relation between the Lord God and creatures but also an image of the very being of God – God existing in the essential relation of Father, Son, and Spirit. Somewhat abruptly, one might think, Barth insists that God is not 'solitary in Himself', which is why his image has to be male and female – all other explanations of the *imago Dei* theme suffer from the fact that they do not do justice to 'this decisive verse' (Gen. 1:27).

In the following volume[27] Barth anticipates much that appears in the Congregation letter. In particular, Barth inveighs against talk of exchange of roles between the sexes, sexlessness, abstract humanity, and so on.

Catholic Critiques of Barth's Anthropology

Barth's interpretation of the image of God in terms of sexual differentiation was, however, regarded as a radical break with centuries of tradition, and certainly not welcomed by Catholics.[28]

In the entry 'Gottebenbildlichkeit' in the *Lexikon für Theologie und Kirche*,[29] the author, Heinrich Gross, regarding Gen. 1:26–7, advises the Catholic reader that Barth's conception of the image of God as residing in the sexual differentiation of the human creature and the relatedness of male and female is to be rejected. For the *Lexikon*, the human creature is image of God as sharing in God's royal authority (see Ps. 8), and as radiating God's majesty.

In the first great work of English-speaking Catholic biblical scholarship, *A Catholic Commentary on Holy Scripture* (1953), Edmund Sutcliffe comments on the verses (Gen. 1:26–7) that 'the immediate context suggests that the likeness is to be found primarily in man's lordship of created things, which bear a relation of subordination to him analogous to that which he bears to his Creator'.[30] This lordship, he adds, 'is founded in man's exclusive posses-

---

[27] Ibid.: III/3: §54.
[28] Angelo Scola, however, is not so opposed: 'Great theologians such as Barth and Balthasar have not hesitated to say that the dual unity of male and female receives its full meaning precisely in view of the relationship between Christ the Bridegroom and the Church his bride. This relationship is visible under the veil of the sacrament of the Eucharist, in which the slain Lamb celebrates his nuptials as the Bridegroom' – perhaps going a little beyond what Barth would have endorsed (*Nuptial Mystery*: 31).
[29] *Lexikon für Theologie und Kirche* edited by Josef Höfer and Karl Rahner (Freiburg: Herder 1957–65), one of the standard works of the day.
[30] *A Catholic Commentary on Holy Scripture*, edited by Bernard Orchard and others (Edinburgh: Thomas Nelson 1953): 183.

sion of intellect and will without which this lordship would be impossible'. This goes beyond the meaning the text would have carried at the time, Sutcliffe allows. That it is in 'these faculties of the spiritual soul that man's likeness to God ultimately rests' took centuries to become clear. Here Sutcliffe refers us to Petavius, *De opificio sex dierum*, for further enlightenment.[31] Clearly, Sutcliffe sees his interpretation in line with a great tradition. He never even mentions that the human creature was made 'male and female'.

The New Jerome Biblical Commentary (1989) takes the same line: 'In the ancient Near East, the king was often called the image of the deity and was vested with God's authority; royal language is here used for the human';[32] while *The Oxford Bible Commentary* (2001), granting that the verse (Gen. 1:27) defines human beings as resembling God in a way that is not the case with the animals, comments that the nature of the resemblance remains unclear: 'hypotheses abound', perhaps in our having 'the unique capacity to communicate meaningfully with God' (*sic*) or our being 'God's representatives or vice-gerents on earth' (the traditional view).[33]

In short, the Christian doctrine of the image of God in terms of sexual differentiation and male–female relationship, proposed by Barth and now in the Congregation *Letter*, may well be both more biblical and more relevant in the climate of modern feminism – it is certainly a break with centuries of tradition.

Nuptiality

For the Congregation *Letter's* interpretation of the creation narratives, the nub of the matter is 'nuptiality'. Their nakedness (Gen. 2:25) reveals the human body, to our first parents, 'marked with the sign of masculinity or femininity' – which 'includes right from the beginning the nuptial attribute'. This 'spousal perspective' allows us to understand how 'woman, in her deepest and original being, exists "for the other"' – as men do too, only it does not come so naturally to them.

This spousal perspective provides the symbolism that is indispensable for understanding the history of salvation as revealed in Scripture: 'God makes himself known as the Bridegroom who loves Israel his Bride' (§6). 'For as a

---

[31] Denis Pétau (1583–1652), French Jesuit historian and theologian.
[32] *The New Jerome Biblical Commentary*, edited by Raymond E. Brown, Joseph A. Fitzmyer and Roland E. Murphy (London: Geoffrey Chapman 1989): 11.
[33] *The Oxford Bible Commentary*, edited by John Barton and John Muddiman (Oxford: Oxford University Press 2001): 43.

young man marries a virgin so shall your creator marry you, and as the
bridegroom rejoices over the bride, so shall your God rejoice over you'
(Is. 62:5), and so on. These images – bridegroom and bride – 'characterize
the dynamic of salvation'. Indeed, they are 'much more than simple metaphors' (§9). They 'touch on the very nature of the relationship which God
establishes with his people'. Christ as bridegroom and the Church as his
bride is a powerful image, explicit in the New Testament, building on the
image of the Lord God's love for his people Israel, and a recurrent theme in
Christian tradition.

What does it mean to say that these terms are 'much more than simple
metaphors'?

Biblically, of course, the marital relation is not the only analogy. God is
also pictured as Judge, much more frequently indeed, such that the human
creature's relationship to God is as much like a trial in a court of law as
encounter in the marriage bed. Many other images of Christ come to mind
besides that of Bridegroom: Word, light, shepherd, vine, living bread, 'the
way, the truth, and the life', and so on.

Thomists might be tempted to put in a word here for the appeal that
Thomas regularly makes to the self-identification of God as 'I am who am'
(Exod. 3:15): ipse esse subsistens, the act of being, far beyond any question of
gender. Metaphors, however rich and imaginative, one might say, need to
be subjected to the ontological interpretation of the divine names in age-
old Catholic tradition.[34] One might appeal, then, to the metaphysics of
causality: God as 'primary cause', creatures as 'secondary causes'.

In the last analysis, the Letter concedes, every human being, man or
woman, is called 'to be for the other'. Yet this is a *feminine* characteristic –
indeed *the* mark of femininity. A woman's physical capacity to give life
structures her personality all the way up:

> It allows her to acquire maturity very quickly, and gives a sense of the serious-
> ness of life and of its responsibilities. A sense and a respect for what is concrete
> develop in her, opposed to abstractions which are so often fatal for the exis-
> tence of individuals and society. It is women, in the end, who . . . keep life
> going (§13).

---

[34] Of course metaphysics has often done harm in Catholic theology: yet, as Cornelius
Ernst liked to point out, St Thomas's approach to the problem of theological interpretation
of Scripture laid down what is surely an inescapable requirement for theologians of any
epoch: namely, 'that their interpretation must exhibit the ontological primacy of God, God
as the ultimately really real' (Cornelius Ernst OP, *Multiple Echo: Explorations in Theology*,
edited by Fergus Kerr OP and Timothy Radcliffe OP (London: Darton, Longman and Todd
1979): 73).

(Presumably men are the ones who go in for the fatal abstractions – who else?) True, 'that which is called "femininity" is more than simply an attribute of the female sex'. This is why men can do it too – 'live for the other and because of the other' (§14).

However, when we turn to the example of the Virgin Mary, we find 'dispositions of listening, welcoming, humility, faithfulness, praise and waiting' – virtues which belong to 'the vocation of every baptized Christian'. Yet, the Letter insists, women live these attributes 'with particular intensity and naturalness' (§15).

Which is why women are indispensable in the Church's life – 'recalling these dispositions to *all* the baptized'. Which is why, also, 'one understands how the reservation of priestly ordination *solely to men* does not hamper in any way women's access to the heart of Christian life' (§16).

Women, in short, are 'called to be *unique* examples and witnesses for *all* Christians of how the Bride is to respond in love to the love of the Bridegroom' (§16).

Men, that is to say, need to acquire the 'femininity' which will allow them to respond properly to the Bridegroom. Men need to discover and develop the dispositions of the bride awaiting her Lord.

Finally: 'The witness of women's lives must be received with respect and appreciation, as revealing those values without which humanity would be closed in self-sufficiency, dreams of power and the drama of violence' (§17). We can see, then, what men are like, without women to show them how to be human.

Conclusion

Thus, in the closing years of the twentieth century an entirely new doctrine of the human creature as 'image of God' is to the fore, with sexual difference as the clue to theological understanding of human nature and destiny. In particular, we owe this doctrine to the reflections of Pope John Paul II. In the background, however, this theology of nuptiality is anticipated by Hans Urs von Balthasar, in obedience to the visions of the mystic Adrienne Kaegi-von Speyr; and the retrieval of the theme of epithalamic mysticism by Henri de Lubac, in medieval and patristic literature – and here Origen is the key figure, with some help from the insights of Pierre Teilhard de Chardin.

On 19 April 2005 Joseph Ratzinger was chosen by his fellow Cardinals to succeed Pope John Paul II, and took the name of Pope Benedict XVI. Obviously, as pope, he will see himself neither as professor nor as Prefect of the Congregation for the Doctrine of the Faith. (Some of those dismayed, and some who were delighted, by his election, seem to assume that he will not see the difference between these posts.)

For centuries new popes have adopted names that signal their conception of their ministry. No doubt we are expected to think of Saint Benedict (c. 480–c. 550), Patriarch of Western Monasticism and Patron of Europe: there is no doubt that this pope will see the re-evangelization of Europe as his priority. We might also think of Pope Benedict XIV (1740–58), remarkable for his sympathetic, albeit not uncritical, attitude to the Enlightenment as well as the realism of his policy of accommodation with the absolutist rulers of the day. Those familiar with the recent history of Catholic theology, however, will think of Pope Benedict XV (1914–22), best remembered no doubt for his vain attempts to bring an end to the First World War. For a theologian who had to rewrite his *Habilitationsschrift* to free it of alleged 'modernist' tendencies, Benedict XVI must be well aware that, since Benedict XV's first act was to put an end to the activities of the *Sodalitium Pianum*, the ugly network of anti-'modernist' vigilance committees in seminaries and universities, his taking the name seems a signal that there will be no danger of what he himself referred to as 'narrow-minded and petty surveillance'.[35]

Dominus Jesus was not well received in some quarters. Yet, the main issue was truth: the philosophical presuppositions that the Congregation theologians feared underlay some of the pluralist theologies of religion, adopted by Roman Catholics as well as proposed by others. We might mention five: the belief that divine truth is so ineffable that nothing can be said about it at all; the relativist attitude to truth which holds that what is true for some people is not necessarily true for others; the radical opposition allegedly existing between the West's logical mode of thought and the symbolic mode of the East; the subjectivism of those who take human understanding to be the only source of knowledge; and the metaphysical emptying of the mystery of the Incarnation.[36]

---

[35] *The Nature and Mission of Theology: Approaches to Understanding Its Role in the Light of Present Controversy* (San Francisco: Ignatius Press 1995; originally published 1993): 66; see E. Poulat, *Intégrisme et Catholicisme intégral: un réseau secret international antimoderniste: 'La sapinière' 1909–1921* (Paris 1969).
[36] Joseph Ratzinger, *Pilgrim Fellowship of Faith: The Church as Communion* (San Francisco: Ignatius Press 2005): 210.

Chapter Twelve

AFTER VATICAN II

The defining event in twentieth-century Roman Catholic theology was the Second Vatican Council. Neoscholastic theology, abandoned in seminaries and universities almost everywhere, has not revived, as yet at any rate. Nevertheless, or as a result, much good work has been done in Catholic theology since Vatican II, pursuing other methodologies and with other aims.[1] As we have seen, in this portrait gallery of the best-known twentieth-century theologians, diversity of approach should not be underestimated. Indeed, even when neoscholastic theology was officially required and widely taught it was never free of internal conflict, not to mention *odium theologicum*. Divisive issues left, or put, on the agenda by Vatican II deserve brief attention, as we conclude our survey: in particular issues relating to church governance, liturgy and sexual ethics.

Dissension

The Roman Catholic Church is not the monolithic entity that her enemies and her most zealous members believe. Beliefs are not held univocally, or with clarity, or across the board. The notion that, 'in Catholic doctrine there exists an order or "hierarchy" of truths, since they vary in their relation to the foundation of the Christian faith',[2] while regarded quite widely as one more Vatican II innovation, a concession to ecumenists, is actually

---

[1]   For an excellent survey see Paul D. Murray, 'Roman Catholic Theology after Vatican II', in *The Modern Theologians: An Introduction to Christian Theology since 1918*, edited by David F. Ford with Rachel Muers (Oxford: Blackwell 2005): 265–86.
[2]   Decree on Ecumenism *Unitatis Redintegratio* 21 November 1964: §11.

only a description of what has always been the case. While no one doubts the place of the Virgin Mary, for example, as articulated in the Marian dogmas, in the Catholic Christian interpretation of the history of salvation, it is perfectly obvious that these dogmas have much more weight in some people's lives than in others', and in some parts of the Church than in others, in relation to faith in Christ – which displays the considerable diversity in Catholic sensibility and devotion. The doctrine of the Trinity, while of course never denied, plays a much more significant part in some people's lives than it does in others'. And so on.

Long before the liturgical texts were revised after Vatican II, Catholics have always prayed at Mass and on other public occasions, for the unity of the Church – meaning, of course, not the reunion of all Christians but unity among Catholics, in a Church which has always included diversities, especially in popular devotion and personal piety, that only too easily give rise to mutual misunderstandings, suspicions of 'orthodoxy', sectarianism and, eventually, dissension and schism.

The aftermath of Vatican II has been turbulent. However, as Newman noted in August 1870, 'there has seldom been a Council without great confusion after it' – he cited five of the first six Oecumenical Councils.[3] More specifically, according to Henri de Lubac, a certain one-sidedness has often prevailed. The Council of Trent, which rejected the *sola scriptura* principle of the Reformation, gave rise to the caricature that Catholics did not need Scripture, since they relied on the living voice of the Magisterium. Vatican I, putting an end to 'conciliarism' once and for all, resulted, to quote de Lubac, in 'the excesses of a curialist papalism'. Now, in 1970, de Lubac sees, as a result of Vatican II's rediscovery of the Church as 'people of God', and so on, 'an integralism of (false) collegiality . . . pushed in the direction of a democratic collectivism'.[4] In each case, the final texts were the product of hard-won compromise: what the minority feared should not be ignored if we are to have a balanced interpretation.

Hans Urs von Balthasar, as we might expect, came out with the outspoken account: 'Within the "Roman Catholic" Church herself there are differences. There are the polarizations in the wake of the Second Vatican Council: left versus right, progressive versus conservative. Some people dissolve allegedly rigid forms until nothing is left but formlessness, while others hold fast to these forms until they actually ossify. Neither is replaced by anything that promises to last, but by things, cobbled together in haste,

---

3   *The Letters and Diaries of John Henry Newman*, XXV (Oxford: Clarendon Press 1979): 175.
4   *The Motherhood of the Church* (San Francisco: Ignatius Press 1982): 165; original 1971.

outdated even before they see the light of day'. 'The Church's internal polarizations' are such that her message, 'a testimony that is so polemically splintered', is not as believable and effective as it should be.[5]

From his election in 1963 Pope Paul VI strove to forestall rejection of the Council's decisions by those outvoted at the final ballot. Most famously, he had an appendix inserted at the last minute, in *Lumen Gentium*, the text on the Church, to reassure the minority that the doctrine of episcopal collegiality was not the diminution of papal authority, which they feared. He kept postponing decisions, especially the vote on religious liberty, as we saw (chapter three), for fear that the minority would be so significant as to discredit the decision. For the rest of his ministry (he died in 1978), he did his best to prevent disputes over the implementation of the Council's decisions from issuing in secessions and schisms. If he showed more tolerance towards 'liberals' and 'progressives' than towards 'traditionalists' and 'conservatives', as some say, no doubt he believed that those who sought more radical reforms than the Council actually countenanced would depart, disillusioned, and so he worried more about those who would reject the Council altogether and stay determinedly in order to restore the pre-Vatican II Church. His policy succeeded: there was no secession comparable with that of the 'Old Catholics', after 1870, refusing to accept the dogma of papal supremacy.

Archbishop Marcel Lefebvre (1905–91) continued to oppose collegiality, ecumenism, religious liberty, liturgical reform, and so on, as he did at the Council, gathering around him a small but significant company of likeminded Catholics. He was excommunicated in 1988.

A sizeable number of Catholics were unhappy with the policies of Paul VI, and some even with those of John Paul II, to the extent that they doubted their legitimacy as popes. While they were happy with the latter's confrontational approach to dissenting theologians they hated what they regarded as John Paul II's indiscriminate friendliness towards heretics, Jews and Muslims – praying in Canterbury Cathedral, at the Wall in Jerusalem, and kissing the Qur'an in Damascus. Worst of all, many Catholics were horrified at the heterogeneous assembly which John Paul II summoned to pray for peace with him at Assisi, on 24 January 2002, the height of his syncretistic folly, as they thought.

A tiny minority of Catholics opt for 'Sedevacantism': Peter's chair (*sedes*) they regard as currently 'vacant'. They flourish in Mexico, but are also to be found in France, Italy, Germany, the Czech Republic, Japan and the United

---

[5] *In the Fullness of Faith: On the Centrality of the Distinctively Catholic* (San Francisco: Ignatius Press 1988): 17–18.

States of America. In the late 1970s and early 1980s many 'sedevacantist' bishops were ordained by Archbishop Pierre-Martin Ngô-Dhinh Thuc (1897–1984).[6] By then he was excommunicated, but, according to Canon Law, these ordinations, though illicit, were not invalid. These are 'real' bishops, who could, and do, ordain priests and more bishops, all of whom are truly ordained, although automatically excommunicated. Thanks to Thuc (who died fully reconciled with Rome), and to over a hundred 'Thuc bishops', thousands of Catholics have these excommunicated clergy to minister to them.[7]

Obviously, such groups are tiny, and some quite crazy. Yet, fringe minorities as they are, their existence touches, however remotely, questions left unresolved at Vatican II. In an obsessional and parodistic manner, they articulate anxieties that many Catholics have felt about the way Catholicism has 'disintegrated', as they would say, in the past half-century.

Papacy and Collegiality

The introduction, or restoration, of the concept of collegiality has not made much difference in practice to how the Church is governed. On the contrary, authority and power seem more concentrated in the Vatican than ever. The ultramontanist minority at Vatican II feared that the status of the pope among the other bishops would decline. Talk of the bishops as a 'college' was suspected of being a coded way of reviving the dreaded spectre of 'conciliarism'. Perhaps the enthusiasm of some in the 'progressive' majority suggested that, in their view, the pope's role should, and would, become more like that of chairing episcopal synods, or executing decisions taken collectively. This would call down the Vatican I anathema against those who would say that 'the Roman pontiff has merely an office of supervision and guidance, and not the full and supreme power of jurisdiction over the whole church, and this not only in matters of faith and morals, but also in those which concern the discipline and government of

---

[6]   The most distinguished 'Thuc bishop' was the former Dominican Michel Louis-Bertrand Guérard des Lauriers (1898–1988). A colleague of Chenu and Congar, he taught philosophy at Le Saulchoir from the 1930s to 1960s: a rigorously speculative version of Thomism with no appeal to history. Convinced that the New Order of the Mass was heretical, he left the Dominicans in 1969 to teach at Lefebvre's seminary at Écône, Switzerland. In 1981 Thuc ordained him bishop. He was excommunicated in 1983 and in 1984 he ordained priests and three bishops (including Robert McKenna, another former Dominican).

[7]   Of course they do not believe that the excommunication is just or valid; it would anyway go against their conscience to celebrate Vatican II rites.

the church dispersed throughout the world'[8] – though many of the bishops who voted in favour of papal supremacy expected to return to balance it with a statement about episcopal authority, and anyway the decision was not unanimous.[9]

In 1995, however, after 17 years of exercising his authority in a conspicuously non-collegial manner, John Paul II surprised everyone, in the encyclical *Ut Unum Sint*, by inviting the pastors and theologians of the Orthodox Church and (even!) of the Catholic Church to help him find a way of exercising the primacy, consistent with how it was practised in the first millennium of Christianity.

This takes us back to the central theme in Yves Congar's theology. Discussing the theological anthropology of the Orthodox tradition, as far back as 1952, he concludes: 'theology is only fully "catholic" when, like a healthy organism, it breathes deeply and uses both its lungs'.[10] This is (I think) the first appearance of the metaphor taken up by Pope John Paul II: 'the Church breathing with both her lungs'.[11]

Perhaps Hans Küng's intemperate attacks on the theory of papal supremacy, as well as on Pope John Paul II's practice, set back dealing with the problem. No one who has looked into the work, say, of Francis Oakley, can doubt that, sooner or later, the Roman Catholic Church will have to come to terms with what was true in the tradition of conciliarism. Yet that remains very much an item on a Western medieval agenda. John Paul II appeals, clearly, to the Eastern tradition. For Yves Congar, the idea of episcopal collegiality rather than pointing to whatever may be true in conciliarism, opens the way to something like a Russian Orthodox conception of 'conciliarity' in terms of *sobornost*'.

Obviously, if the Roman Catholic Church were to find a way in which the Petrine ministry would be practised in accordance with Orthodox demands, that would not necessarily satisfy churches in the Reformation tradition. Congar's pessimism about bridging that gap may remain relevant.

---

[8] *Decrees of the Ecumenical Councils*, edited by Norman P. Tanner SJ (London: Sheed and Ward 1990), vol. 2: 814.

[9] On 13 July 1870, the last serious vote, out of 601, 88 were against the definition, 62 were in favour but wanted amendments; thus one in four was unhappy with the definition, without adding in the 76 still in Rome but mysteriously absent from the ballot. In the end, on 18 July 1870, at the final ceremonial ballot, 535 were present and all but two voted in favour (Riccio of Cajazzo in the Kingdom of Naples and Fitzgerald of Little Rock, Arkansas) – while about 140 had left Rome, including most of the English bishops.

[10] Yves Congar, 'The Human Person and Human Liberty in Oriental Anthropology', *Dialogue between Christians* (London: Chapman 1966): 232–45.

[11] B. Petra, 'Church with "Two lungs": adventures of a metaphor', *Ephrem's Theological Journal* 6 (2002): 111–27.

'Strife' over Liturgy

Among other unresolved issues left over from Vatican II affecting ordinary Catholics, there is the problem of the liturgy. This was not an issue at Vatican I: it never occurred to anyone then that the liturgy, and in particular the Mass, needed reform. Indeed, even in the 1950s, few of us expected or wanted substantial changes.

Even those of us who remember scenes of petty rage in the sacristy, and baleful scowls at the altar, over infringements of rubrics and the like, would not have believed how rancorous conflict over the 'changes' would become after Vatican II. The Constitution on the Sacred Liturgy, *Sacrosanctum Concilium*, was promulgated on 4 December 1963. The reforms that followed, supposedly implementing the Constitution, seem, to a significant number of Catholics in western Europe and in the English-speaking world, to have done such harm to the liturgy and especially to the Mass, that there is now talk of 'reforming the reform',[12] and of 'recatholicizing the reform'.[13] Back in 1981 Cardinal Ratzinger, as he then was, referred to 'the strife and dissension, which have arisen sconcerning the liturgy'.[14] No dispute since Vatican II has been so acrimonious.

One benefit of abandoning neoscholastic theology, it seemed to some, was that a Catholic theology more directly inspired by Scripture would interact more fruitfully with the liturgy. Neoscholastic theology, some even claimed, was a reassertion of exactly the way of doing theology that led to the (supposed) decline of liturgy in the later Middle Ages: analytic, cerebral, rationalistic. Eminent liturgiologists might be cited in support of this version of history. Thomas Aquinas, it was generally supposed, had no feeling for liturgy; his theology had nothing to contribute to the standard seminary liturgy course.[15] While in one sense a return to the Middle Ages, neoscholastic theology remained isolated from the cult of medievalism to be found in

---

[12] Klaus Gamber, *The Reform of the Roman Liturgy: Its Problems and Background* (San Juan Capistrano, CA: Una Voce Press and Harrison, NY: Foundation for Catholic Reform 1993).

[13] M. Francis Mannion, 'The Catholicity of the Liturgy: Shaping a New Agenda', in *Beyond the Prosaic: Renewing the Liturgical Movement*, edited by Stratford Caldecott (Edinburgh: T&T Clark 1998): 11–48.

[14] Joseph Cardinal Ratzinger, *The Feast of Faith: Approaches to a Theology of the Liturgy* (San Francisco: Ignatius Press 1986): 147.

[15] Few knew the wonderful essay by Ignatius Mennessier OP (1902–65), 'L'Idée du sacré et le culte d'après S. Thomas', *Revue des Sciences Philosophiques et Théologiques* 19 (1930): 63–82 or consulted his editions of the relevant questions in the *Summa Theologiæ*; recently, however, we have David Berger, *Thomas Aquinas and the Liturgy* (Naples, FL: Sapientia Press 2004) and Peter M. Candler, Jr., 'Liturgically Trained Memory: A Reading of *Summa Theologiæ* III.83', *Modern Theology* 20 (2004): 423–45.

the English Gothic Revival, for example, in the European Romantic Movement in general, and in much ordinary Catholic piety and ecclesiastical architecture. These movements reasserted feeling, intuition and imagination over against the rationalism that (supposedly, anyway) marked the Enlightenment. During the modernist crisis, neoscholastic Thomism was directed precisely *against* feeling, imagination and symbolism. The harbingers of Romanticism in Catholic theology were the theologians of the Tübingen School – which was why strict Thomists hated them. Chenu's interest in Möhler, as we saw, was one of the most significant objections to him.

When Vatican II undertook 'the reform and promotion' of the liturgy, it did so, of course, 'to impart an ever-increasing vigour to the Christian lives of the faithful, to adapt more closely to the needs of the present age those institutions which are subject to change; to encourage whatever can promote the union of all who believe in Christ; to strengthen whatever serves to call all of humanity into the church's fold' (*Sacrosanctum Concilium* §1). Few, in 1963, expected the degree of change that was to come. Even at the time, some questioned the wisdom of adapting the liturgy to promote Christian reunion and even to attract non-Catholics in off the street. While a place was to be 'allotted to the vernacular', in the Mass, the natural meaning of the text confines this to the parts that the congregation say or sing, and goes on to insist that they should be able to say or sing all these in Latin also (§54). Nobody expected the celebrant to be saying Mass in English in a couple of years. Again, Vatican II 'warmly recommended' that the congregation receive Holy Communion from hosts consecrated at that Mass, and not from the reserved sacrament, as was generally the custom. Communion under both kinds may be granted when the bishops think fit – which might extend to the newly baptized, for example, in the Mass that follows their baptism (§55). Again, nobody expected that, ten years later, it would be taken for granted, throughout the English-speaking world, that communicants receive from the chalice if they so desire. Again, we read that concelebration, 'an appropriate way of manifesting the unity of the priesthood', a practice that 'has remained in use to this day in the church both in the east and in the west', should be extended to occasions when a large number of bishops and priests are gathered – with the caveat that every priest retains the right to celebrate Mass on his own (§57). The connection with the past seems a little strained when we learn that 'a new rite for concelebration' will be created (§58).[16] The laws about the design and construction of altars, and the positioning of the

---

[16] It had already been: concelebration took place for the first time on 3 October 1963, at the Council; even more revolutionarily, on 11 October, the lay auditors were granted permission to receive communion at the principal Mass.

eucharistic tabernacle, are to be revised, and laws which 'seem less suited to the reformed liturgy' should be 'corrected or abolished' (§128). There is no hint that churches would be reordered internally to allow for the eucharist to become more like a meal, and for the celebrant to face the people.

The constitution on the liturgy was the first to be passed at the Council, at the end of the second session.[17] Already, on 14 November 1962, after no more than three weeks of relatively strife-free debate, the vote was 2,162 in favour of permitting reform, and 46 against. As the tiny number who questioned the text even at this early stage shows, few anticipated how radical the reforms would be. However, judging by their speeches, many of the bishops regarded liturgy as so secondary that their interest, let alone suspicion, was never engaged. Mainly, the draft was so carefully prepared, under the guidance of Annibale Bugnini, that, unlike all the other drafts, it was never seriously challenged, let alone sent back for rewriting.

Anyone who remembered Pope Pius XII's zeal for liturgical reform, the sympathy with the desire for the use of the vernacular he expressed in the encyclical *Mediator Dei* (1947), the commission he set up in 1948 for general liturgical reform, the reform of the entire Holy Week liturgy starting with the restoration of the Easter vigil in 1951, the relaxation of fasting before communion and the introduction of evening Masses (1957), and so on, should have sensed how things might go.[18]

In the English-speaking world, when Latin gave way to the vernacular, some expected existing Anglican translations of the Roman liturgy to be adapted and even adopted.[19] The Vatican authorities, however, decreed that

[17] According to Christopher Butler, 'one of the best documents presented to the Council', *The Theology of Vatican II* (London: Darton, Longman and Todd 1981): 14; but he doubts 'whether the assembled bishops, who had usually attained to their office for reasons remote from a pure passion for theology, always understood precisely what they were sanctioning by their votes, or at least the theological motivation behind the documents they had been debating'; cf. 175. His own preference 'would rather be for a silent Latin Mass of the old type, in which the priest prayed quietly the prayers of the Missal and the faithful could either read their missals, or say the rosary or practise mental prayer', *A Time to Speak* (Southend-on-Sea: Mayhew-McCrimmon 1972): 53.

[18] Alcuin Reid OSB, *The Organic Development of the Liturgy* (London: Saint Michael's Abbey Press 2004); see also Lauren Pristas, 'Theological Principles that Guided the Redaction of the Roman Missal', *The Thomist* 67 (2003): 157–95.

[19] With the Alternative Service Book in 1980, and the abandonment of the Book of Common Prayer by many parishes, Anglicans became irreconcilably divided over liturgical language, some blaming the ASB for trying 'ecumenically' to accommodate the dumbed-down Roman missal: in a vast literature see *Ritual Murder: Essays on Liturgical Reform*, edited by Brian Morris (Manchester: Carcanet Press 1980); and *No Alternative; The Prayer Book Controversy*, edited by David Martin and Peter Mullen (Oxford: Blackwell 1981), particularly 'Personal Identity and a Changed Church', by David Martin, in the latter, 12–22.

fresh versions should be made, and, more contentiously, that they were to be usable wherever English is spoken. Problematic as this is, in cultures in which the language has developed quite distinctively (in American English, for example, the word 'men' now means only male human beings), two equally fundamental matters of dispute need to be noted – the eucharist as a meal, and the celebrant facing the people.

The Mass on the Analogy of a Meal

In the Catechism (1992) the eucharist is described as the sacrifice of thanksgiving and praise addressed to God the Father; the memorial of the Paschal sacrifice of Christ; and the presence of Christ in the eucharistic species (§§1356–81).

For most post-Vatican II Catholics, in the English-speaking world, the Mass is 'the sacred meal that Christians eat in common'. Previously, according to Herbert McCabe, one of the finest recent Catholic theologians, the Mass appeared to be

> a sacred rite conducted by a priest set apart by his special clothing and his position facing away from the audience, speaking sacred words in a beautiful and ancient hieratic language unknown to the people. At one point in the ceremony some of the people are privileged to approach the holy place to receive from the priest a private share in his mysteries; they return to their places with bowed heads and half-closed eyes, oblivious of those around them.

In contrast, the Mass now, for most of us, is seen 'first of all as the common meal of the Christian community' – and here we appeal initially to 'the natural symbolism of eating and drinking'.[20]

However, three or four decades on, the approach to the Mass which is gaining authority is that, though what Christ established at the Last Supper took place within the framework of a Jewish Passover meal, what he commanded his disciples to repeat was not the meal but the sacrifice.[21] At solemn meals in Antiquity, it is pointed out, guests did not sit round the table, anyway, as we now do; they sat or reclined on the same side of the table, leaving the other side for the servants to approach. If the Last Supper

[20] Herbert McCabe, *The New Creation: Studies on Living in the Church* (London: Sheed and Ward 1964): 70–8.
[21] Joseph Ratzinger, *The Spirit of the Liturgy* (San Francisco: Ignatius Press 2000): 78–9.

were to be the model for the Mass then we should not have the celebrant as host facing the congregation as the guests.[22]

What has happened, so Joseph Ratzinger maintains, is an 'unprecedented clericalization'. In the eucharistic rite now, the focus is on the celebrant: people have to see him, respond to him, engage in what he is doing, and so on. Indeed, when he lifts the consecrated host for us to adore, the celebrant often holds it at his own eye level – which, from the congregation's point of view, makes his face into a monstrance. Moreover, with the priest facing the people, so Ratzinger says, the worshipping community turns into a self-enclosed circle, no longer opened out on what lies ahead and above, the eschatological and the transcendent – at some risk of being no more than a gathering of decent people gazing at one another.

This is, of course, a caricature. No doubt there are eucharists in which the participants celebrate the community that they feel with one another, at least in the first place (papal Masses come to mind, with thousands of people from near and far, the travel and the waiting and enduring the weather already a 'bonding'). Surely this sense of companionship need not exclude or diminish the focus on the transcendent. Ratzinger's point is that when the priest had his back to the people he was not so important. He was just part of the furniture, his personality (affable or morose) did not matter – though again, papal Masses come to mind: the focus was always on the crucifix and the elevation of sacred host and chalice, yet it would be ridiculous to say that John Paul II's face did not matter.

Facing the People

Given all the upheavals in the liturgy since Vatican II, so Ratzinger says, it would not be right to press for further external changes.[23] The reordering of churches that would be required to retrieve the ancient tradition of praying towards the east would be too much to undertake.

There is face-to-face dialogue during the first part of the liturgy, when we listen to the readings and to the homily; but in the second, strictly eucharistic part, we turn to the Lord, looking away from one another. The Mass is not an event in which we eat and drink together, facing one another then; it is an event in which we turn together to face in the direction from which we expect the Light to come – namely from the east. For centuries,

---

[22] Louis Bouyer, *Liturgy and Architecture* (Notre Dame IN: University of Notre Dame Press 1967): 53–4.
[23] *Feast of Faith*: 139.

churches have been constructed so that this is taken for granted. This 'east-ward position' for the celebrant is no doubt derived from a pagan habit of praying towards the dawn; Christians, anyway, want the eucharistic celebration to focus, symbolically, on Christ the Light, Christ the Rising Sun. That is the story.

To some Catholics this is a matter of enormous significance.[24] In its way, obviously, restoring 'orientation' in Catholic churches would be quite 'ecumenical', at least in the 'inter-faith' sense. The congregation in the synagogue turns towards Jerusalem, the faithful in the mosque towards Mecca, so when the celebrant at the eucharist faces east – with his back to the people – the entire worshipping community would be focused on expecting and adoring the One who comes. This would exhibit the eschatological-parousial dimension of the eucharist.

Moreover, the liturgy is also cosmic: the eucharist celebrated this way would be 'inviting the sun to be a sign of the praise of God and a sign of the mystery of Christ for the assembled community'.[25] This would help in rediscovering a spirituality that takes in the whole of creation.

These are issues over which Catholics, at least in the West, were they confronted with them in practice, would be hopelessly divided. For the majority, the very idea that Christians should face east, or in any particular direction, when they pray, would be unintelligible. For most Catholics now, the eucharist is by analogy primarily a kind of meal, such that it would be unintelligible for the celebrant to face the same way as the congregation, *versus Orientem* – with his back to them, as they would see it. We need to be discouraged from regarding the eucharist as *merely* a meal, as a communal celebration of the friendship we feel for one another (if that is a temptation). We can do without priests who 'animate' the eucharistic celebration by intruding their personalities. Whatever side of the table guests sat at in Antiquity, and whatever the arguments of the liturgiologists (not altogether free of *odium theologicum*), it seems out of the question now that Catholics at large would give up the analogy of a meal and the custom of Mass 'facing the people'. For better or worse, for most of us, it would simply not make sense.[26] Celebrating Mass facing the congregation came about as the natural

---

[24] Uwe Michael Lang Cong Or, *Turning towards the Lord: Orientation in Liturgical Prayer* (San Francisco: Ignatius Press 2004).

[25] *Feast of Faith*: 143.

[26] The celebration of Mass 'facing the people' was not a Vatican II innovation, as most of us assumed at the time; little-read rubrics in the Roman Missal of 1920 take for granted the possibility that the altar may be *versus populum*, such that the celebrant, standing behind the altar, is *versa facie ad populum*; as pilgrims and travellers knew, it was always possible to find ancient churches where the Tridentine Mass was celebrated 'facing the people'.

and spontaneous consequence of the dialogue Mass in the vernacular, legitimized while Vatican II was still in session – whatever the scholarly debates.[27]
A small, though significant minority of priests ordained in the past few
years, likely to augment under the pontificate of Benedict XVI, will celebrate the eucharist, whenever possible, in Latin and adopting the eastward
position for the Canon. For the great majority of ordinary Catholics,
however, in Europe and North America, the idea of Mass celebrated with
the priest's back to them (as they would say) seems bizarre.

The End of Marriage

There are several other issues over which Catholics simply have to agree to
disagree, however reluctantly, since one side or the other finds a certain
position quite unintelligible. In some parts of the Church, for example,
especially in the United States of America, Catholics are deeply divided
over the rights and wrongs of capital punishment. Recent papal teaching,
and the Catechism of 1992, are explicitly against resort to the death penalty
in most cases of convicted murderers – but the majority of US Catholics
remain in favour. Perhaps minds may be changed in due course: one side
does not find the other's position completely *unintelligible* – only utterly *mistaken*, which means that rational argument remains possible.

On the question of the use of contraception, however, it looks as if the
majority of Catholics in the West now find the basic principle of the inseparability of the unitive and procreative dimensions of sexual activity simply
unintelligible – and yet the teaching of the Catholic Church rests on that
principle. Catholics, in western societies, do not have significantly more
children than anyone else. It seems unlikely that they all practise natural
family planning methods. This is by far the most significant division of
opinion, to put it mildly, in the Church.

In the encyclical *Humanæ Vitæ* (1968) Paul VI condemned what of
course he knew are widely used methods of 'depriving conjugal acts of
their fertility' (§14). He was only reaffirming the stance taken by his predecessors, Pius XI (in *Casti Connubii*, 1930), Pius XII (on several occasions),
John XXIII (in *Mater et Magistra*, 1961) and at Vatican II, in the pastoral

---

[27] Cf. Otto Nussbaum, *Der Standort der Liturgen am christlichen Altar vor dem Jahre 1000* (Bonn:
Hanstein 1965), which seems to show that celebration facing the people is widely attested;
and S. deBlaauw, *Cultus et decor: liturgia e architettura nella Roman tardoantica e medievale* (Vatican:
Bibliotheca Apostolica Vaticana 1994), claiming that *versus populum* is 'the classic Roman disposition', 95.

constitution *Gaudium et Spes* (§50). Popes do not condemn things that they believe seldom or never happen; on the contrary, it is precisely because certain things they judge wicked take place on a grand scale that they issue their challenge.

Not everyone found it easy to accept the teaching that 'each and every marriage act must remain open to the transmission of life' (*Humanæ Vitæ* §11) and that, accordingly, anything that interfered with that act or its procreative consequences was *intrinsece inhonestum* (§14).

For one thing, by the 1960s, a large number of married couples, rightly or wrongly, doubted the competence of the bishops or the pope or any celibate person to understand the matter, let alone to decide or rule on its moral status.

Anyway, at Vatican II, unprecedented emphasis was placed on the dignity and responsibility of the laity. The pastors in the Church would be 'enabled to judge more clearly and more appropriately in spiritual and in temporal matters' if they allowed themselves to be 'helped by the experience of the laity' (*Lumen Gentium* §37). Much else no doubt comes into it (diocesan and parish finances at least), yet it is hard to see how the 'experience of the laity', *laicorum experientia*, would not include marriage and sexual experience. The 'judgement' remains with the pastors, here, no doubt, as elsewhere; but pastoral judgements, in at least some intimate matters, may be expected to defer to 'experience' that by definition only lay people ever have.

Moreover, though few would put it in these philosophical terms, the encyclical takes for granted a focus on the moral value of a single act, taken by itself, whereas, in ethics at large, there has been a shift towards an approach which emphasizes the intention of the agent and the circumstances. This shift, in academic philosophy, is by no means uncontroversial. On the one hand, some philosophers doubt whether it makes sense to speak of moral acts that are right or wrong absolutely, in themselves, independently of whatever the agent's intention or the circumstances. Most people, on the other hand, prior to being affected by philosophical theories about it, would happily allow that certain acts are simply wrong, whatever the agent's intention or the circumstances. We might not agree as to which specific acts or courses of action are in the category of those that are absolutely unacceptable – whatever the circumstances or the agent's motives. In some circumstances, we may be able to excuse the agent, to the extent that the subjective culpability may seem almost non-existent – though what was done, we may think, was objectively absolutely wrong. However, that an act of contraceptive intercourse in marriage falls into the category of intrinsically immoral, whatever the motivation or the circumstances, seems quite implausible to an increasing number of people, Catholics included.

The main problem, however, is that the longstanding assumption that every marriage act should be open to the transmission of life has become unbelievable. Having children is no longer the primary purpose of marriage. While Catholics and Christians in general, as well as Jews, Muslims and many other religious people, hope and intend to have children as the result of getting married, the age-old assumption that sexual intercourse is primarily for procreation has become unintelligible.[28]

While most Catholics rule out contraceptive methods that they regard as manifestly abortifacient and so grievously sinful to use, many find it unintelligible to equate *all* contraceptive intercourse, morally, with abortion. Admittedly, many Catholics may be less solid nowadays in their opposition to abortion. However, this may only mean that, while they condemn the sin, they find it much easier to excuse the sinner and even those who collude with her. In itself, this line need not differ from the traditional position in moral theology: sins that are objectively very grave may, subjectively, be easy enough to excuse (and forgive). On the other hand, the belief that, before a disputable number of weeks, the human embryo is not a person at all, is so widespread in western societies that many Catholics too accept it. What was once a metaphysical theory, a highly contestable account of subjectivity, consciousness and personal identity, has now seeped into general acceptance by people who have no background whatsoever in philosophy.[29]

Marriage at Vatican II

The belief that the primary end of marriage was procreation – 'increase and multiply' (Gen. 1:28) – became questionable in the 1920s. Until then, deliberate attempts to exclude having children seemed gravely sinful. Indeed, a marriage in which the couple decided never to risk having a child is not a marriage. On the other hand, from the first years of the Church, as history shows, a great range of contraceptive methods was always available – the *pharmakeia* denounced by Paul may refer to abortifacient drugs (Gal. 5:20). These methods were repeatedly condemned as sinful – which shows how widely they were practised.

---

[28]   See Leslie Woodcock Tentler, *Catholics and Contraception: An American History* (Ithaca, NY: Cornell University Press 2005); and for the longer view, John T. Noonan, Jr., *Contraception: A History of Its Treatment by the Catholic Theologians and Canonists*, enlarged edition (Cambridge, MA, and London: Harvard University Press 1986).

[29]   See David Albert Jones, *The Soul of the Embryo: An Enquiry into the Status of the Human Embryo in the Christian Tradition* (London: Continuum 2004).

At Vatican II, however, in the chapter on marriage and family in the constitution *Gaudium et Spes*, the terminology of primary and secondary ends of marriage, hitherto standard in moral theology textbooks, was quietly dropped, with typical creative amnesia. Marriage is proclaimed to be a kind of friendship, a free and mutual gift which the spouses make of themselves to each other, 'a gift proving itself by gentle affection and by deed', a mutual self-giving which is 'uniquely expressed and perfected through the marital act' (§49). Certainly, as we are reminded in the next section, on 'the fruitfulness of marriage', 'marriage and conjugal love are by their nature ordained toward the begetting and educating of children' – yet we are reassured that having children 'does not make the other purposes of marriage of less account', indeed, we are told, quite explicitly, that marriage is 'not instituted [by God, that is to say] solely for procreation' (§50).

Marriage, indeed, 'persists as a whole manner and communion of life, and maintains its value and indissolubility, even when offspring are lacking – despite, rather often, the very intense desire of the couple' (§50). Marriages which turn out to be infertile, through no action on either spouse's part, are true marriages. The couple wanted offspring; it was not their doing that their attempts were in vain. The man who would seek an annulment of the marriage on the grounds that his wife has borne him no son and heir was – at last – deprived of all putative grounds for doing so.

There is more to marriage than having children. Couples who cannot have children of their own enjoy the kind of friendship which is uniquely expressed in their love-making. Conjugal love as worthwhile in itself, involving the good of the whole person (§49), was at last established as a Catholic value. Half-buried Manichean fears that sex was intrinsically evil, or marriage at best a concession to concupiscence, or valid only for procreation, were rejected, once and for all.

Surprising as this might seem, it was felt necessary to say that sexual love, in human beings, is to be clearly distinguished from 'the dispositions of lower forms of life' (§51).

From the outset, however, the document notes that only 'certain key points' are being considered. Footnote 14 makes it clear that the question of the morality of certain contraceptive technologies was reserved, by Pope Paul VI's decision on 23 June 1964, to a special commission and was not to be debated, let alone decided, by the bishops at the Council. Clearly Paul VI understood how divisive the debate would be.

A great deal is said about the responsibility that couples need to exercise in starting a family. There is reference also to the divine law that 'reveals and protects the integral meaning of conjugal love, and impels it toward a truly human fulfilment' (§50). In connection with abortion, the text goes on, 'the

Church issues the reminder that a true contradiction cannot exist between the divine laws pertaining to the transmission of life and those pertaining to the fostering of authentic conjugal love' (§51). Such remarks obviously allude to birth control methods.

It seems likely that, when they voted in favour of this chapter of *Gaudium et Spes*, many of the bishops expected the papal commission to recommend a widening of permissible contraceptive methods beyond the so-called natural method dependent on the woman's cycle, to include the use of certain drugs to prolong her natural periods of infertility (at least that). Yet, as the angry exchanges in the aula over the text that was finally passed show, at least a significant number of the bishops were deeply opposed to any change in the Church's teaching. 'Responsible parenthood', in the sense that couples should verify the existence of conditions which make having a child at a given time a responsible act of mature Christians, seemed to some nothing but a refusal of divine providence and a failure in faith. The strongly 'personalist' tone of the emphasis on conjugal love, so natural to those who composed the text, seemed to others merely sentimentalism, an echo of the cult of 'experience' attributed to the modernists.

Cardinal Ottaviani, for example, Prefect of the Holy Office, arguing that the text placed far too much emphasis on the conscience of the spouses in deciding how many children to have, mentioned that he was the eleventh child in a family of twelve, his father (*sic*) being a man who trusted in divine providence. Cardinal Browne recommended the older language – that the primary end of the marriage act is procreation, while the secondary end is both the mutual help of the spouses and a remedy for concupiscence.

At the vote on the chapter on marriage taken on 16 November 1965, a total of 1,569 of the Council fathers were satisfied, but 556 still had reservations to some degree or other.[30]

---

[30] The literature is immense; but see *On Human Life: An Examination of 'Humanæ Vitæ'* by Peter Harris and others (London: Burns and Oates 1968), which includes the text of the Theological Report dated 26 June 1966: 224–44, composed by six theologians and ratified by the commission under the presidency of Cardinal Ottaviani: while not liberalizing the traditional teaching in so many words, the means of preventing conception is left to the judgement of the couple. Paul VI did not accept this advice but the fact, known almost at once, that a majority of cardinals, bishops and theologians approved of this document (Wojtyla was absent, choosing solidarity with his colleague Cardinal Wyszynski whose passport was withdrawn) has left the Roman Catholic Church in a state of quasi-schism over this issue for 40 years.

Marriage since Vatican II

Persuaded that anything that the Church had taught for so long could not be wrong, Paul VI disregarded the majority on the commission he had set up to study the question and decreed that acts of love-making in marriage were intrinsically immoral if the couple used drugs or barriers of whatever kind to prevent the wife's becoming pregnant.

Cardinal Karol Wojtyla, a member of the commission, was not present when they finally voted. His advice to Paul VI seems to have been decisive. In turn, he was advised by his friend Wanda Poltawska, a psychiatrist in Krakow, married and with children, who has written a good deal in the following vein:

> When a couple really understand human fertility, contraception becomes unnecessary for them, since conception is possible only at a given time in each menstrual cycle. Contemporary man can consciously control his fertility: one might say that human fertility has become truly human only today, when it can be placed under the control of his intellect and will.[31]

In 1992 Pope John Paul II authorized the publication of the Catechism of the Catholic Church: it declares that conjugal love, evidently valued in itself, naturally tends to fecundity, and reaffirms the unbreakable connection between union and procreation in the marriage act, citing *Humanæ Vitæ* and *Casti Connubii* (§2366). It goes on to describe any form of regulation of births other than periodical continence and natural methods as 'intrinsically evil' (§2370).

What bishops and popes teach is clear; what most of the laity do seems equally clear. There is little sign that the two 'sides' engage in debate, or try very hard to persuade one another. The millions of young Catholics who sang their admiration and affection for Pope John Paul II at the many great assemblies during his pontificate did not all accept his teaching on this matter, of which they could not have been ignorant. There is what some describe as a silent schism. If it is true that the basis of the disagreement lies in the rejection by many Catholics of the ancient belief in the inseparability

---

[31] 'The Psychology and Psychopathology of Fertility', in *Natural Family Planning: Nature's Way – God's Way* (Milwaukee, WI: De Rance 1980). In 1962 Poltawska was diagnosed with cancer of the colon, surgery was scheduled and the prognosis unhopeful; Wojtyla sought Padre Pio's prayers and she was cured 'instantaneously'; Padre Pio (1887–1968), the Capuchin stigmatic, was canonized by John Paul II in 2002, see Jonathan Kwitny, *Man of the Century: The Life and Times of Pope John Paul II* (London: Little, Brown and Company 1997): 179.

of the unitive and procreative in sexual intercourse, it is difficult to see how the two views are ever to be reconciled.

Since it is widely regarded as a foregone conclusion, there are few authors, theologians or other, who argue against the magisterial teaching. In the days when such arguments were necessary none was better than *Birth Regulation and Catholic Belief*, by P.J. FitzPatrick.[32]

There are, on the other hand, theologians who defend the Church's official teaching, often with great philosophical skill. The argument against contraception was set out classically, in 1968, by Elizabeth Anscombe: 'You can have sex without children: Christianity and the new offer'.[33] Roger Scruton, another fine philosopher, in an impressive, much-criticized defence of traditional sexual morality, finds the argument unpersuasive. If the thought is that, since the normal sexual act is intrinsically generative, all other forms of sexual intercourse are morally wrong, he finds this 'a result which is extremely counter-intuitive'. For one thing, it would mean, in logic, that the sexual act performed by people ignorant of the facts of human reproduction would be intrinsically immoral. Mainly, however, he appeals to experience; 'our disposition to divorce the sexual act from reproduction has brought about a vast, and morally significant, change in the project of love-making'. The moral significance, on the view taken in *Humanæ Vitæ* and in the teaching of Pope John Paul II, is of course entirely negative: ever-increasing promiscuity and irresponsible sexual activity. Granting that 'practices which remove the likelihood that new and wholly overwhelming personal responsibilities will issue from an act can change the moral nature of the act', Scruton seems open to the possibility that there may be changes for the better, 'in the project of love-making'. He thinks, anyway, that such facts cannot be used as the sole basis for the ethics of something as complex as human sexual behaviour. Whatever we are to conclude about the morality of 'infertile' acts, he argues, 'must depend upon far wider assumptions about human nature, and cannot be derived from the fluctuating intentionality of infertile intercourse'.[34]

More recently, there has been some impressive argument in favour of

[32] *Birth Regulation and Catholic Belief: A Study in Problems and Possibilities* by G. Egner [P.J. FitzPatrick] (London and Melbourne: Sheed and Ward 1966).
[33] Reprinted in her *Collected Philosophical Papers III: Ethics, Religion and Politics* (Oxford: Basil Blackwell 1981): 82–96.
[34] Roger Scruton, *Sexual Desire: A Philosophical Investigation* (London: Weidenfeld and Nicolson 1986): 286–7. 'Human love involves an inevitable tendency to seek out and be with the other, to involve one's destiny completely and inseparably with his' (242), a feature we might call 'nuptiality'; sexual desire is itself inherently 'nuptial', it involves concentration upon the embodied existence of the other (339) which Scruton takes from John Paul II (407 note 32).

natural family planning.[35] On the whole, however, this body of work, conducted with philosophical skill and appealing to medical and psychological evidence in a humane and sophisticated way, seems to have little impact.

As we have seen, in the work of Hans Urs von Balthasar, of Pope John Paul II, and of the Congregation for the Doctrine of the Faith while under Cardinal Ratzinger's stewardship, the new emphasis on the doctrine of nuptiality, as the key to authentic Catholic self-understanding, includes a reaffirmation of the traditional belief in the unbreakable link between the unitive and the procreative in marital love-making. In effect, according to Balthasar, only Catholic Christians have much chance of understanding the challenging doctrine taught by successive popes, and, among them, he concludes, perhaps only the minority of married couples who practise the asceticism required by following the various natural methods can fully understand.[36] In other words, only those couples who have this understanding of human fertility and practise this asceticism are truly Catholic. Others, for all that they love God and neighbour, send their children to Catholic schools, go to Mass every Sunday, and so on, are either such grave sinners that they should not be taking Holy Communion (the teaching prior to Vatican II), or so confused by modern beliefs about sexual activity, personal relationships, and so on, that they cannot even begin to make sense of the authentically Catholic understanding of marriage. The majority of Catholics, on this account, are simply in 'invincible ignorance'.[37] And if it follows that only a tiny minority of us are 'real' Catholics, then perhaps we shall have to live with that.

Conclusion

Catholics, like all Christians, know that we are sinners. As far back as Novatianism, the rigorist movement which started in Rome in the mid-second century, deprecating concessions to those who had compromised with paganism under persecution, and Donatism in the African Church in the

[35] Janet E. Smith, *Humanæ Vitæ: A Generation Later* (Washington, DC: The Catholic University of America Press 1991); and *Why Humanæ Vitæ Was Right: A Reader*, edited by Janet E. Smith (San Francisco: Ignatius Press 1993). More practically, see Catherine Pepinster, 'Doing What Comes Naturally', *The Tablet,* 3 December 2005: 16–17.

[36] 'A Word on *Humanæ Vitæ*', originally a lecture at a symposium in San Francisco, 1978; in *New Elucidations* (San Francisco: Ignatius Press 1986): 204–28.

[37] An indispensable concept, in neoscholastic moral theology, as indeed in Suárez and Aquinas, cf. 'Ignorance', in *Dictionnaire de Théologie Catholique*, vol. 7 (1922): cols 731–40; and K.E. Kirk, *Ignorance, Faith and Conformity* (London: Longmans Green 1925).

early fourth century, much the same thing, there have always been people in the Church ready to excommunicate others for lack of orthodoxy, often ending by going into schism in order to preserve, as they believed, 'the true Church'. Perhaps one of the lessons we have learnt since the cruel way in which the modernists were treated a century ago is that we have to live with some quite deep divisions and intractable rifts within the Catholic Church, over morals and liturgy especially. The official word for such conflict is 'confusion': we have had nothing but confusion over these issues, at least since the close of Vatican II. Some will say that we have learnt, at last, to fudge issues, to avoid confrontations, to leave judgement too easily to God.

Perhaps we might agree, at least, to recall the beautiful words of the 'Te igitur' in the ancient Roman Canon of the Mass, and pray that, through Jesus Christ, the Father may 'accept and bless these gifts', offered in the first place for the Holy and Catholic Church, 'which Thou mayst vouchsafe to pacify, guard, unite and govern throughout the world' – *quam pacificare, custodire, adunare et regere digneris toto orbe terrarum* – a prayer for peace and unity, within the Catholic Church, which there is no reason to believe will ever become redundant, this side of history.[38]

---

[38] 'Tridentine', of course; but these words are cited by Pope Vigilius (537–55) as already long part of the Canon in his day (cf. *Patrologia Latina*, vol. 69 column 22).

Appendix

THE ANTI-
MODERNIST OATH

Prescribed in the *motu proprio, Sacrorum Antistitum*, issued by Pope Pius X, 1 September 1910, abrogated only in 1967, treated effectively as the formulary of orthodoxy for clerics throughout the first half of the century, the Oath went as follows:

I, _____, firmly embrace and accept all and each of the things defined, affirmed and declared by the inerrant Magisterium of the Church, mainly those points of doctrine directly opposed to the errors of our time. And in the first place I profess that God, beginning and end of all things, can be certainly known, and therefore also proved, as the cause through its effects, by the natural light of reason through the things that have been made, that is, through the visible works of creation. Second, I admit and recognize as most certain signs of the divine origin of the Christian religion the external arguments of revelation, that is, the divine deeds, and in the first place the miracles and prophecies. And I maintain that these are eminently suited to the mentality of all ages and men, including those of our time. Thirdly, I also firmly believe that the Church, guardian and teacher of the revealed word, was immediately and directly instituted by the real and historical Christ himself, while dwelling with us; and that it was built upon Peter, prince of the apostolic hierarchy, and his successors till the end of time. Fourthly, I sincerely accept the doctrine of the faith handed on to us by the Apostles through the orthodox Fathers, always with the same meaning and interpretation; and therefore I flatly reject the heretical invention of the evolution of dogmas, to the effect that these would change their meaning from that previously held by the Church. I equally condemn every error whereby the divine deposit, handed over to the Spouse of Christ to be faithfully kept by her, would be replaced by a philosophical invention or a creation of human consciousness, slowly formed by the effort of men and to be henceforward perfected by an indefinite progress.

Fifthly, I maintain in all certainty and sincerely profess that faith is not a blind feeling of religion welling up from the recesses of the subconscious, by the pressure of the heart and of the inclination of the morally educated will, but a real assent of the intellect to the truth received from outside through the ear, whereby we believe that the things said, testified and revealed by the personal God, our creator and lord, are true, on account of the authority of God, who is supremely truthful. I also submit myself with due reverence, and wholeheartedly join in all condemnations, declarations and prescriptions contained in the encyclical *Pascendi* and in the decree *Lamentabili*, mainly those concerning the so-called history of dogmas. Likewise I reprove the error of those who affirm that the faith proposed by the Church can be repugnant to history, and that the Catholic dogmas, in the way they are understood now, cannot accord with the truer origins of the Christian religion. I also condemn and reject the opinion of those who say that the more learned Christian has a two-fold personality, one of the believer and the other of the historian, as if it would be lawful for the historian to uphold views which are in contradiction with the faith of the believer, or to lay down propositions from which it would follow that the dogmas are false or doubtful, as long as these dogmas were not directly denied. I likewise reprove the method of judging and interpreting Holy Scripture which consists in ignoring the tradition of the Church, the analogy of faith and the rulings of the Apostolic See, following the opinions of rationalists, and not only unlawfully but recklessly upholding the critique of the text as the only and supreme rule. Besides, I reject the opinion of those who maintain that whoever teaches theological history, or writes about these matters, has to set aside beforehand any preconceived opinion regarding the supernatural origin of Catholic tradition, as well as the divine promise of a help for the perpetual preservation of each one of the revealed truths; and that, besides, the writings of each of the Fathers should be interpreted only by the principles of science, leaving aside all sacred authority, and with the freedom of judgement wherewith any secular monument is usually studied. Lastly, I profess myself in everything totally averse to the error whereby modernists hold that there is nothing divine in sacred tradition, or, what is much worse, that there is, but in a pantheistic sense; so that nothing remains there but the bare and simple fact to be equated to the common facts of history, namely, some men who through their work, skill and ingenuity, continue in subsequent ages the school started by Christ and his apostles. Therefore I most firmly retain the faith of the Fathers, and will retain it up to the last gasp of my life, regarding the unwavering charisma of the truth, which exists, has existed and will always exist in the succession of bishops from the Apostles; not so that what is maintained is what may appear better or more suitably adapted to the culture of each age, but so that the absolute and unchangeable truth preached by the Apostles from the beginning may never be believed or understood otherwise.

All these things I pledge myself to keep faithfully, integrally and sincerely, and to watch over them without fail, never moving away from them whether in teaching or in any way by word or in writing. Thus do I promise, thus do I swear, so help me God, etc.

INDEX

Note: *n* after a page reference indicates
a note on that page

Action Française, 10, 34–5
Adam, Karl, 7–8, 53, 190
Alternative Service Book, 210n
Anscombe, G.E.M., 220
Anti-Modernist Oath, 1–2, 223–5
Aquinas, St Thomas, 1, 9, 11–12, 18,
    21–4, 24, 28–9, 35, 67, 78–9, 107,
    132, 142
    on faith, 26–7
    on the human body, 180
    on image of God, 194
    on liturgy, 208n
ARCIC, 50–1
Aristotle, 11–12, 18, 28–9, 117, 133,
    197
Augustine, 18, 23, 29, 81, 88, 132, 185,
    194
De Auxiliis, 115, 125n

Baader, Franz, 191
Balthasar, Hans Urs von, 58, 78,
    121–44, 147, 148n
    on animals, 127–8
    and Barth, 123, 129–31, 198n
    on descent into hell, 134–5
    on eucharist and sexual intercourse,
    141
    on *Humanæ Vitæ*, 140–1, 221
    on infallibility, 160n
    on language, 128–9

on de Lubac, 75
    on nuptiality, 135–7
    on polarizations in the Church,
    204–5
    and Rahner, 88, 91–2, 94, 104, 122,
    142n
    and Adrienne von Speyr, 122n, 124,
    134–5, 141
    on Suárezianism, 124–6
    on supersexuality in God, 142–4
baroque scholasticism, 21–3, 115,
    125
Barth, Karl
    and Balthasar, 129–31
    on image of God, 197–8
    and Kirschbaum, 134n
    and Küng, 147–50
    on Marianism, 84
    on Molinism, 80n
    and Song of Songs, 135, 197
Benedict XV (Della Chiesa), 21, 202
Benedict XVI, 202; *see also* Ratzinger,
    Joseph
Bernard of Clairvaux, 69, 81, 83, 101,
    152
Billot, Louis, 10–11, 21
Blondel, Maurice, 24, 68n, 73, 78
Bonaventure, 8, 18, 101, 132, 185
Boston Letter, 95–7
Bouyer, Louis, 10n, 89, 105n, 146
Browne, Michael, 19n, 20, 36, 44, 47,
    48, 54, 218
Buber, Martin, 184, 190

Bugnini, Annibale, 210
Bulgakov, Sergius, 82
Bultmann, Rudolf, 61
Butler, Christopher, 105–6, 210n

cardinals, 38n
Carey, George, 175
Catherine of Siena, 41
Chenu, Marie-Dominique, 10, 17–33, 35, 54n, 59, 70n, 125, 131
    on Aquinas, 27–9
    cited by Balthasar, 132
    cited by de Lubac, 78
    on Wolffianism, 29–32
Chesterton, G.K., 62, 168
Claudel, Paul, 84, 190
Clement of Alexandria, 78, 88
Coakley, Sarah, 102n
collegiality, 43–5, 50, 156–7
concelebration, 89, 209
conciliarism, 154–7, 207
Congar, Yves, 10, 34–51, 54n, 151, 175, 207
    Cambridge worse than Colditz, 36
    on collegiality, 43–5
    on ecumenism, 38–40
    on nuptiality, 43
    on reception, 49–51
    on religious liberty, 45–8
Constance, Council of, 154–6
contraception, 176, 182, 214–21
Cook Wilson, John, 108–9
Cossa, Baldassare (John XXIII), 154, 155n

Daly, Mary, 1n
Damaskinos, 183
Daniélou, Jean, 80n
Delp, Alfred, 87n
Denifle, Heinrich, 27
Denys, 18, 23, 29, 130, 132
De Petter, Dominikus, 52–3, 58
Descamps, Albert, 57
Descartes, René, 13, 112, 127, 131, 169
Dezza, Paola, 9, 146
Dignitatis humanæ, 45–8
Döllinger, Ignaz von, 187n

Dominus Jesus, 183, 192, 202
Dulles, Avery, 34

Eagleton, T.F., 2n
ecumenism, 38–40, 171–2
Emery, Gilles, 33
Ernst, Cornelius, 91, 200n
experience
    Balthasar on, 129n
    John Paul II on, 177–8
    and laity, 215, 220
    Lonergan on, 117–19
    modernist cult of, 218
    Ratzinger on, 191
    Schillebeeckx on, 58–9, 61–5
    suspicion of, 2, 4n, 6, 14–16
experiential-expressivism, 92–3, 118–19

Feeney, Leonard, 96–7
feminism, 138–40, 143, 193, 200–1
Fenton, Joseph C., 7
Fernandez, Aniceto, 44, 47
Fides et Ratio, 1, 169–70
Fiorenza, Francis P., 91
First Amendment, 46
FitzPatrick. P.J., 220
Flick, Maurizio, 9
Florus of Lyons, 72
Frings, Josef, 186

Galot, Jean, 57
Gandhi, Mahatma, 176
Garrigou-Lagrange, Réginald
    Bouyer on, 10
    Chenu on, 21–2, 27, 59
    fears modernism, 19, 93
    model neothomist, 10–18
    and Pinckaers, 33
    and Wojtyla, 165–6
Gaudium et Spes, 21, 77, 187n, 215, 217–18
Giles of Rome, 180
Gilson, Etienne, 30, 68, 112, 191
Gredt, Joseph, 9–10
Gregory XII (Correro), 155
Gregory of Nyssa, 142
Gross, Heinrich, 198
Guardini, Romano, 7–9, 87, 89, 191

Guérard des Lauriers, Michel, 206n
Gumpel, Peter, 146

Hackeborn, Mechthild von, 138
Hasler, August, 158
Hegel, G.W.F., 13, 91, 100
Heidegger, Martin, 53, 87–8, 100, 133,
    138, 169, 191
Hello, Ernest, 10
Hemmerle, Klaus, 142
Hoenen, Peter, 107–9
Honecker, Martin, 88n
Hopkins, G.M., 132–3
Hügel, Friedrich von, 24, 71, 105
Humanæ vitæ, 140–1, 158, 176, 179,
    181, 214–20
Humani generis, 59, 65, 75–6, 145
Hume, David, 13
Husserl, E., 13, 52–3, 167

Ignatius of Loyola, 6, 119, 125
image of God, 79, 193–6, 197
indulgences, 49n
infallibility, 43, 159–161
Ingarden, Roman, 167
intégrisme, 41
invincible ignorance, 221n

Jeremias, Joachim, 64
Joachim of Fiore, 77n, 185
John of the Cross, 21, 132, 137, 165
John XXIII see Cossa
John XXIII (Roncalli), 6–7, 36–7, 151,
    171–2, 214
John Paul II, 1, 10, 201, 205
    on Aquinas, 168–70
    commitment to ecumenism, 171–2,
        175
    and Humanæ Vitæ, 176–9, 180–2
    Küng on personality cult, 146n
    and Padre Pio, 219n
    reform of papacy, 170–5
    theology of the body, 175–9
    see also Wojtyla, Karol
Jones, David Albert, 216n
Joseph, H.W.B., 107–8
Josephology, 186n
justification, 147–50

Kant, Immanuel, 64, 111–12, 164, 169
Kasper, Walter vii
Keeler, L.W., 110
Kenny, Anthony, 9, 107n
Kolnai, Aurel, 181
König, Franz, 151
Krebs, Engelbert, 8n
Kreling, G., 58
Küng, Hans, 145–62
    on Barth, 147–50
    meets Benedict XVI, 151–2
    and conciliarism, 154–8
    Congar on, 151n
    and infallibility, 158–161

Lagrange, M.J., 22
Läpple, Alfred, 184
Lash, Nicholas, 105n
Lefebvre, Marcel, 205
Leibniz, Gottfried, 26, 30
Lennan, Richard, 93–4
Leo XIII (Pecci), 2, 18, 24, 152
Leo the Despot, 84
Lepidi, A., 9, 23
Levering, Matthew, 33
liberation theology, 90n, 192
Lindbeck, George, 92–3, 118–19
Lonergan, Bernard, 105–20
    on Aquinas, 109–10, 115
    and Cook Wilson, 108–9
    and language, 113–14
    and natural theology, 116–17
Lubac, Henri de, 67–86
    on Aquinas, 72–4, 78–9
    and corpus mysticum, 71–2
    on image of God, 79
    mocked as Thomist, 68
    and 'mother church', 83
    on nature and grace, 74–5
    and Origen, 80–2, 84
    and Song of Songs, 81
    Lumen Gentium, 7, 77, 95–6
Luther, Martin, 131, 153, 188

McAleer, G.J., 180
McCabe, Herbert, 211
MacIntyre, Alasdair, 2
MacKinnon, Donald, 130

Maier, F.W., 185
Maréchal, Joseph, 111
Marian doctrine, 84, 137–8, 153–4, 186
Maritain, Jacques, 34, 168, 181
Marshall, Bruce D., 93
Martelet, G., 186–7
Martin V (Colonna), 154–6
men, as defective women, 140
Mercier, Désiré, 5–6, 164
Merleau-Ponty, M., 53, 169, 191
metaphysics, vii, 11–12, 11–12, 166–9
Metz, J.B., 89, 188–9
Meynell, Hugo, 108
Migne, J.-P., 72n
Milbank, John, 75, 190n
modernism, 1–2, 5, 41
Möhler, J. A., 15, 20, 191
Molinism, 15, 83, 115–16
Montcheuil, Yves de, 71
Motte, R.A., 28
Murray, Paul D., 92n, 203n

neoscholasticism, vii, 1–2, 9, 22, 52n,
    73, 126, 159, 187, 208
Newman, John Henry, 105
    1877 Preface, viii n
    on Novatianism, 41
    shocked by Dominican neglect of
        Aquinas, 67n
Nouvelle théologie, 31, 76, 85, 150
nuptiality, 81–3, 135, 175–9, 197,
    199–201, 220n, 221

O'Hara, Charles W., 107
O'Meara, T.F., 2
O'Rourke, Fran, 18n
Oakley, Francis, 207
Origen, 80–4, 101–2, 122, 136
Ottaviani, Alfredo, 37, 46, 77, 186, 218
Otto, R., 119

Patfoort, Albert, 57
Paul VI (Montini), 47, 123, 140–6, 171,
    205, 217
Peddicord, Richard, 30
Péguy, Charles, 133
Pepinster, Catherine, 221n
Philippe, Paul, 56

Philippe, Thomas, 20n
Phillips, G., 156
Philo of Alexandria, 95
Pico, Giovanni, 77n, 85
Pinckaers, Servais, 33
Pio, Padre, 219
Pius X (Sarto), 2, 14, 41, 171
Pius XII (Pacelli), 42, 72, 151, 152, 171,
    214
    zeal for liturgical reform, 210
Plato, 110, 133
Poltawska, Wanda, 219
pragmatism, 14–15
Prignon, A., 44
Przywara, Erich, 121

Rahner, Hugo, 87n
Rahner, Karl, 87–104
    and anonymous Christianity, 94–8,
        124, 189
    on Aquinas, 90–1, 99–101
    and Balthasar, 88, 91–2, 104
    on infallibility, 160–1
    Lindbeck on, 92on
    makes mental reservation, 56–7
    and Origen, 101
    Ratzinger on, 103, 186, 189
Ramsey, A.M., 39, 157n
Ratzinger, Georg, 187n
Ratzinger, Joseph, 183–202, 208, 212
    avoids neoscholasticism, 190
    Congar on, 187n
    enthusiasm for Teilhard, 192
    on God, 191
    and Söhngen, 185
reception, 49–51
Ricoeur, Paul, 55, 175
Rocca, Gregory P., 33
Rougier, Louis, 13n
Rousselot, Pierre, 23, 68, 100
Ruffini, Ernesto, 7
Rupert of Deutz, 69–70
Rushd, Ibn, 180
Rutherford, Samuel, 82–3

Sacrosanctum Concilii, 208–10
Scheeben, M.J., 136–7
Scheler, M., 13, 166n

Schillebeeckx, Edward, 52–66
    on Aquinas, 57–9
    on Chenu and Congar, 54n
    defended by Rahner, 56
    on Easter, 62–4
    reconstructs Christology from NT,
        59–62
Schmaus, Michael, 185
Scola, Angelo, 195n, 198n
Scotus, John Duns, 110, 125, 133
Scruton, Roger, 220
sedevacantism, 205–6
Siewerth, Gustav, 122, 144
Sigismund, 154–5
Smith, Janet E., 221n
sobornost', 42, 43n, 207
Söhngen, Gottlieb, 100, 105, 148, 185,
    191
Soloviev, Vladimir, 132
Song of Songs, 81–3, 135–6, 138, 197
Speyr, Adrienne Kaegi-von, 122n,
    129n, 134, 141–2
Spir, A.A., 30
Steuchus, A., 25
Stirnimann, H., 149
Suárez, Emmanuel, 20
Suárez, Francisco, 124–5
Suárezianism, 5, 67–8, 107, 110, 124,
    126
Sutcliffe, Edmund, 198
Sweeney, Garrett, 161n

Teilhard de Chardin, Pierre, 69, 76, 84,
    132, 192
Thomistic Theses, 2, 3–4, 21, 24, 168,
    191
Thuc, P.-M., 206
Til, Cornelius Van, 148n
Tillich, Paul, 119

Torrell, J.-P., 33
Tracy, David, 111n
Tromp, Sebastian, 37, 55
Tübingen School, 7n, 15, 20, 53, 209
Tymieniecka, Anna T., 167
Tyranowski, Jan, 165
Tyrrell, George, 5–7, 56, 68, 93

ultramontanism, 6, 55, 173, 206
Ut Unum Sint, 171–5, 207

Vatican I, 117, 158, 207n, 208
Vico, G.B., 190n
Vigilius, 222n

Wais, K., 164
Weigel, George, 176, 187
William of St-Thierry, 69
Williams, A.N., 18n
Williams, G.H., 163n, 168
Wilmsen, A., 184
Wittgenstein, Ludwig, 13, 92–3, 102,
    108n, 128, 169, 191
Wojtyla, Karol, 71, 163–82
    on Aquinas, 168–70
    on the body, 180–1
    on contraception, 219–21
    on Maritain, 168
    and phenomenology, 166–8
    and Poltawska, 219
    and Tyranowski, 165
    see also John Paul II
Wolff, Christian, 30, 117
Wolffianism, 23, 30–1, 127
women, 102, 200–1

Yannaras, C., 82

Zigliara, T.M., 9, 23

31215134R00136

Made in the USA
Middletown, DE
22 April 2016